TOURISM IN PERIPHERIES
Perspectives from the Far North and South

TOURISM IN PERIPHERIES
Perspectives from the Far North and South

Edited by

Dieter K. Müller

*Department of Social and Economic Geography,
Umeå University, Sweden*

and

Bruno Jansson

CABI

www.cabi.org

CABI is a trading name of CAB International

CABI Head Office
Nosworthy Way
Wallingford
Oxfordshire OX10 8DE
UK

Tel: +44 (0)1491 832111
Fax: +44 (0)1491 833508
E-mail: cabi@cabi.org
Website: www.cabi.org

CABI North American Office
875 Massachusetts Avenue
7th Floor
Cambridge, MA 02139
USA

Tel: +1 617 395 4056
Fax: +1 617 354 6875
E-mail: cabi-nao@cabi.org

A catalogue record for this book is available from the British Library, London, UK.

A catalogue record for this book is available from the Library of Congress, Washington, DC.

ISBN-10: 1 84593 067 1777
ISBN-13: 978 1 84593 17773

Produced and typeset by Columns Design Ltd, Reading, UK
Printed and bound in the UK by Athenaeum Press, Gateshead

Contents

Contributors

Alistair R. Anderson, *Aberdeen Business School, Robert Gordon University, Aberdeen, UK; e-mail: a.r.anderson@rgu.ac.uk*

Don Carney, *Scottish Centre of Tourism, Aberdeen Business School, Robert Gordon University, Aberdeen, UK; e-mail: d.carney@rgu.ac.uk*

Suzanne de la Barre, *Faculty of Physical Education and Recreation, University of Alberta, Edmonton, Alberta, Canada; e-mail:* sd@ualberta.ca

C. Michael Hall, *Department of Management, University of Canterbury, Christchurch, New Zealand; e-mail: michael.hall@canterbury.ac.nz*

Tom Hinch, *Faculty of Physical Education and Recreation, University of Alberta, Edmonton, Alberta, Canada; e-mail: tom.hinch@ualberta.ca*

Wilson Irvine, *Aberdeen Business School, Robert Gordon University, Aberdeen, UK; e-mail: w.irvine@rgu.ac.uk*

Bruno Jansson, *Department of Social and Economic Geography, Umeå University, Sweden; e-mail: bruno.jansson@geography.umu.se*

Berit C. Kaae, *Danish Centre for Forest, Landscape and Planning, KVL, Hørsholm, Denmark; e-mail: bck@kvl.dk*

Kumaran Krishnan, *Scottish Centre of Tourism, Aberdeen Business School, Robert Gordon University, Aberdeen, UK; e-mail: k.krishnan@rgu.ac.uk*

Günter Löffler (d. 2005), *Department of Geography, University of Würzburg, Germany*

Brent Lovelock, *Department of Tourism, University of Otago, Dunedin, New Zealand; e-mail: blovelock@business.otago.ac.nz*

Andrew Martin, *Scottish Centre of Tourism, Aberdeen Business School, Robert Gordon University, Aberdeen, UK; e-mail: a.martin@rgu.ac.uk*

Peter Mason, *Department of Tourism, Leisure and Human Resource Management, University of Luton, UK; e-mail: peter.mason@luton.ac.uk*

Dieter K. Müller, *Department of Social and Economic Geography, Umeå University, Sweden; e-mail: dieter.muller@geography.umu.se*

Robert Nash, *Scottish Centre of Tourism, Aberdeen Business School, Robert Gordon University, Aberdeen, UK; e-mail: r.nash@rgu.ac.uk*

Jarkko Saarinen, *Department of Geography, University of Oulu, Finland; e-mail: jarkko.saarinen@oulu.fi*

Klas Sandell, *Department of Geography and Tourism, Karlstad University, Sweden; e-mail: klas.sandell@kau.se*

Philip Ulrich, *Department of Social and Economic Geography, Umeå University, Sweden*

Malin Zillinger, *ETOUR – European Tourism Research Institute, Mid-Sweden University, Östersund and Department of Social and Economic Geography, Umeå University, Sweden; e-mail: malin.zillinger@etour.se*

Preface

Editing a book on tourism in peripheries is not really an innovative idea, but it remains a challenge anyway. Considering the amount of existing literature on the topic, it is obviously not possible to review it in total and, hence, one can wonder whether there is a need for additional contributions. Of course, we think there are many questions not even formulated and not answered yet. Moreover, focus has been on peripheries in developing countries rather than on peripheries in higher latitude and developed countries.

Particularly from our Nordic perspective, tourism development forms a major challenge. Governments expect tourism to contribute towards achieving viable solutions for sustaining rural communities. Hence, the question is high on the political and scientific agenda. The conference 'Perspectives on Tourism in Nordic and other Peripheral Areas' held in August 2004 in Umeå, Sweden, aimed to assess tourism's role in solving this problem and this book appears as a consequence of this conference. We would like to thank the people at CABI for accepting the book for publication in their appreciated book series.

Organizing conferences and publishing books is a resource-consuming task. We would thus like to acknowledge the support from the following: (i) the International Geographical Union Commission on Tourism, Leisure and Global Change; (ii) the Department of Tourism, University of Otago, New Zealand; (iii) Umeå University, Sweden; (iv) the Västerbotten Tourist Board; (v) the Bank of Sweden Tercentenary Foundation; and (vi) the Skoglund Foundation.

On a more personal level a number of people have particularly contributed to making the conference – and also this publication – possible. Michael Hall volunteered as keynote speaker and contributed in various ways to the conference and the book. Johan Persson and Lotta Brännlund managed practical matters and introduced us to the fine art of taking payment by credit card. Other people to be acknowledged are Maritta Holmberg, Ulf Wiberg (dean of the Faculty of Social Science) and all those at the Department of Social and Economic Geography, Umeå University.

These lines were written shortly after we learnt of the decease of Günter Löffler, one of the contributors to our book. We therefore would like to dedicate it to his memory.

Dieter K. Müller and Bruno Jansson
Umeå, Sweden, November 2005

Part I
Tourism in Peripheries: an Introduction

1

The Difficult Business of Making Pleasure Peripheries Prosperous: Perspectives on Space, Place and Environment

DIETER K. MÜLLER AND BRUNO JANSSON

Department of Social and Economic Geography, Umeå University, Sweden

Introduction

By the 1960s Christaller (1964) had identified peripheries as areas where people from various European centres spend their vacations. Besides the northern peripheries, the Mediterranean areas were mentioned among such regions. However, 40 years later, these realms are dramatically distinguished by development. Many southern destinations with assets such as a favourable climate and good swimming conditions have developed successfully and have sometimes even experienced stagnation, consolidation and rejuvenation stages, as outlined by Butler (1980). In fact, some areas are hardly considered to be peripheries any longer.

Meanwhile, tourism development in the northern peripheries differs considerably from development in southern areas. Often they do not dispose of assets, allowing them to compete with typical 3S (sun, sea and sand)-destinations. Less favourable climatic conditions, limited population numbers, restricted accessibility and many other factors prevent them from becoming true mass tourism destinations. Nevertheless, tourism is increasingly considered as being a tool for providing economic growth, employment and welfare in peripheries (Hall and Jenkins, 1998). Moreover, few positive accounts of tourism development are available (for an exception, see Müller and Ulrich, this volume, Chapter 6); the rhetoric of tourism development is preached like a mantra, with its expectations of changing the poor development cycles characterizing many peripheral areas, despite tourism having failed to deliver the desired development (see Hall, this volume, Chapter 2).

Considering previous negative experiences with tourism development, one might wonder why tourism has once again been put high on the agenda of regional policy. Focusing on tourism development partly appears to be clutching at the last straw. The failure of other policy schemes and the recent deindustrialization of the peripheries in developed countries owing to an increasingly internationalized competition has forced governments to find 'new' solutions for sustaining peripheral communities (Townsend, 1997). Tourism is a welcome response to this pressure, particularly because this industry is promising service employment with relatively low entrance barriers, superficially open to a wide range of the labour force. Moreover, tourism employment is considered to be attractive to young people, which also appears to be favourable, considering the often problematic demographic structures with a dominance of older people.

Finally, it could be argued that tourism appears to be a good solution for peripheral labour markets, simply because central governments do not have the expertise required in assessing the potential for tourism development in the periphery. Tourism merely appears to be an easy and cheap solution to regional problems. Tourism development schemes also offer fast action and promise quick changes.

However, peripheral locations are also sometimes viewed as opportunities promising exclusiveness and combining high yields with a minimum of impact. In particular, the development of ecotourism has entailed expectations of finally developing high-yield products suitable for peripheral locations.

It is this tension between an often recognized lack of tourism development and a rejuvenated interest in peripheral tourism that constitutes the point of departure for this book. Reviewing tourism development in locations in Northern Europe, North America and New Zealand, it is asked whether there are new trends in tourism development that can turn around cycles of failing development.

The ambition of this chapter is to review some of the ideas and issues that have been forwarded regarding peripheries and tourism development. The focus is on peripheries within the developed world and specifically on areas featuring a cold climate. There have been several previous attempts at defining and understanding tourism in peripheries (e.g. Hall and Johnston, 1995; Price, 1996; Butler et al., 1998; Brown and Hall, 2000) and, hence, this chapter does not aim at providing a comprehensive review of previous writings (see instead Hall, this volume, Chapter 2). Instead, it addresses a selection of issues that appear to be important restrictions in the conversion of the periphery into a pleasure periphery. Finally, this chapter outlines the contents of this book.

Tourism in the Pleasure Periphery

Many peripheries are today populated to an extent that has not previously been seen. This is partly as a result of political action in history aiming at securing state territory and leading to the foundation of settlements and military bases, and partly due to economic interests in natural resources. Finally, indigenous people such as the Sami in the Nordic countries and the Inuit in North America have traditionally settled in these areas, but they have also adapted to Western lifestyles. In particular, the extraction of natural resources such as minerals, forests and fish has historically caused a need to relocate labour to the periphery. However, recent economic restructuring has entailed deindustrialization or, at least, a more effective and less labour-intensive extraction of resources. Hence, many peripheries today are characterized by high unemployment and out-migration.

It is in this context that governments struggle with defining new visions for peripheries. Obviously, it is difficult to rewind the clock of development and withdraw from peripheries. Instead, the decision is usually to retain the population in these areas. The reasons for these decisions can probably be found both in nostalgia and in political realities such as the struggle for votes. The resulting strategies are paradoxical with respect to government intervention in current mobility. Governments do not choose to actively depopulate peripheral regions, since such a governmental intervention would be controversial in many countries. Instead, governments intervene to sustain peripheral communities by supporting peripheral job creation, which is obviously less controversial. However, even this remains a governmental intervention aiming at influencing internal migration patterns and these have seldom been successful in a long-term perspective (Boyle *et al.*, 1998).

A viable and popular vision for peripheral areas is that, with their supply of a pristine nature, these areas can cater for the recreational demand of visitors from all over the world and, hence, considerable support is put into developing an infrastructure for tourism. By increasing accessibility, it is assumed that tourism in these areas can enter a more mature stage and finally develop into a successful 'pleasure periphery'.

The term pleasure periphery was coined by Turner and Ash (1975) in their book The Golden Hordes: International Tourism and the Pleasure Periphery. The title also reveals a perspective. The term Golden Hordes refers to the Huns, who once threatened Europe by invading from the East. There are thus a number of connotations shared by many regarding these hordes: uncivilized, wild, brutal, ruthless. Hence, tourism to the periphery is here not mirrored as a possibility but as a threat. The periphery, on the other hand, is the playground for these hordes, allowing them to have pleasure outside the restraining obligations of home. Turner and Ash (1975) delimited their pleasure periphery as a zone a few hours' flight away from the industrial centres and usually towards the south. In Europe, the Mediterranean fits into this zone as does Florida in the USA.

However, the idea of a pleasure periphery was already outlined by Christaller (1964). In an attempt at locating sites for tourism in Europe, Christaller argued that peripheries disposed of qualities, allowing people from central places and areas to relax and recreate. The argument followed thoughts already pinpointed in his central place theory, acknowledging the concentration of service and labour to central places. Thus, tourism was considered a development alternative for peripheral areas.

The idea of tourism as a tool for regional development is rooted in and inspired by the academic writings of, for example, Hirschman (1958), Myrdal (1963) and Friedmann (1966), and has recently been reviewed by Sharpley (2002) and Telfer (2002a, b). In particular, the idea of a centre–periphery dichotomy appears to be crucial for the idea that tourism can be used as tool for creating economic growth and employment in the periphery, by breaking existing economic structures. However, Britton (1982, 1991) claims that peripheral destinations lack control over tourism and thus are dependent on external agents supplying infrastructure and capital. Tourism is thus only just another expression of a capitalist system of accumulation. Similarly, Mowforth and Munt (1998) challenge the idea in the context of tourism in the Third World. Accordingly, even new alternative forms of tourism are just another way of sustaining colonial dependency patterns, for example by dictating how to manage destinations and still claiming large shares of the economic revenue.

The question of how to destroy these patterns of peripheral dependency largely remained unanswered. Nevertheless, ideas of developing tourism in peripheries are mainly related to increasing problems of marginality caused by economic restructuring comprising a decline in agriculture, forestry and fishing, a deindustrialization owing to increasing international competition and a decline in public sector employment in many industrialized countries. This results in a need for new employment opportunities (e.g. Wanhill, 1997; Jenkins *et al.*, 1998; Saarinen, 2003, 2005; Hall and Boyd, 2005; Lundmark, 2005).

However, peripherality implies numerous restrictions for tourism development. Hall and Boyd (2005) have recently provided a useful review of problems present in peripheries. Among other factors they identify lack of access to transportation, information, political power and capital as strong obstacles to a successful development. Particularly in high latitudes, there are strong seasonal climatic variations delimiting the tourist season. Winter conditions and polar nights have put natural limits to tourism development, although they are also increasingly seen as attractions in themselves. Still, they usually restrict the access – particularly for car-based tourists – and largely remain an expensive tourism product.

Images of Peripheries

In contrast to these constraints, perceptual images of peripheries are often positively loaded. Ideas and stories of frontier, pioneer life and adventures in the great outdoors have certainly contributed to the mystique of peripheries and their inhabitants. Writings by authors such as Jack London have for long depicted the polar areas as a great challenge, as did the expeditions in search of the Northwest Passage or the South Pole. By the 19th century northern destinations had become popular. For example, the Swedish/Norwegian King Oscar II – accompanied by many members of international royalty – visited the North Cape in 1873 during his coronal voyage and contributed to the establishment of the North Cape as a tourist destination (Jacobsen, 1997). Moreover, even the explorer Robert Everest paid a visit to this spot and both thus added to a perception of the North as the end of the world.

These perceptions of a frontier have remained until today. Travelling to the end of the world is still a popular venture, whether to the northern or southern hemisphere. In the northern hemisphere, the Arctic Circle poses an imaginary border that must be stepped over. On the other side of this border exist wilderness and its inhabitants, the Sami. As has been shown in other contexts, wilderness has traditionally been perceived as positively associated with aspects such as religion, solitude, escapism and challenge (Hall and Page, 2002). This image of the periphery is often added to by national tourist boards. Hence, the North Calotte is usually featured as Europe's last wilderness and similar images are even reproduced regarding North America and New Zealand. Hence, Pedersen and Viken (1995) claim that these areas are increasingly converted into global playgrounds for adventure seekers living their imaginary vision of the periphery.

Issues in Peripheral Tourism

Access to peripheries

Access to peripheries is a main threshold for developing tourism. Time–space restrictions entail additional time in reaching peripheries and, hence, location becomes a major disadvantage (Jansson, 1994; Hall, 2005). Lundgren (1982) illustrates this in a model depicting a spatial hierarchy of tourist flows. Accordingly, tourist flows between metropolitan destinations are most intensive, while peripheral rural destinations and remote wilderness areas generate the least intensive flows, often requiring air transportation. This is particularly true for extreme peripheries such as Antarctica, to which all visits require rather long flights or boat trips (Hall and Johnston, 1995). Besides time constraints, travelling to peripheral destinations tends to be expensive, although some governments provide subsidies and guarantee access within regional policy frameworks.

The availability of connections to the peripheries varies in different parts of the world. Lundgren (1995) demonstrated that the penetration of northern space by transport infrastructure took different forms in Europe and North America, entailing the availability of more comprehensive tourism services all over Scandinavia, while the situation in America is characterized by a declining supply in the northernmost areas. However, access to major service and tourism centres by car and train is possible in many cases.

The existing airport infrastructure provides an impression of great demand, not usually mirrored in actual passenger figures (Lundgren, 2001). Attempts at establishing charter connections to peripheral destinations have often failed as has, for instance, been shown for Sweden, where an

EU-sponsored project – Short Breaks in the North – aimed at developing a charter tourism concept by channelling central European tourists to Northern Sweden (Johansson and Bergdahl, 1999), was unsuccessful. Although popular during the project period, the project failed to survive after public economic support had been withdrawn. Problems with service quality, organization and leadership spelled the end for this attempt at turning the north into a charter destination.

However, there are exceptions; in 2004, Santa Claus' official airport in Rovaniemi (in northern Finland and close to the Santa Center at the Arctic Circle) received 105,000 international passengers in total, 103,000 of whom were charter tourists (Civil Aviation Administration, 2004). Similarly, Kittilä airport – close to several winter sports centres in Finnish Lapland – attracted 66,000 international charter passengers. Hence, these peripheral airports nationally rank number two and three, respectively, in terms of arriving charter passengers. In Kiruna, Northern Sweden, the popularity of the Icehotel entailed the entrance of a competing airline on the market and dramatically increased the number of available seats on scheduled flights. Obviously, uniqueness helps overcome distance (Prideaux, 2002).

Moving in peripheries

The penetration of the periphery by transport infrastructure does not only depend on access to the periphery, but also on the opportunities to travel within the periphery (Lundgren, 1995). In Europe's peripheral areas, road networks are usually well maintained and allow for access to all permanent settlements and, thus, to most of the touristic supplies. In contrast, peripheries in North America or Asia are more remote in terms of access. The existing transport infrastructure is geared towards connections to the centres, but not within the periphery.

In Europe, this problem is targeted by various INTERREG projects in trying to overcome the focus on south–north transport corridors by developing alternative corridors between the west and the east. These projects are an EU initiative which aims to stimulate interregional cross-border cooperation within the EU. For example, within the Trans-Barents Highway project, community art work was used to foster a shared identity by creating pieces of Art along the Barents Highway, which leads from Bodø in northern Norway, via Luleå on the Swedish coast of the Baltic Sea, to Murmansk on the Kola Peninsula (The Trans Barents Highway Symposium of Art, 2004). Similarly, the maintenance of ferry connections between the cities on both sides of the Bothnian Sea is always contested because of small passenger volumes, and hence they are heavily financially supported by EU development schemes.

Road standards are also an issue. As reported by Lundgren (1995), the penetration of the north by road infrastructure is far more advanced in Europe, while access to northern Canada is less developed. In Europe, major road projects were finished during the 1980s, making even rather remote nature areas accessible to tourists (Bäck and Bäck, 1986). In Norway, tunnel constructions have made even islands comfortably accessible by car. Hence the North Cape, located on the island of Mageröy, can nowadays be reached without using a ferry. Thus, all major traffic arteries are paved and gravel roads are often private but also made accessible for the public. Nevertheless, winter conditions make car use less attractive to drivers not used to snow- and ice-covered roads. Moreover, frost damage on the road surface makes roads bumpy, even during the summer season.

New road development also creates new tourists flows. The opening of the road between Narvik and Kiruna opened up the Northern Scandinavian Mountain Range for motorized tourists. Similarly, paving the road into Lagmannalaugir, a national park in southern Iceland, also created increased tourism traffic to the area, causing negative impacts on the environment and degrading the experience of pristine nature (Sæþórsdóttir, 2004). Hence, upgrading of existing and creation of new road infrastructure is not undisputed with regard to tourism development. The famous Icelandic K1 gravel road crossing the interior of the country is still unpaved and thus allows its use only during a short summer season and with four-wheel drive vehicles. An upgrading of the road quality would certainly open up the area to a larger number of tourists. However, a potentially negative impact on the environment and a lack of touristic infrastructure can be listed as arguments against such a development.

Besides car-based tourism, buses are a viable means of transport which allow for travel within in the periphery. In the northern hemisphere, scheduled public bus connections are widely available, while tourists in New Zealand, for example, can choose bus tours more specifically catering for tourist demands. In the northern hemisphere, railway connections are mainly available between major settlements, but other transportation is often required to reach tourist facilities.

Peripheral places

Many peripheral settlements are characterized by the small size of the community. These communities were often originally established due to forestry, mining, hunting or as trading posts. Economic restructuring has, however, caused unemployment and a selective out-migration, not least of younger households. This development often entails negative feedback and deters both in-migration and new investment. In this context, governments try to break these cycles of failing development by creating employment within new industries such as tourism. However, it has previously been shown that tourism development does not always entail a positive situation for the destination communities (Singh *et al.*, 2003). Instead, appropriate planning, including participation of the local community, is assumed to be central for achieving successful development (Timothy and Tosun, 2003).

Although many share the vision that tourism is a tool for sustaining rural and peripheral communities, there is considerable controversy regarding the means of achieving this. Particularly in cases where outsiders and other marginal community members are involved, visions can collide and cause setbacks. Sandell (1995) reports, for example, on a failed national park establishment in northern Sweden. Here, the local community perceived the park plans as a threat to the upholding of traditional outdoor activities. Strong local opinion finally stopped all plans forwarded, without any comprehensive community involvement by the Swedish Environmental Protection Agency.

This is only one example, however. In many cases, local communities do not utilize their resources of power to make their own decisions. Instead, they are dependent on central decision making and funding (Hall and Boyd, 2005). Hence, tourism becomes a field of complex negotiations between different levels of governance and agencies (Hall, 2000).

Besides these issues related to negotiating tourism development between local community and regional and national institutions, there are many other factors preventing a successful tourism development. A crucial factor is often the lack of skilled labour. The existing labour force is seldom educated in services and the adaptation from often physically demanding jobs in industrial production, agriculture, forestry or mining is difficult (Jussila and Järviluoma, 1998). Moreover, employment in tourism is not even attractive, since it does not provide significant incomes. Instead, tourism offers part-time or seasonal employment. Additionally, old-fashioned perceptions of gender roles imply that many men are reluctant to accept employment in the service industries, despite low entrance barriers (Jussila and Järviluoma, 1998).

Hence, despite a positive tourism development, high unemployment may remain since labour demand is satisfied by a seasonal workforce (Lundmark, 2005). Exceptions can be found in areas that are also attractive to amenity migrants (Müller, 2006). Here, tourism offers jobs and opportunities for making a living. After some years, many amenity migrants move on to other occupations outside tourism.

One way of getting involved in tourism is by entrepreneurship, which is not always possible, particularly in communities that were previously dominated by industrial production. Smith (1989) claimed that many tourism entrepreneurs are marginal in relation to their host community; they are recruited from in-migrants or set aside in various other ways within the local community, which can imply difficulties in starting a business, particularly in cases where the local community forms an important ingredient of the tourism product (Keen, 2004). For example, Pettersson (2004) argued that many entrepreneurs among the indigenous Sami were young men who could not make a living in reindeer herding, or women who had lost their traditional roles in the industry due to modernization and automatization. Thus, these groups had increasingly become marginalized within their traditional livelihood.

Another field of tension arises because of diverging visions regarding tourism development. Governmental institutions usually consider tourism as a tool for creating new employment and thus axiomatically assume that entrepreneurs are interested in expanding their businesses. However, it has been shown that many entrepreneurs have chosen tourism for lifestyle motives and, thus, they are reluctant to employ any workforce besides their family and friends (Getz *et al.*, 2004; Hall and Rusher, 2004; Komppula, 2004; Shaw and Williams, 2004). Instead, they try to fulfil visions related to self-fulfilment, independence and living environment. Thus, many entrepreneurs are not committed to growth and are reluctant to invest more comprehensively in their businesses.

Moreover, the multiple social relationships within the local community are of importance for creating networks and cooperation between different stakeholders (Clarke, 2005). Tourism entrepreneurs can primarily consider their competitors as threats to their own business and, thus, do not participate in common activities such as marketing. Varying business practices can also cause irritation and disagreement. Particularly in cases where municipalities act as tourism businesses themselves by owning and running tourism facilities such as campgrounds and hotels, there is an obvious risk of disloyal competition, where the public stakeholders have superior access to information and resources. Moreover, common activities within the local business community can also be utilized by stakeholders favoured but not economically involved. This free-rider problem can lead to a split appearance on the market, but also to a more passive strategy towards the demand market.

Overcoming these conflicts, which are more often the norm than the exception (Hall, 2003), is sometimes seen as an important step towards a successful development. Hall (2000) also points to the role of local champions who can take the lead in tourism development. Hence, planning and decision making are complex processes involving both social and power relations. The smallness of peripheral communities does not necessarily contribute to making these relationships more easily managed and planned (Hall, 2003). Instead, peripheral places seem to concentrate power into the hands of a few, which provides continuity even regarding the maintenance of conflicts.

Peripheral economies

Access to capital is another issue that is forwarded as an obstacle for tourism development (Botteril *et al.*, 2000; Hall and Boyd, 2005). The absence of risk and investment capital needed for tourism infrastructure and promotion often requires the involvement of other stakeholders. Sometimes local governments support tourism ventures economically by financial aid or ownership.

In the context of winter sports destinations, however, Flagestad and Hope (2001) argue that public ownership of alpine facilities often prevents a successful development due to lack of market orientation. The opposite case, i.e. a strong involvement by powerful corporations willing to invest in tourism, is put forward, but has turned out to have other negative impacts.

This has been illustrated for the mountain resort Hemavan in northern Sweden (Arell, 2000); here, a powerful tourism corporation purchased the local tourism infrastructure, including hotels and alpine facilities. The corporation made significant investments, but without listening to the local community. Moreover, in a destination development project aiming at gathering stakeholders around a common vision, the corporation finally left the discussion table unwilling to accept the diverging ideas of local stakeholders. So, instead of increased development, the major outcome was a split community.

Lack of both competence and networks are other issues with a negative influence on tourism development. In particular, connections to major demand markets are often weak and peripheral enterprises lack access to major marketing channels. This is partly due to a lack of resources, and partly to the scope of the peripheral products that do not allow competition for major markets. Internet access has been seen as a solution to this isolation, and the Internet has also been used as a marketing tool; the competence of many entrepreneurs is limited and counteracts an efficient use of this tool (Eichhorn, 2002; Evans and Parravicini, 2005).

Besides these issues directly related to tourism entrepreneurs and tourism development, the general development of many peripheral communities constrains tourism development. Many peripheral communities increasingly suffer from a weak supply of services and goods. Hence, multiplier effects remain small and leakage increases, particularly when outside ownership is involved. Hence, even ideas related to ecotourism requiring local engagement and involvement risk becoming obsolete, since local products cannot be purchased.

Environmental issues

Pristine environments have been considered as a major asset of peripheral areas. However, as shown by, for example, Irvine and Anderson (this volume, Chapter 7) with regard to the foot-and-mouth crisis, environmental quality is a volatile factor. Nevertheless, ecotourism development is forwarded as a major trait for many peripheral communities (Fennell, 2002). Ecotourism is appealing because it is considered to unite sustained environmental quality with high-yield and environmentally aware tourists, which appears suitable considering location disadvantages and sensitive environments (Price, 1996). An increasing body of literature acknowledges and forwards this development option (see, for instance, Fennell, 2002).

However, it is reasonable to contest whether tourism is a good development option from an environmental point of view. Protected areas are major points of attraction in the periphery. It has been shown that these areas are often fragile and also difficult to manage (Eagles and McCool, 2002). In this context, tourism development usually means a considerable increase in the number of visitors, although at a low level. However, the opposite scenario is often that of almost no tourism at all and, hence, tourism development implies physical impacts that would otherwise never occur. Therefore, tourism opens new spaces to physical degradation. It is sometimes stated that this is compensated by the educational dimension of ecotourism, leading to a greater environmental awareness (Fennell, 2003).

When considering environmental issues, the focus is often on the destination only. Issues related to transportation to and from the destination are usually neglected (Gössling and Hall, 2006). This should be particularly true for peripheral destinations.

Outline of this Book

This book is structured in five parts. This first part is compiled by Hall, who employs a comparative approach and asks why tourism development has often failed to deliver new employment and economic development in the past. After addressing significant issues for this situation, he concludes that tourism must be seen as an integrated part of more comprehensive development strategies and not, as recently, as an isolated field of action.

In Part II, the focus is on economic issues in regional development. Saarinen provides evidence for Hall's theoretical overview by reviewing tourism development in Northern Finland. Although there are some positive trends within nature-based and second-home tourism, seasonality and lack of strategy are major weaknesses. Hence, Saarinen suggests that there is a need for an integrated strategy – putting tourism into the context of wider local and regional development.

The following chapter addresses a specific means of regional development in Europe, i.e. EU regional development schemes. Zillinger describes a network initiated to enhance cooperation and market access among tourism entrepreneurs in Norrbotten County in Northern Sweden. She concludes that networking is indeed increasingly perceived as positive. However, the studied network also includes entrepreneurs with no knowledge of the aims and means of tis cooperation. Hence, she concludes that networking in peripheral areas with large distances between the different actors is a difficult task, not only concerning the practical issues of meetings but, particularly, concerning communication within the network.

In the subsequent chapter, Löffler addresses the economic impact of tourism on the supply of goods and services in peripheral areas. He assesses this question by analyzing data on retail trade and detects that tourism indeed contributes significantly in sustaining rural retail stores. Hence, tourism development is identified as a key component of sustaining rural communities.

Part II is concluded by Müller and Ulrich, who employ a labour market perspective on tourism development in Sweden since 1960. They argue that tourism development has been central for many rural labour markets, not least in peripheral parts of the country where tourism in some locations in fact constitutes more than 50% of all employment. They conclude that this development is mainly due to the improvement of infrastructure and mobility.

Part III addresses challenges to tourism development in peripheral areas. First, Irvine and Anderson provide a review of the effect of the foot-and-mouth crisis on rural tourism development in Scotland. In particular, they point to the vulnerability of a superficially stable industry branch by comparing two areas that were hit by the crisis in very different ways. One area in fact recorded the disease and, thus, its tourism was directly affected by the closing of the countryside, while the other was not affected by the disease. Nevertheless, even in the latter area tourism suffered because of the spoilt image of countryside in general.

In the following chapter, the focus is then shifted to the southern hemisphere. Lovelock examines domestic and international tourists' perceptions of naturalness in peripheral New Zealand, particularly regarding 'pest' species. This study shows that while international visitors have a similarly moderate to high level of understanding of New Zealand's natural ecosystems as compared to domestic visitors, there were significant differences in how they felt the ecosystem should be managed. Generally, international visitors were less supportive of more radical management practices aimed at eradicating pest species.

In the next chapter, Sandell reviews conflicts between tourism development and the interests of local stakeholders in the context of a proposed national park in northern Sweden. He presents a human ecology framework of analysis and the specific Nordic background, namely the public right of access. He argues that the conflict over tourism development is not only between centre and periphery; instead, conflict is caused by various 'eco-strategies' representing different interrelationships between man and environment. Thus, he concludes that community-based management approaches promise more success, as has also been seen in other peripheries worldwide.

Part III ends with a chapter by Mason addressing visitor management systems in polar regions. Visitor management has traditionally been largely concerned with visitor impacts and an emphasis has been placed on managing the negative consequences of tourism. While the approach of managing impacts has its merits, it has tended to assume that negative impacts are inevitable. This approach has tended to ignore the role of visitor experience in relation to visitor management. This chapter discusses a number of 'hard' and 'soft' approaches to visitor management, specifically focusing on interpretation and self-regulation using codes of conduct, and it concludes that, in fact, little is known about the impact of different tourism management schemes in these areas.

The fourth part of the book addresses opportunities for peripheral tourism development. Nash *et al.* address issues related to wind farms, wind farm perceptions and wind farm development in Scotland. The attitudes of the general public and the press to wind farming are outlined and the attitudes of tourists to the development of such farms and their likely impact on tourism are also discussed. The findings indicate that wind farms can indeed contribute to an increasing visitation of the rural periphery, although they are not solely capable of attracting tourists.

However, due to their novelty, they open a window of opportunity allowing for strategic tourism development.

The following chapter deals with indigenous issues and tourism in a Canadian context. Hinch and de la Barre focus on three different sporting events as tourist attractions. They highlight the potentials and risks associated with the development of sports tourism in an indigenous setting and conclude that tourism development should not only be seen in the light of commercial development, but also with respect to its ability to sustain local culture.

An epilogue follows, featuring two chapters. First, Kaae provides an assessment of tourism research addressing Greenland. She states that identified needs as regards tourism research often involve market research, but seldom address more academic problems. Moreover, a scattered research structure – including a dominance of natural science research and a lack of national and international research coordination – prevents the successful development of a knowledge base regarding tourism in peripheral areas. Finally, Jansson and Müller provide a short conclusion stating, among other things, that tourism in peripheries will certainly entail further research considering recent changes in society.

References

Arell, N. (2000) The evolution of tourism in the Tärna mountains: arena and actors in a periphery. In: Brown, F. and Hall, D. (eds) *Tourism in Peripheral Areas*. Channel View, Clevedon, UK, pp. 114–132.

Bäck, L. and Bäck, E. (1986) *Effekterna av ett vägbygge – väg 98 mellan Kiruna och Riksgränsen: en studie av friluftslivet i Norrbottensfjällen 1979–1985*. Uppsala Universitet, Uppsala, Sweden.

Botterill, D., Owen, R.E., Emanuel, L., Foster, N., Gale, T., Nelson, C. and Shelby, M. (2000) Perceptions from the periphery: the experience of Wales. In: Brown, F. and Hall, D. (eds) *Tourism in Peripheral Areas*. Channel View, Clevedon, UK, pp. 7–38.

Boyle, P., Halfacree, K. and Robinson, V. (1998) *Exploring Contemporary Migration*. Longman, Harlow, UK.

Britton, S.G. (1982) The political economy of tourism in the Third World. *Annals of Tourism Research* 9, 331–358.

Britton, S.G. (1991) Tourism, dependency and place. *Environment and Planning D: Society and Space* 9, 451–478.

Brown, F. and Hall, D. (eds) (2000) *Tourism in Peripheral Areas*. Channel View, Clevedon, UK.

Butler, R. (1980) The concept of a tourist area cycle of evolution: implications for management of resources. *Canadian Geographer* 24, 5–12.

Butler, R., Hall, C.M. and Jenkins, J. (eds) (1998) *Tourism and Recreation in Peripheral Areas*. Wiley, Chichester, UK.

Christaller, W. (1964) Some considerations of tourism location in Europe: The peripheral regions – underdeveloped countries – recreation areas. *Papers in Regional Science* 12 (1), 95–105.

Civil Aviation Administration (2004) *CAA's Air Traffic Statistics 2004*. Vaanta, Finland.

Clarke, J. (2005) Effective marketing in rural tourism. In: Hall, D., Kirkpatrick, I. and Mitchell, M. (eds) *Rural Tourism and Sustainable Business*. Channel View, Clevedon, UK, pp. 87–102.

Eagles, P.F.J. and McCool, S.F. (2002) *Tourism in National Parks and Protected Areas: Planning and Management*. CAB International, Wallingford, UK.

Eichhorn, V.M. (2002) *European Union-funded IT projects: a chance for small and medium-sized tourist enterprises to obtain a sustained competitive position? A project evaluation using the case of Västerbotten/Sweden*. MA thesis, ETM, Bournemouth University, UK.

Evans, G. and Parravicini, P. (2005) Exploitation of ICT for rural tourism enterprises: the case of Aragon, Spain. In: Hall, D., Kirkpatrick, I. and Mitchell, M. (eds) *Rural Tourism and Sustainable Business*. Channel View, Clevedon, UK, pp. 103–118.

Fennell, D. (2003) *Ecotourism*. 2nd edn, Routledge, London.

Flagestad, A. and Hope, C.A. (2001) Strategic success in winter sports destinations: a value creation perspective. *Tourism Management* 22, 445–461.

Friedmann, J. (1966) *Regional Development Policy: a Case Study of Venezuela*. MIT Press, London.

Getz, D., Carlsen, J. and Morrison, A. (2004) *The Family Business in Tourism and Hospitality*. CAB International, Wallingford, UK.

Gössling, S. and Hall, C.M. (eds) (2006) *Tourism and Global Environmental Change: Ecological, Social, Economic and Political Interelationships*. Routledge, London.

Hall, C.M. (2000) *Tourism Planning: Policies, Processes and Relationships*. Pearson Education, Harlow, UK.

Hall, C.M. (2003) Politics and place: an analysis of power in tourism communities. In: Singh, S., Timothy, D.J. and Dowling, R.K. (eds) *Tourism in Destination Communities*. CAB International, Wallingford, UK, pp. 99–114.

Hall, C.M. (2005) *Tourism: Rethinking the Social Science of Mobility*. Pearson Education, Harlow, UK.

Hall, C.M. and Boyd, S. (2005) Nature-based tourism in peripheral areas: introduction. In: Hall, C.M. and Boyd, S. (eds) *Nature-based Tourism in Peripheral Areas: Development or Disaster?* Channel View, Clevedon, UK, pp. 3–17.

Hall, C.M. and Jenkins, J.M. (1998) The policy dimension of rural tourism and recreation. In: Butler, R., Hall, C.M. and Jenkins, J. (eds) *Tourism and Recreation in Rural Areas*. Wiley, Chichester, UK, pp. 19–42.

Hall, C.M. and Johnston, M.E. (eds) (1995) *Polar Tourism: Tourism in Arctic and Antarctic Regions*. Wiley, Chichester, UK.

Hall, C.M. and Page, S.J. (2002) *The Geography of Tourism and Recreation: Environment, Place and Space*. 2nd edn, Routledge, London.

Hall, C.M. and Rusher, K. (2004) Risky lifestyles? Entrepreneurial characteristics of the New Zealand bed and breakfast sector. In: Thomas, R. (ed.) *Small Firms in Tourism: International Perspectives*. Elsevier, Amsterdam, pp. 83–98.

Hirschman, A. (1958) *The Strategy of Economic Development*. Yale University Press, New Haven, Connecticut.

Jacobsen, J.K.S. (1997) The making of an attraction: the case of North Cape. *Annals of Tourism Research* 24, 341–356.

Jansson, B. (1994) *Borta bra men hemma bäst*. Department of Social and Economic Geography, Umeå University, Sweden.

Jenkins, J.M., Hall, C.M. and Troughton, M. (1998) The restructuring of rural economies: rural tourism and recreation as government response. In: Butler, R., Hall, C.M. and Jenkins, J. (eds) *Tourism and Recreation in Rural Areas*. Wiley, Chichester, UK, pp. 43–68.

Johansson, M. and Bergdahl, S. (1999) Kortsemester i Norra Europa. *ETOUR Working Paper* 1999:20. ETOUR, Östersund, Sweden.

Jussila, H. and Järviluoma, J. (1998) Extracting local resources: the tourism route to development in Kolari, Lapland, Finland. In: Neil, C. and Tykkyläinen, M. (eds) *Local Development: a Geographical Comparison of Rural Community Restructuring*. United Nations University Press, Tokyo, pp. 269–289.

Keen, D. (2004) The interaction of community and small tourism businesses in rural New Zealand. In: Thomas, R. (ed.) *Small Firms in Tourism: International Perspectives*. Elsevier, Amsterdam, pp. 139–152.

Komppula, R. (2004) Success and growth in rural tourism micro-businesses in Finland: financial or lifestyle objectives? In: Thomas, R. (ed.) *Small Firms in Tourism: International Perspectives*. Elsevier, Amsterdam, pp. 115–138.

Lundgren, J.O.J. (1982) The tourist frontier of Nouveau Quebec: functions and regional linkages. *Tourist Review* 37 (2), 10–16.

Lundgren, J.O.J. (1995) The tourism space penetration processes in Northern Canada and Scandinavia: a comparison. In: Hall, C.M. and Johnston, M.E. (eds) *Polar Tourism: Tourism in Arctic and Antarctic Regions*. Wiley, Chichester, UK, pp. 43–61.

Lundgren, J.O.J. (2001) Canadian tourism going north: an overview with comparative Scandinavian perspectives. In: Sahlberg, B. (ed.) *Going North: Peripheral Tourism in Canada and Sweden*. ETOUR, Östersund, Sweden, pp. 13–46.

Lundmark, L. (2005) Economic restructuring into tourism in the Swedish mountain range. *Scandinavian Journal of Hospitality and Tourism* 5, 23–45.

Mowforth, M. and Munt, I. (1998) *Tourism and Sustainability: New Tourism in the Third World*. Routledge, London.

Müller, D.K. (2006) Amenity migration and tourism development in the Tärna mountains, Sweden. In: Moss, L.A.G. (ed.) *The Amenity Migrants: Seeking and Sustaining Mountains and their Cultures*. CAB International, Wallingford, UK.

Myrdal, G. (1963) *Economic Theory and Under-developed Regions*. University Paperbacks, London.

Pedersen, K. and Viken, A. (1996) From Sami nomadism to global tourism. In: Price, M.F. (ed.) *People and Tourism in Fragile Environments*. Wiley, Chichester, UK, pp. 69–88.

Pettersson, R. (2004) *Sami Tourism in Northern Sweden: Supply, Demand and Interaction*. ETOUR, Östersund, Sweden.

Price, M. (1996) *People and Tourism in Fragile Environments*. Wiley, Chichester, UK.

Prideaux, B. (2002) Building visitor attractions in peripheral areas – can uniqueness overcome isolation to produce viability? *International Journal of Tourism Research* 4, 379–389.

Saarinen, J. (2003) The regional economics of tourism in northern Finland: the socio-economic implications of recent tourism development and future possibilities for regional development. *Scandinavian Journal of Hospitality and Tourism* 3, 91–113.

Saarinen, J. (2005) Tourism in the northern wilderness: wilderness discourses and the development of nature-based tourism in northern Finland. In: Hall, C.M. and Boyd, S. (eds) *Nature-based Tourism in Peripheral Areas: Development or Disaster?* Channel View, Clevedon, UK, pp. 36–49.

Sæþórsdóttir, A.D. (2004) Adapting to change: maintaining a wilderness experience in a popular tourist destination. *Tourism Today* 4, 52–65.

Sandell, K. (1995) Access to the North – but to what and for whom? Public access in the Swedish countryside and the case of a proposed national park in the Kiruna mountains. In: Hall, C.M. and Johnston, M.E. (eds) *Polar Tourism: Tourism in Arctic and Antarctic Regions*. Wiley, Chichester, UK, pp. 131–146.

Sharpley, R. (2002) Tourism: a vehicle for development? In: Sharpley, R. and Telfer, D.J. (eds) *Tourism and Development: Concepts and Issues*. Channel View, Clevedon, UK, pp. 11–34.

Shaw, G. and Williams, A.M. (2004) From lifestyle consumption to lifestyle production: changing patterns of tourism entrepreneurship. In: Thomas, R. (ed.) *Small Firms in Tourism: International Perspectives*. Elsevier, Amsterdam, pp. 99–114.

Singh, S., Timothy, D.J. and Dowling, R.K. (2003) *Tourism in Destination Communities*. CAB International, Wallingford, UK.

Smith, V.L. (1989) Eskimo tourism: micro-models and marginal men. In: Smith, V.L. (ed.)

Hosts and Guests: The Anthropology of Tourism. 2nd edn, University of Pennsylvania Press, Philadelphia, Pennsylvania, pp. 52–88.

Telfer, D.J. (2002a) The evolution of tourism and development theory. In: Sharpley, R. and Telfer, D.J. (eds) *Tourism and Development: Concepts and Issues*. Channel View, Clevedon, UK, pp. 35–78.

Telfer, D.J. (2002b) Tourism and regional development issues. In: Sharpley, R. and Telfer, D.J. (eds) *Tourism and Development: Concepts and Issues*. Channel View, Clevedon, UK, pp. 112–148.

The Trans Barents Highway Symposium of Art (2004) The Trans Barents Highway Project, Haparanda, Sweden.

Timothy, D.J. and Tosun, C. (2003) Appropriate planning for tourism in destination communities: participation, incremental growth and collaboration. In: Singh, S., Timothy, D.J. and Dowling, R.K. (eds) *Tourism in Destination Communities*. CAB International, Wallingford, UK, pp. 181–204.

Townsend, A.R. (1997) *Making a Living in Europe: Human Geographies of Economic Change*. Routledge, London.

Turner, L. and Ash, J. (1975) *The Golden Hordes: International Tourism and the Pleasure Periphery*. Constable, London.

Wanhill, S. (1997) Peripheral area tourism. *Progress in Tourism and Hospitality Research 3*, 44–70.

2 North–South Perspectives on Tourism, Regional Development and Peripheral Areas

C. Michael Hall

Department of Management, University of Canterbury, Christchurch, New Zealand

Introduction

It has now become something of a truism to say that tourism is a significant tool for regional development. Unfortunately, the fact that it is has been explicitly recognized for over 50 years (e.g. Ullman, 1954; Cornwall and Holcomb, 1966) is matched by the fact that tourism has also frequently failed to deliver what has been promised, for it has been around for just as long.

The sad reality is that tourism's role in regional development remains relatively poorly understood as it is often given only a cursory examination by those in regional planning and public policy analysis, while the tourism literature itself often fails to place tourism in its broader economic and social environment. It is not the purpose of this chapter to single-handedly 'solve' problems of tourism and regional development in peripheral areas; however, it does intend to focus on several key policy themes that need to be better understood if progress is to be made as to the contribution that tourism may be able to bring to peripheral areas.

Places are constantly undergoing change, but the rate of change and the nature of such change are not the same throughout the world. Moreover, the lessons of contemporary globalization reinforce the fact that places do not occur in isolation – they are connected through a variety of natural and human systems to other places (Harvey, 2000). However, the nature of such connections do change over time, with implications for all places within the global economic, political and environmental system The notions of change and the relativity of places are of significance as they highlight the role of time in assessing the peripherality of a place – what is peripheral at one time may not be at another – plus, they also stress the issue of 'peripheral to what?'

It is a well-established geographical principle that places possess different degrees of accessibility and that such accessibility is hierarchical in nature. The global system of cores and peripheries is therefore steadily changing in response to innovations in regulatory structures, governance, transport and communications technology and to shifts in demand and supply for various goods and services, as well as to the movement of people.

Yet, although such realities are accepted in an historical perspective they seem much more difficult to accept in policy terms, particularly when one lives in such a periphery that is losing services as a result of consolidation and centralization, so that those services supposedly become more efficient and effective in their delivery, or, if one is politically responsible for such an area. What may be economically rational is not necessarily politically rational, particularly when one adopts a philosophy that the 'public good' is not necessarily to be equated with 'economic good'.

This, therefore, means that governments at various levels will often seek to find means to 'support' peripheral regions. At one time this was often undertaken by the national state for strategic military and political reasons, particularly in Europe and the Americas, but also in northern Australia and the various outposts of empire as well. However, with the demise of the Cold War and the growth of new political philosophies that embrace a lessening of national and international regulatory structures, many peripheral areas are seeking other reasons to survive. Indeed, the question may indeed be asked from a regional public policy perspective: why should we support peripheral areas at all?

The first response to the above is that such places are important. They serve as both a significant unit of analysis as much as firms, individuals or the state and, perhaps importantly from our desire to understand processes of regional development, they help us understand the situation within which individuals, firms and institutions are actually embedded. Moreover, within contemporary globalization notions of 'place', 'region', 'locales' and the 'local' have assumed even greater significance through their capacity to be commodified, marketed and promoted in order to attract mobile investors, capital, people (of the right kind) and tourists. The rhetoric of place is therefore deeply embedded in processes of capital accumulation in which competitive places try to secure a development niche (Hudson, 2000, 2001).

However, places are also about people. Places are constituted by the web of social relations that exist within a specific locale. This is not to say that economic relations are unimportant, rather that they must be recognized in relation to the role of people and their social networks, a factor clearly recognized in economic development terms through concepts such as social capital and the emphasis given to the development of trust in business network development. And, from a public policy perspective, people – and their attachment to place – clearly matter.

There are undoubtedly many people who believe that there should be no intervention or central government support for peripheral regions and that they should be allowed to decline in a neo-Darwinian battle of the 'survival of the fittest'. The issue of the appropriateness of state support for peripheral areas will, in great part, depend on political and economic philosophies. However, a number of reasons can be offered that may serve as the basis, as justification, for intervention in peripheral areas from the perspective of the national interest:

- Significant social and environmental costs may arise as a result of migration out of peripheral areas.
- There are often substantially sunk costs in peripheral areas, particularly in terms of infrastructure, that would potentially be permanently lost if they were not supported.
- There are usually substantial stocks of natural and biophysical resources that need to be managed for a range of economic, social and environmental values.
- Support for peripheral areas may also serve as a means of intra- and inter-generational equity that serves to keep economic, environmental and social options open in the future.
- There is a significant human welfare value in maintaining support for peripheral areas.

Although such values may have appeal to some, the harsh realities are that economic and intellectual capital is becoming increasingly con-centrated in urban centres throughout most of the developed world and that the extent of economic transfers from the centres to the periphery is not as great as previously. Therefore, peripheral regions are seeking to find new ways of competing in the global race for mobile capital and people (Hall, 2005).

Peripherality and Regional Development

The notion of peripherality is an essentially contested concept, with the term being open to interpretation from spatial, economic, social and political perspectives. The concept is closely related to ideas of marginality, which is a condition of disadvantage that may arise from unfavourable environmental, cultural, social, economic and political factors.

Mehretu *et al.* (2000), in their review of the concept of marginality, noted that the literature on uneven development and social polarization treats the phenomenon of marginality as a generic concept of socio-economic disadvantage in which inequality and inequity are treated as synonymous. Arguably, similar perspectives can be traced in the literature on peripherality. At the scale of 'place', four different notions of marginality could be applied to peripheral regions: contingent, systematic, collateral and leveraged (see Table 2.1).

In the case of this particular paper, with respect to the role of tourism in peripheral areas, the issue of contingent marginality is clearly a major consideration because of the role that distance and accessibility play in the relative attractiveness of locations for tourism. However, in some jurisdictions it is apparent that other concepts of marginality will be more significant.

Table 2.1. Typology of marginality in relation to place (from Mehretu *et al.*, 2000).

Type of marginality	Description	Examples
Contingent	A condition that results from competititve inequality in which communities are placed at a disadvantage because of the dynamics of the market. Vulnerability to contingent marginality is generally based on disadvantages that develop because of social, cultural, locational and environmental limitations in dealing with the market. Reasons may be such factors as unattractive locations, distance decay, inadequate labour skills, cultural barriers to diffusion of innovations and lack of information about opportunities	(i) Poor location in terms of access to transport and communication networks – e.g. northern Canada (ii) Environmental constraints on farming combined with poor relative location to market – e.g. northern Scandinavia (iii) Behavioural constraints in dealing with information technology – e.g. Amish
Systematic	A condition that results from disadvantages that communities experience in a socially constructed system of inequitable relations within a hegemonic order that allows one set of individuals and communities to exercise undue power and control over another set. May be expressed through markers such as class, culture, race, ethnicity, age, immigration status and gender	(i) Often associated with colonial and neo-colonial regimes in the less developed world, e.g. South Africa during apartheid (ii) Tribal-/ethnic-based marginalization, e.g. Rwanda, Sudan
Collateral	A derivative form of disadvantage that depends on the existence of contingent and/ or systematic marginality. A condition experienced by communities who are marginalized – primarily on the basis of their social or geographic proximity to communities that experience either contingent or systematic marginality. They suffer marginality by 'contagion'	(i) Concerns about collateral marginality may discourage FDI[a] and tourist flows into peripheral regions in sub-Saharan Africa, South and Central Asia, the Middle East and Central and South America.
Leveraged	A derivative form of contingent and/or systematic disadvantage that communities experience when their bargaining position as labour and suppliers to advanced enterprises is weakened by transnational enterprises who possess the ability to be flexible and spatially mobile and hence create competitive bidding between places that seek their business. Vulnerability to leveraged marginality depends on location and standards of living.	(i) Relocation of production to less unionized areas or areas that show greater workforce flexibility and/or lower wage rates (ii) Relocation to areas that provide better concessions in terms of rents, taxes, repatriation of profits, infrastructure

[a] Foreign direct investment.

Vulnerabilities to contingent marginality are generally regarded as amenable to amelioration with strategies to benefit from the opportunities of the competitive market (e.g. Gustafson, 1994; Wiberg, 1994; Gibbs and Tanner, 1997; Kousis, 1998). Hence, places will often try to change their relative accessibility via development of new transport and communication infrastructure and/or networks as well as incentives to use such networks.

However, there are a range of innovative responses to peripherality that operate at different scales and in different sectors according to different policy measures and to the nature of the policy environment within which peripheral regions are located. It is also important to emphasize that in most of the developed world the responses of places to peripherality will often involve responses from the state (be it national or local), as well as the actions of firms and individuals. Yet even the actions of firms and individuals are often related to state strategies, notwithstanding that they are not explicitly connected through formal public–private partnerships, with many policy settings being developed and implemented with assumptions being made about the way that firms and individuals will behave.

The policy settings with respect to peripheral areas are usually established with several goals in mind, including the following:

- generating employment;
- generating economic development;
- maintaining or increasing the local population base;
- maintaining or increasing the local tax base;
- maintaining or increasing local services;
- diversifying the local economy;
- enhancing quality of life through extending leisure and cultural opportunities; and
- conserving natural resources.

However, it must be emphasized that these goals operate over various time horizons and policy goals may not always be mutually compatible. Moreover, actions in one part of government with respect to peripheral areas may often run counter to that of other areas.

For example, in a number of peripheral regions support has been cut for public transport. Simultaneously, policies in the tourism field are often initiated to encourage more free and independent travellers to visit peripheral regions. However, unless they have their own means of transport they are often unable to reach those businesses that have been given support to meet such a market. Nevertheless, it is within this context that tourism has now been placed consciously by government at various levels in the developed world as a response to the changed economies of peripheral regions.

Peripheral regions in the developed world tend to share a number of common characteristics (Hall and Boyd, 2005). They are marked by relatively simple economies that tend to be natural resource-based (extensive agriculture and grazing, timber, hydroelectricity); mineral extraction is often highly significant (though short-term) and energy is cheap – it has often been used to attract processing plants, particularly for pulp and paper, as well as smelting operations. The production of high-value products and services tends to be low. Peripheral regions also tend to have limited transport infrastructure as, almost by definition, they are located at the end of transport networks.

In recent years peripheral regions have also lost significant state services as well as suffering from out-migration. By virtue of their relative inaccessibility and low population base they are nevertheless usually blessed with high natural amenity values that are often perceived as a potential basis for nature-based tourism and wilderness conservation (Fig. 2.1). It is these high natural values, along with the potential to transform former industrial centres into heritage tourism attractions, which provide part of the reason for state and community interest in tourism. To put it crudely, if we can't economically farm it, cut it, mine it or dam it, it may as well be turned into a tourist attraction (and/or a national park).

The other major justification for state interest in tourism is that it is often seen as a low-skill industry with low-entry levels that can easily provide alternative employment for those who have lost jobs in other sectors. Unfortunately, such perspectives have also often been misplaced.

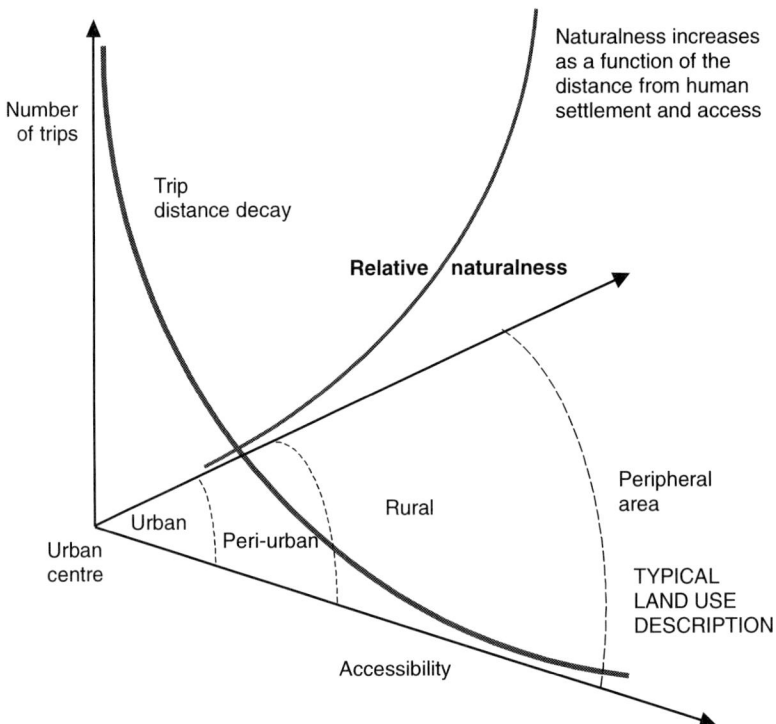

Fig. 2.1. Tourism in peripheral areas; relationship to accessibility, naturalness and trip distance decay from a major urban centre.

From Peripheral Places to Destinations

The periphery has long been an important concept in tourism studies. For example, Christaller (1963), in his highly influential account of tourism development, distinguished between pleasure travel – which he saw as primarily oriented towards peripheral areas – and business and education travel, which were regarded as primarily an urban tourism function. Christaller observed that tourism not only made use of peripheral lands that could not otherwise be used for agriculture or forestry but that: 'It is typical for places of tourism to be on the periphery ... during certain seasons peripheral places become destinations for traffic and commodity flows and become seasonal central points' (Christaller, 1963, p. 96).

Indeed, this notion was later taken up by Turner and Ash (1975) in one of the more influential textbooks on tourism of the 1970s, when they referred to the idea of a 'pleasure periphery' for international tourism (in light of the increased mobility of people in the developed world). However, the initial consideration of tourism peripherality by Christaller was grounded in economic location theory and the spatial relationships that exist between metropolitan and peripheral areas. By the time of Turner and Ash (1975), the notion had expanded to include a core-periphery model which not only reflected the spatial organization of human and economic activity but grounded the reasons for such structures in neo-colonial relationships that reflected the unequal distribution of power.

More recently, peripheral areas have become the subject of study in their own right, particularly in the European context, as a result of the use of tourism as a response to economic and political restructuring in such areas (Botteril et al., 1997; Buhalis, 1997; Hall, D., 2004; Hall, D. et al., 2005).

Peripheral areas are characterized by a number of interrelated features that impact the development of tourism, as well as other industry sectors:

1. Peripheral areas, by definition, are geographically remote from mass markets. This not only implies increased transportation costs to and from the core areas but may also increase communication costs with suppliers and the market as well (Hall, 2005).
2. Peripheral areas tend to lack effective political and economic control over major decisions affecting their well-being. They are particularly susceptible to the impacts of economic globalization and restructuring through the removal of tariffs and the development of free trade regimes (Jenkins et al., 1998). In addition, the political and economic decisions made by firms whose headquarters lie elsewhere and by political institutions in the national capital or at the supranational level may lead to a situation where 'organizations and individuals within the periphery often feel a sense of alienation, a feeling of governance from afar and a lack of control over their own destiny' (Botterill et al., 1997, p. 3).
3. Internal economic linkages tend to be weaker at the periphery than at the core, thereby potentially limiting the ability for achievement of high multiplier effects because of the substantial degree of importation of goods and services (Archer, 1989).

4. In contemporary society migration flows tend to be from the periphery to the core. This is a major issue for many peripheral and rural regions because of the impact that this can have not only on the absolute population of a given area but on its profile as well. For example, migration outflows tend to be younger people looking for improved employment and education opportunities for both themselves and/or their children. The loss of younger members of communities can then have flow-on affects in terms of school closures, thereby further reinforcing such a vicious cycle of out-migration. In addition, out-migration can also lead to a loss of intellectual and social capital.

However, for some peripheral areas new forms of in-migration may occur, with respect to retirement and second-home development, although this will tend to be with respect to older age groups. In some situations, although such developments may inject economic and human capital into peripheral areas, they may also place further strain on health and social services (Hall and Müller, 2004).

5. Botterill *et al.* (1997) have argued that peripheries tend to be characterized by a comparative lack of innovation as new products tend to be imported rather than developed locally. However, there has been little empirical examination of this issue.

6. Because of the economic difficulties experienced by peripheral regions the national and local state may play a relatively greater interventionist role than in core regions (Hall and Jenkins, 1998). This is illustrated through the establishment of local economic development agencies, the development of special grant schemes for peripheral areas as in the case of the European Union, and/or agricultural subsidy programmes (Jenkins *et al.*, 1998). However, again there is a need for closer examination of such assertions as state interventions occur with respect to both urban and regional uneven development, not just in the periphery.

7. Information flows within the periphery and from the periphery to the core are weaker than those from the core to the periphery (Botterill *et al.*, 1997). Such information flows may have implications for political and economic decision making undertaken in core regions as well as for the broader perceptions of place, given the difficulties that may exist in changing existing images of the periphery (Hall, 1997).

8. Peripheral regions often retain high aesthetic amenity values because of being relatively underdeveloped in relation to core areas. Such high natural values may not only serve as a basis for the development of nature-based tourism but may also be significant for other types of tourism and leisure developments, such as that associated with vacation homes (Hall and Müller, 2004; Hall and Boyd, 2005).

Destinations are locations of tourist consumption. More than that, destinations are commodified through the place competition process and the activities of the state, which actively encourages tourist consumption within its borders, invariably in cooperation with the private sector. Destinations are regulated and often highly commodified spaces that are an outcome of shifts in the nature of the consumption and production process that have been accompanied by broader changes in regulation, governance and state intervention, as well as being the focus on the region as an economic unit.

Destinations also have to be placed within the set of global relations of international capital and demand and supply chains (see Fig. 2.2). As Logan and Molotch (1987, pp. 43–44) note:

> A place is defined as much by its position in a particular organizational web – political, economic, and culture – as by its physical makeup and topographical configuration. Places are not 'discovered', as high school history texts suggest; people construct them as a practical activity.

Importantly, it must be recognized that the construction of place is a contested activity. Many such conflicts owe their origins to changing tastes and preferences amongst the ever-changing user populations of peripheral areas and to the shifting spatial influences of exogenous economic and political forces, as well as to consumption patterns (e.g. Fountain and Hall, 2002). They also have origins in the same conflicts between exchange value and use value noted above. For example, in Norway, as in a number of countries, conflict exists between the commercial interests of farmers and timber producers on the one side and the experience interests of hikers, campers and recreational visitors on the other (Larsen, 2001). They compete for utilization of the same areas for mutually exclusive activities.

The establishment of national parks is controversial for the same reason, as is the construction of dams and river piping for electricity generation. Larsen (2001) noted that, over time, there will be a growing number of such conflicts as society demands areas and resources for both commercial and experience production.

The question therefore arises in an era of place competition: do we need to attract tourists to survive and assist 'our place'? While the social and environmental impacts of tourism are undoubtedly important, the reality is that it is the perceived economic benefits of tourism – such as employment and regional development – that drive the desire to attract tourists to destination regions (Shaw and Williams, 2004). The policies of the national and local state are geared around the search for economic growth. It is extremely rare that a destination will put up a 'No Tourists' sign, even if some of the people who live there would like to at times.

The reality is that nearly everywhere on the planet believes that mobility – albeit in some places more regulated than others – is good for them, and if tourists come to your locale, you are told that it is good for you. Nevertheless, despite being told that it's good for you, tourism often fails to achieve the expectations of it in terms of economic development. Several reasons can be put forward for this phenomenon (Hall, 2005).

First, is the tendency by both government development agencies and many tourism researchers to fail to see tourism within the larger development context and policy environment. Most significantly, while recent government initiatives have sought to address peripheral area problems by way of local and/or regional tourism development

Global Production Networks

International tourism and place distribution and promotion channels, Transnational networks, customers

National Production Networks

Institutions, including national tourism and promotional agencies; firms; growth coalitions; customers

Strategic coupling process

Dependency and transformation

Regions/communities

Growth Coalitions: institutions, firms, business associations, networks, labour; Place marketing

Regulatory and institutional structure of the region/ community

Commodified space as regional asset

POTENTIAL OR ACTUAL CONTESTATION

Use value   Exchange value

Local residents   Members of growth coalition

Local firms

Connectivity and relations to other places

Regional/local space

Economic, human and natural capital, relative accessibility, capacity for innovation

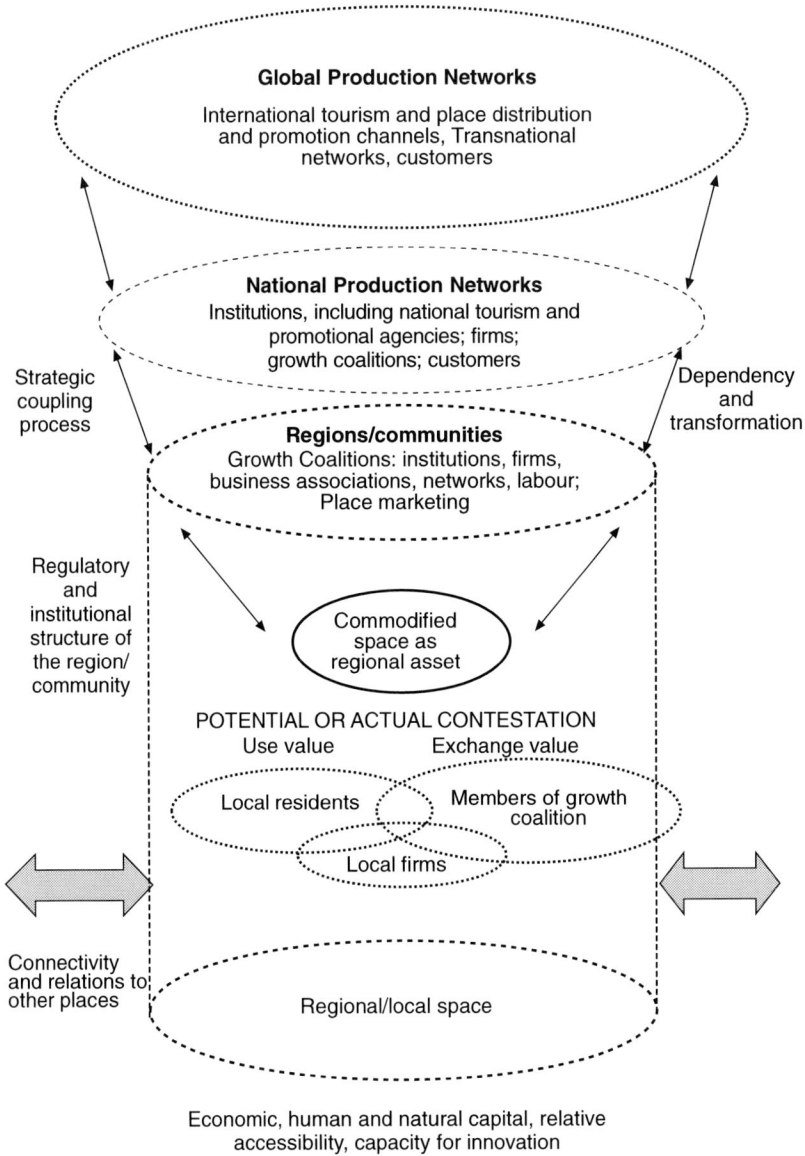

Fig. 2.2. A framework for analysing peripheral place commodification within regional and global production networks.

programmes, simultaneously, many governments have adopted restrictionist economic policies which have compounded the difficulties of peripheral areas in adjusting to economic and social restructuring (e.g. by means of centralization of financial, health and transport services). In such instances policy-makers also appear to be struggling with national *versus* local priorities (e.g. the restructuring and deregulation of agriculture and other industries *versus* subsidy provision), a point that also raises the issue of conflict in the values and objectives of the nation state as opposed to the local state (Jenkins *et al.*, 1998).

A second reason for the relative lack of success of tourism development in peripheral areas is that policy-makers are also confronted with inadequate (and sometimes misleading) knowledge of peripheral area issues, and therefore a restricted capacity to identify appropriate policy instruments to select, promote and support industries and other productive capacities as viable and sustainable alternatives. Indeed, in many peripheral areas there are a number of industries (e.g. aquaculture, horticulture, specialist timber and furniture manufacturing), as well as tourism, that appear to offer opportunities for diversification of the regional economic base, and for stemming the leakage and transfer of labour and capital (and thus community services and infrastructure) from peripheral economies to metropolitan areas.

Nevertheless, some forms of tourism development and a focus on specific markets may actually preclude other development alternatives that may be more extractive in nature. Tables 2.2 and 2.3 detail some of the macro- and microeconomic measures that the state may use to intervene in regional development policy.

A third reason for perceived policy failure is that the initial expectations for tourism as a means of regional development were too high. Arguably this is particularly the case with nature-based tourism which, almost by definition, tends to be very small-scale, often highly seasonal, and fails to attract the large numbers of tourists characterized by mass pleasure tourism (Hall and Boyd, 2005).

Indeed, policy realism often appears to be lacking with respect to nature-based tourism. Nevertheless, at a local scale such developments can still be extremely significant in allowing population and lifestyle maintenance and possibly even a small amount of growth, although not the dramatic improvements that many regions and their politicians seek;

Table 2.2. Macroeconomic policy measures with regional implications (from Armstrong and Taylor, 1985; Chisholm, 1990).

Category	Regional effect
Fiscal	
Automatic stabilizers	Progressive taxes and income support measures, especially unemployment benefits
Discretionary	Regional variation in taxes and central government expenditure (including infrastructure and procurement)
Monetary	Geographical variation in interest rates and credit control
Import controls and tariffs	Protect specific industries, which may be localized
Export controls and tariffs	Assist specific industries, which may be localized
Currency exchange rate	Affects the competitiveness of domestic production and exports relative to imports
Public investment	Differential regional impact

Table 2.3. Microeconomic regional policy measures (from Armstrong and Taylor, 1985; Chisholm, 1990).

Policies	Measures
Policies for reallocation of labour	
In situ reallocation	Occupational training and retraining
	Educational policies
	Journey-to-work subsidies
Spatial reallocation	Migration policies
	Housing assistance
	Employment information
	Improvements in efficiency of labour market
Policies for reallocation of capital	
Taxes and subsidies: inputs	Assistance with capital investment
	Wage subsidies
	Operational subsidies
	Research and development assistance, including new product and product differentiation
Taxes and subsidies: output	Export rebates
	Price subsidies
	Marketing and promotion assistance
Taxes and subsidies: technology	Research and development
	Innovation
	Communication access assistance
Improved efficiency of capital markets	Loan guarantees
	Export credit guarantees
	Venture capital
Administrative controls	Controls on location of investment
	Planning controls
	Reduced administrative controls

however, for some individuals and communities such small development are regarded as sufficient.

The fourth, and arguably most important, factor is that tourism and visitor growth is often seen as an end in itself, rather than posing the question of what is the best contribution that tourism can make to an area given other development opportunities in time and space, resource limitations, innovations, competition and long-term options. Such an approach means that the focus is placed, for example, on the relative yield of different types of visitors, the broader costs and benefits of tourism and the extent to which tourism is integrated within broader economic strategies, particularly with respect to inter-sectoral relations. Such a comment may be obvious, but the reality is that this is not the strategy that is usually adopted with respect to regional development in peripheral areas.

Strategies

At first glance the 'answer' to the problem of peripherality is improved access. Undoubtedly, access is a significant issue which is a focus of much place competition. Historically, places competed for railways in the 19th century, motorways in the 20th century and airports (and airlines) in the 21st. New transport connections have been vital for developing second homes and attracting visitors to a number of locations in Europe that have previously not been able to attract such development. However, it should also be noted that as accessibility to a peripheral location improves, not all of the effects will be positive (Hall, 2005).

Obviously, accessibility may not only increase the market area of any destination but, additionally, it can also mean that it becomes easier for the residents of an area to travel, thereby affecting the overall travel budget (inbound *versus* outbound). Just as critically, some firms in the destination will have the cost structures of their supply chain affected by new transport costs, while the changed accessibility patterns will probably lead to new market entrants developing in competition with existing tourism firms (Krugman, 1991). New entrants may have better linkages to tourism-generating regions and, therefore, have distinct competitive advantages over existing local firms.

Regional development through tourism is established not only by the stock of its human-made capital (e.g. transport and energy infrastructure, housing, production of goods) or of its natural capital (wilderness, natural resources, national parks, green space, high value species) but also by its human capital (professional skill, training, individual knowledge, education) and social capital (subjects' ability to coordinate their own actions and choices in view of common goals). Human and social capital therefore both become critical requirements for sustainable nature-based tourism development as they are not the consequence of development, but rather its prerequisite. A region is rich if it has human capital and social capital because these are the means by which other forms of capital are produced and specific aspects of the natural environment turned into tourism resources.

Nevertheless, the relative absence of human and social capital also becomes one of the greatest development challenges of many regions (Hall and Boyd, 2005). In the case of the development and transfer of intellectual capital in tourism, some prospects may exist with respect to the deliberate location of tourism education and research facilities in peripheral areas, but there is little empirical research in the value of such an approach.

Perhaps in many economically peripheral areas the creation of some jobs is better than no jobs at all but, given the substantial amounts of money that governments place in regional development schemes, a closer examination of the redistributive effects of tourism development within a region is warranted (Hall, 2005). For example, while tourism may be relatively labour intensive compared to some other industries, it is that labour input which is most vulnerable to minimization by owners in order to restrict costs, therefore creating the situation in which employment is often casual, contract, part-time, low paid and, often, heavily centred on women because of a gendered understanding of the nature of service.

In the situation in which tourism is promoted as an alternative to other economic activities, such as marginal agricultural or forestry operations or the mining industry, the ability of employees to transfer from those sectors to the tourism industry is somewhat limited unless there is both substantial investment in retraining schemes and dramatic shifts in traditional gender roles. Therefore, in many situations, the ability for tourism to provide an employment alternative is actually quite limited, particularly when the seasonal nature of tourism production and consumption is taken into account (Shaw and Williams, 2004).

One of the greatest difficulties in developing tourism in peripheral areas is in understanding the factors by which tourism firms locate successfully (see Table 2.4). If tourist firms are publicly owned then some of the commercial pressures that influence business location in market-optimal as opposed to social- or place-optimal conditions can be resisted, although there are still usually demands for returns to shareholders.

Decision-making with respect to business location in tourism has not been fully examined. However, there is substantial evidence to suggest that, for many smaller businesses, lifestyle and amenity considerations play an important factor in decision-making. This is not to suggest that profit is not important for such businesses; it is, yet their entrepreneurial goals are geared towards satisfying lifestyle goals as well as gaining sufficient return on investment. Indeed, their central business problem is actually in keeping the business sustainable within a particular size range (Hall and Rusher, 2004).

Furthermore, many tourism microbusinesses in peripheral areas are highly seasonal and constitute just one income stream for their owners and employees. Significantly, in many peripheral areas such operators have

Table 2.4. Relative importance of factors in explaining the distribution of the tourism industry.

Important	Moderately important	Not important
Accessibility	Firm networks	Access to research
road	Infrastructure	Industry organization
aviation/airports	Local linkages	Unionization
railway	Business services	Headquarters function
communication	Wage rates	Skilled labour
pedestrian	Government intervention	Destination promotion
Exchange rate	land and premises	
Amenity values	land prices and rents	
	loans, grants and tax reductions	
	planning	
	advice and assistance	
	support from various levels of government	

often returned to the region following a period of working in larger urban centres or overseas. This may represent a significant input of intellectual capital into peripheral areas, although the capacity of regions to adopt such knowledge will usually depend on the degree of institutional openness in communities. Indeed, such openness also becomes a significant factor with respect to the role that second homes may play in peripheral communities.

Where there is capacity in the housing market, as there usually is in peripheral as opposed to peri-urban or daytrip regions, second-home development represents significant opportunities not only for economic returns but also for the development of new social and economic networks that may have links to metropolitan areas. In some cases such second-home relationships are almost diasporic networks as they serve to link people back to their home region even though they spend the majority of their time elsewhere.

Networks and the associated concept of clusters are being seen as increasingly important to peripheral regions and network development, and collaboration has received substantial attention in recent years (e.g. Rosenfeld, 1997; Waits, 2000). In areas that may suffer from a relative lack of human capital and intellectual capital in particular, networks may offer substantial value in knowledge development as well as the more mundane values such as cooperative marketing (Hjalager, 2000; Hall, 2005).

Although one of the lessons of cluster development programmes around the world 'is that there is no precise, "right" (one size fits all) formula for developing industry clusters' (Blandy, 2000, p. 80), a number of factors have been recognized as significant in the development of clusters and the associated external economy which serves to reinforce the clustering process. These include:

- the life cycle stages of innovative clusters;
- government financing and policies;
- the skills of the region's human resources;
- the technological capabilities of the region's R&D activities;
- the quality of the region's physical, transport, information and communication infrastructure;
- the availability and expertise of capital financing in the region;
- the cost and quality of the region's tax and regulatory environment; and
- the appeal of the region's lifestyle to people that can provide world class resources and processes.

Hall (2001, 2002) identified several other factors that may be significant in cluster and network success:

- spatial separation – the existence of substantial spatial separation between elements of a cluster that inhibit communication;
- administrative separation – the existence of multiple public administrative agencies and units within a region;
- the existence of a 'champion' to promote the development of a network; and

- the existence of substantial spatial separation between elements of a cluster may lead to communication difficulties.

The further development of social capital through the creation of networks is extremely important in terms of its capacity to reduce the level of uncertainty for entrepreneurs in the creation of new businesses. Network-based relationships can provide entrepreneurs with critical information, knowledge and resources. Social and intellectual capital, including access to prior experience can therefore be used to maximize the scarce capital available to some small tourism businesses, as well as to better leverage relations between businesses in different sectors, particularly with respect to tourism and the agricultural sector (Hall, C.M., 2004).

In a number of peripheral areas high levels of social capital have assisted in the development of trusting relationships, which has allowed various network members to overcome issues of smallness and newness through their affiliation with prestigious and well-established businesses within the overall context not only of network membership but also of brand association. Such a strategy represents a classic model of resource acquisition by new small business ventures (Starr and MacMillan, 1990; McGee et al., 1995), the significance of which has been little recognized in studies of tourism networks and entrepreneurship and their contribution to peripheral area development (Hall, C.M., 2004).

Conclusions

Tourism and Regional Development: on the Periphery?

This chapter has outlined a number of significant issues with respect to the relationships between tourism, regional development and peripheral areas. It has highlighted several aspects of the problematic relationship between tourism and regional development, particularly with regard to expectations of tourism as a development mechanism, to the poor understanding of tourism and to the poor understanding of the policy environment within which tourism is operating.

Perhaps, most significantly, it has emphasized that tourism needs to be integrated with other potential development possibilities if it is to make a positive contribution to peripheral areas. Several development strategies were also discussed, including accessibility improvement, changes to the capital base and the development of clusters and networks. Fundamental to all of these is the need for realistic assessment of what tourism can bring to the periphery. Tourism is integrated into a wide range of contemporary local economic development strategies (see Table 2.5) (Imbroscio et al., 2003).

However, what is judged as being most important of all for innovation and development is the growth of the human and intellectual capital in peripheral regions. Tourism mobility and the nature of some tourism entrepreneurs may be able to assist here in some small way. Nevertheless,

Table 2.5. Typology of local economic development policies as a response to globalization.

Policy type	Characteristics
Locational	Lower production factor costs (land, labour, capital) relative to other places, i.e. tax incentives, subsidies, act to increase accessibility via improvements to transport and communication networks
World-class community	Developing innovative production capacities to gain a niche in global economy via public private partnerships, encouragement of research and development, attraction of entrepreneurs and skilled labour, and attracting foreign and domestic investment
Entrepreneurial mercantile	Building on local resources to encourage indigenous (often small) businesses to form and grow rapidly, i.e. by providing seed capital and technical marketing assistance
Human capital	Building the level of skills and work-related aptitudes held by the local workforce, i.e. through job training, retraining and the educational system; where appropriate, seeking to attract return migration
Place-based ownership	Enterprises are contolled in a more collective or community-oriented fashion in order to give enterprises a rootedness in place so as to act as a buffer against the capital hyper-mobility of globalization, i.e. community-owned corporations, non-profit corporations, municipal enterprises, consumer cooperatives, employee ownership and community development corporations

perhaps most pressing are a more effective and thorough understanding of the processes of tourism and regional development and the transfer of relevant knowledge and intellectual capital.

Arguably, the responsibility for the development of such understandings lies squarely at the feet of the tourism academy. Although there is much microlevel research on tourism sites there is little coherent understanding of what happens at a regional scale and how such processes interrelate with other regions. For the sake of improving the conditions of those who live in peripheral areas as well as for those who develop regional policy it is to be hoped that such imbalances will begin to be corrected in the not too distant future.

References

Archer, B. (1989) Tourism and island economies: impact analysis. In: Cooper, C. (ed.) *Progress in Tourism, Recreation and Hospitality Management Vol. 1.* Belhaven Press, London, pp. 124–134.

Armstrong, H. and Taylor, J. (1985) *Regional Economics and Policy.* Philip Allan, Oxford, UK.

Blandy, R. (2000) *Industry Clusters Program: A Review.* South Australian Business Vision 2010, Government of South Australia, Adelaide, Australia.

Botterill, D., Owen, R.E., Emanuel, L., Foster, N., Gale, T., Nelson, C. and Selby, M. (1997) Perceptions from the periphery: the experience of Wales. In: *Peripheral Area Tourism:*

International Tourism Research Conference, Bornholm, Sweden, 8–12 September 1997, Unit of Tourism Research at the Research Centre of Bornholm, Bornholm, Sweden.

Buhalis, D. (1997) Tourism in the Greek Islands: the issues of peripherality, competitiveness and development. In: *Peripheral Area Tourism: International Tourism Research Conference*, Bornholm, Sweden, 8–12 September 1997. Unit of Tourism Research at the Research Centre of Bornholm, Bornholm, Sweden.

Chisholm, M. (1990) *Regions in Recession and Resurgence*. Unwin Hyman, London.

Christaller, W. (1963) Some considerations of tourism location in Europe: the peripheral regions – underdeveloped countries – recreation areas. *Regional Science Association Papers* 12, 95–105.

Cornwall, G.W. and Holcomb, C.J. (1966) *Guidelines to the Planning, Developing, and Managing of Rural Recreation Enterprises*. Bulletin 301, Cooperative Extension Service, Virginia Polytechnic Institute, Blacksburg, Virginia.

Fountain, J. and Hall, C.M. (2002) The impact of lifestyle migration on rural communities: a case study of Akaroa, New Zealand. In: Hall, C.M. and Williams, A.M. (eds) *Tourism and Migration: New Relationships Between Production and Consumption*. Kluwer, Dordrecht, Netherlands, pp. 153–168.

Gibbs, D. and Tanner, K. (1997) Information and communication technologies and local economic development policies: the British case. *Regional Studies* 31, 765–774.

Gustafson, G. (1994) PIMA research: theoretical framework. In: Wiberg, U. (ed.) *Marginal Areas in Developed Countries*. CERUM, Umeå University, Umeå, Sweden, pp. 13–23.

Hall, C.M. (2001) The development of rural wine and food tourism networks: factors and issues. In: *New Directions in Managing Rural Tourism and Leisure: Local Impacts, Global Trends*, Scottish Agricultural College, Ayr, UK.

Hall, C.M. (2002) Local initiatives for local regional development: the role of food, wine and tourism. In: Arola, E., Kärkkäinen, J. and Siitari, M. (eds) *The 2nd Tourism Industry and Education Symposium, 'Tourism and Well-being'*, 16–18 May 2002, Jyväskylä, Finland, pp. 47–63.

Hall, C.M. (2004) Small firms and wine and food tourism in New Zealand: issues of collaboration, clusters and lifestyles. In: Thomas, R. (ed.) *Small Firms in Tourism: International Perspectives*. Elsevier, Amsterdam, pp. 167–181.

Hall, C.M. (2005) *Tourism: Rethinking the Social Science of Mobility*. Prentice-Hall, Harlow, UK.

Hall, C.M. and Boyd, S. (2005) *Tourism and Nature-based Tourism in Peripheral Areas: Development or Disaster*. Channel View Publications, Clevedon, UK.

Hall, C.M. and Jenkins, J. (1998) Rural tourism and recreation policy dimensions. In: Butler, R., Hall, C.M. and Jenkins, J. (eds) *Tourism and Recreation in Rural Areas*. John Wiley, Chichester, UK, pp. 19–42.

Hall, C.M. and Müller, D.K. (2004) *Tourism, Mobility and Second Homes: Between Elite Landscape and Common Ground*. Channel View Publications, Clevedon, UK.

Hall, C.M. and Rusher, K. (2004) Risky lifestyles? Entrepreneurial characteristics of the New Zealand bed and breakfast sector. In: Thomas, R. (ed.) *Small Firms in Tourism: International Perspectives*. Elsevier, Amsterdam, pp. 83–97.

Hall, D. (1997) Sustaining tourism development in the fragile Balkan periphery of Europe. In: *Peripheral Area Tourism: International Tourism Research Conference*, Bornholm, Sweden, 8–12 September 1997. Unit of Tourism Research at the Research Centre of Bornholm, Bornholm, Sweden.

Hall, D. (2004) *Tourism and Transition: Governance, Transformation and Development*. CAB International, Wallingford, UK.

Hall, D., Kirkpatrick, I. and Mitchell, M. (2005) *Rural Tourism and Sustainable Business*. Channel View Publications, Clevedon, UK.

Harvey, D. (2000) *Spaces of Hope*. University of California Press, Berkeley, California.

Hjalager, A.-M. (2000) Tourism destinations and the concept of industrial districts. *Tourism and Hospitality Research* 2 (3), 199–213.

Hudson, R. (2000) *Production, Places and the Environment: Changing Perspectives in Economic Geography.* Prentice Hall, Pearson Education, Harlow. UK.

Hudson, R. (2001) *Producing Places*, Guildford Press, New York.

Imbroscio, D.L., Williamson, T. and Alperovitz, G. (2003) Local policy responses to globalization: place-based ownership models of economic enterprise. *Policy Studies Journal* 31 (1), 31–52.

Jenkins, J., Hall, C.M. and Troughton, M. (1998) The restructuring of rural economies: rural tourism and recreation as a government response. In: Butler, R., Hall, C.M. and Jenkins, J. (eds) *Tourism and Recreation in Rural Areas.* John Wiley, Chichester, UK, pp. 43–68.

Kousis, M. (1998) Ecological marginalisation in rural areas: impacts, responses. *Sociologia Ruralis* 38, 86–110.

Krugman, P. (1991) *Geography and Trade.* Leuven University Press, Leuven, Belgium and MIT Press, Cambridge, UK.

Larsen, E.R. (2001) *Revealing Demand for Nature Experience Using Purchase Data of Equipment and Lodging.* Discussion Papers No. 305, Statistics Norway, Research Department, Oslo.

Logan, J.R. and Molotch, H.L. (1987) *Urban Fortunes: the Political Economy of Place.* University of California Press, Berkeley, California.

McGee, J.E., Dowling, M.J. and Megginson, W.L. (1995) Cooperative strategy and new venture performance: the role of business strategy and management experience. *Strategic Management Journal* 16, 565–580.

Mehretu, A., Pigozzi, B.W. and Sommers, L.M. (2000) Concepts in social and spatial marginality. *Geografiska Annaler* 82B (2), 89–101.

Rosenfeld, S.A. (1997) Bringing business clusters into the mainstream of economic development. *European Planning Studies* 5 (1), 3–23.

Shaw, G. and Williams, A.M. (2004) *Tourism and Tourism Spaces.* Sage, London.

Starr, J.A. and MacMillan, I.C. (1990) Resource cooptation and social contracting: Resource acquisition strategies for new ventures. *Strategic Management Journal* 11, 79–92.

Turner, L. and Ash, J. (1975) *The Golden Hordes: International Tourism and the Pleasure Periphery.* Constable, London.

Ullman, E.L. (1954) Amenities as a factor in regional growth. *Geographical Review* 54, 119–132.

Waits, M.J. (2000) The added value of the industry cluster approach to economic analysis, strategy development, and service delivery. *Economic Development Quarterly* 14, 35–50.

Wiberg, U. (1994) Swedish marginal regions and public sector transformation. In: Wiberg, U. (ed.) *Marginal Areas in Developed Countries.* CERUM, Umeå University, Umeå, Sweden, pp. 259–268.

Part II
Tourism and Regional Development Issues

3 Tourism in Peripheries: the Role of Tourism in Regional Development in Northern Finland

Jarkko Saarinen

Department of Geography, University of Oulu, Finland

Introduction

Tourism is widely called the world's largest and fastest growing industry, and there is no indication that its growth is likely to end. In Finland, too, especially in northern Finland, the tourism industry plays an important, growing and crucial role in the regional economies and in everyday life. Tourism and tourists provide more employment opportunities in Finnish Lapland, for example, than any other field of the economy that makes direct or indirect use of natural resources. In the year 2000 the estimated employment effect of tourism was approximately 4000 full-time jobs in Lapland (Saarinen, 2001).

The growing economic role of tourism has also made it a social and political issue, and tourism has been increasingly used as a medium for many socio-cultural and economic goals and changes at the regional and local levels. Change is a constant feature in tourism, but the destinations of tourism and local communities – including a sense of place and identity – are now being influenced and transformed much more rapidly and on a more non-local basis than before. As a result, this increasing spatial differentiation has also caused socio-economic insecurity, with growing competition for production and consumers between, and within, tourist destinations and related communities (Montanari and Williams, 1995).

In spite of the fact that tourism is an international and global activity and a process that has a wide variety of effects on different locations and spatial scales, tourism and its impacts are not entirely evenly distributed (Hall and Page, 1999, p. 1; Milne and Ateljevic, 2001). The core–periphery system plays an important role in the regional patterns of tourism. This system and related societal processes also make tourism a highly polarized and fragmented activity whose regional impacts are not easily evaluated. Especially in peripheries, the impacts and role of tourism in regional systems are challenging tasks to estimate and value.

This chapter discusses the role of tourism in regional development and provides an overview on the recent tourism development in northern Finland. The regional economy of tourism in northern Finland is approached by using municipality level data. The economic significance of tourism is approached at municipality level by utilizing the so-called Nordic Model. Finally, the role of tourism planning within regional development is discussed, with an emphasis on the stronger integration between the tourism industry and other local livelihoods, which has been noted as a crucial issue in the context of sustainable and locally beneficial tourism development (Inskeep, 1994, pp. 6, 31; Hall and Page, 1999, p. 253; Walpole and Goodwin, 2002).

There is an urgent need to reconsider the role of destination regions and communities in tourism planning and how the places and spaces of tourism could be integrated more closely with regional development in order to reduce the potential process of regionally and uneven social development. In the recent discussion on tourism and its contributions to well-being and the quality of life in destination regions, one perspective for development of the benefits of tourism on the regional scale has been the notion of social capital in destination communities and how to 'create' or maintain existing social capital for destination regions through tourism development.

According to Putnam (1995), social capital has a collective character, referring to the features of social systems such as networks, norms and trust that facilitate both actions and cooperation from mutual benefits. The implications of that in tourism planning and its relation to localities in northern Finland will be discussed at the end of this chapter.

Regional Economies of Tourism

Especially in peripheral and rural areas, tourism has been used as a tool for economic growth, welfare and promotion of jobs. In Finland and other Nordic countries the economic and political significance of tourism for regional development has increased considerably in recent years, to the extent that in some peripheral regions it has become a crucial policy issue. Tourism is commonly looked on as having favourable economic and social impacts, introducing new, external sources of income and opportunities for employment (Archer, 1982; Murphy, 1985; Roehl, 1998), and large amounts of public money are being spent nowadays on the development of tourism in peripheries. However, tourism may also have social, economic and environmental costs at the peripheral places and spaces of tourism (Butler, 1999), which are often disregarded in regional development discourses.

Generally, the regional economics of tourism consist of direct, indirect and derivative effects brought to bear on incomes, employment, earnings and tax revenues. Tourists spend money on services and thereby generate direct income and employment effects, whereupon the companies benefiting from this direct income in turn purchase services and goods from other companies and actors, giving rise to indirect income and employment effects in other parts of the economic structure (Archer, 1982).

The resulting transaction chains may vary greatly in length depending on the structure of the region and its business network, and may continue still further in the form of personal purchases made by those gaining employment directly or indirectly from the tourist industry, constituting derivative, or induced, effects. A certain proportion of the income from tourism will find its way out of the system, i.e. there will be 'leaks' in the regional economy (Murphy, 1985, pp. 77–103).

Since the development of tourism in a region will provide new business activity, tourism and the support given to it will tend to be viewed from the regional development perspective not merely as a matter of competing for consumers, but also as a forum competing for investors and attracting new capital. Meanwhile, the important issue for the public sector economy is to know what the effects of the investments and inputs are in relation to the income gained from tourism and what kind of development tourism empowers in the region. It should be noted that the desired goals of regional development are not necessarily the same as the tourism industry's outcomes are as a specific economic activity, which is, in many cases, based on non-locally set priorities, values, needs and goals (Saarinen, 2001; Shapley and Telfer, 2002).

Tourism can be a means of providing economic development in peripheral regions like northern Finland. In the context of core–periphery system, tourism can transfer wealth from the richer, urbanized areas to the poorer peripheral regions, which have often fallen below national averages on social and economic indicators related to well-being and quality of life (Telfer, 2002). Tourism can also act as a promoter of modernization in less developed regions but, in order to do so, the region as a whole should also benefit economically from tourism. Therefore, it is imperative to integrate tourism planning into regional and local development goals: to put tourism and its economic and other impacts in the perspective of larger regional socio-economic contexts (Simmons, 1994; Hall and Page, 1999, p. 253).

Recent Tourism Development in Northern Finland

An overview on the regional structure of tourism

In the past few years tourism has developed intensively in northern Finland. On the basis of the tourism statistics, however, the development has been more moderate than rapid. The reason for this seemingly slow growth, especially in Lapland, is the nature of the statistical system in tourism in Finland: only larger units, i.e. more than 10 rooms, cottages or caravan places per enterprise, are included in the statistical system. Thus, smaller accommodation capacity – private, semi-private (e.g. timeshare systems) or commercial cottages and second homes – and changes in their use – are mostly unknown as is their total number in terms of tourist beds.

Tourism statistics indicate a total of over 3.6 million overnight visits in northern Finland, and almost 1.8 million person/nights spent in tourist accommodation in Lapland during the year 2003 (Tourism Statistics, 2004). In Kainuu, and especially in north Ostrobothnia, the statistics imply a clear increase in the numbers of visitors in the late 1990s. In the past 5 years the growth has been steady: in north Ostrobothnia the number of tourists has increased by almost 300,000 overnight visits and in Kainuu by over 100,000.

On the municipality scale tourism development follows a larger trend. Statistics indicate a moderate growth, or relatively stable development (Table 3.1). The major tourist destinations in northern Finland are situated in the municipalities of Inari (Saariselkä, approximately 11,000 tourist beds), Kittilä (Levi, approximately 15,000), Kolari (Ylläs, approximately 10,000) and Kuusamo (Ruka, approximately 14,000). In addition to those, the cities of Oulu and Rovaniemi are also among the major tourist destinations.

In addition to 'statistical tourist beds' the growth of cottage and other second-home capacity has been very intensive during the 1990s. In almost half of the municipalities in northern Finland the cottage capacity has been increased by more than 30% during that period. There is also a clear growth of tourism in the numbers of passenger arrivals at the airports of northern Finland (e.g. Ivalo, Kittilä, Kuusamo and Rovaniemi). In Kittilä airport, for example, the passenger arrivals have increased by over 700% during the past 10 years. The increase in tourism regarding use of airports and flights, however, does not necessarily indicate the absolute growth of tourism, but rather the change in the tourism system.

The present mode of travelling in tourism and the current challenging work environment emphasizes shorter vacations. This trend has been concretized in northern Finland, where long weekend journeys using flights are nowadays a possible and commonly used form of vacation. The trend is evident both internationally and domestically. The Rovaniemi and Levi regions, for example, are increasingly being used for day or weekend trips

Table 3.1. Tourist overnight visits in selected municipalities in northern Finland, 1995–2003 (from Tourism Statistics 1996–2004).

	Year				
	1995	1997	1999	2001	2003
Enontekiö	99,045	93,193	92,910	94,688	111,916
Inari	279,829	304,365	306,037	298,090	312,696
Kittilä	192,455	190,222	200,491	223,673	253,001
Kolari	148,010	139,252	131,148	124,621	181,629
Kuusamo	224,227	195,781	222,969	270,383	289,768
Muonio	53,041	75,221	78,275	96,298	96,331
Oulu	302,633	337,865	358,845	402,524	427,525
Pelkosenniemi	46,261	43,902	52,560	50,777	54,349
Pudasjärvi	35,817	55,590	82,086	–	44,849
Rovaniemi	282,534	262,517	292,415	295,827	331,440
Salla	48,849	61,882	87,193	–	69,650
Sodankylä	67,458	57,565	79,816	99,041	102,504
Taivalkoski	33,215	29,285	29,125	–	–

by British tourists. During the winter season 2004–2005, both Rovaniemi and Kittilä (Levi) airports handled 200 international charter flights, which were mainly from the UK. In addition, the large numbers of privately owned second homes and cottages have increased the need for repeat weekend trips to the north by domestic tourists.

The majority of the tourists in northern Finland are domestic visitors on holiday. In 2003 the rate of domestic overnight visits in Lapland was approximately 60%, and the rate of leisure tourism was over 80% (Tourism Statistics, 1996–2004). The growing international tourism is concentrated on larger cities and some major resorts, such as Levi, Ruka and Saariselkä, and in certain tourism seasons such as Christmas. In general, the tourism trade in northern Finland is a highly seasonal one. In addition to Christmas, the peak season is spring (mid-February to the end of April), with activities such as Nordic skiing, slalom and snowmobiling. The other, but recently less important seasons, are summer (mid-June to August) and autumn (early and mid-September).

Tourism and its regional structure, including seasonality, are strongly embedded in the core–periphery systems on the international, national and regional level (Butler, 1994): the seasonality and regional differentiation are the intrinsic features of tourism. Most of the tourists live in the centres (cores) and other urban areas, while (some) peripheries and rural regions represent destination regions for vacation and pleasure purposes for urban inhabitants. Centres are also important destinations, however, for people from other urban areas, as well as for those living in peripheries. In this context, the difference between the centres and peripheries as tourist destinations is related to the general travel motivation: the centre attracts both business travellers and, increasingly, leisure-oriented tourists (Toivonen, 2002), while the periphery represents mainly a vacationscape for leisure-oriented tourists. Therefore, the structure of tourism in peripheries is strongly based on the holiday seasons and needs of urban dwellers.

Regional impacts of tourism on incomes and employment

In Finland, tourism income and employment figures are based on estimations at the national level and on specific surveys at the regional and local levels. Based on the national level estimations, the tourism industry provided over €1.5 billion from foreign tourism and about €5 billion from domestic tourism in 1998 (Valtioneuvoston periaatepäätös, 2001). The employment effect was approximately 98,000 jobs (full-time employment throughout the year).

The so-called Nordic Model (Vuoristo and Arajärvi, 1990) has been widely used at both the larger regional and local municipality levels in Finland. Table 3.2 shows direct income and employment figures from selected municipalities in northern Finland. Estimated in accordance with the Nordic Model, direct income from tourism in the municipality of Kuusamo in 1997 was almost €52 million and in Inari €47.5 million.

Table 3.2. Regional economics of tourism in selected municipalities in northern Finland (from Alakiuttu and Juntheikki, 1999; Hätälä and Kauppila, 1999; Saarinen and Kauppila, 2002).

Municipality	Direct tourism income[a] (euros)	Recreational and other services (%)	Direct employment effect[b] (total number of jobs)	Direct employment effect outside municipality[b] (total number of jobs (%))
Inari (1997)	47,522,600	6.8	421	95 (23)
Kuusamo (1997)	51,825,000	20.4	465	37 (8)
Pelkosenniemi (1999)	7,851,500	1.3	103	42 (41)
Pudasjärvi (1997)	16,114,200	16.6	93	6 (6)
Salla (1999)	5,355,700	–	79	7 (9)
Taivalkoski (1997)	6,533,800	20.4	47	1 (2)

[a] Figures include VAT and are rounded to the nearest 100 euros; [b] employment is calculated on a full-time, 12 months per year basis.

In the other municipalities where academic studies on the tourism economy have been conducted, the economic effects were much lower. There are no calculations on indirect or induced effects in all the municipalities but, in the case of Kuusamo, the indirect effects were €6.2 million and in Inari €2.4 million (Alakiuttu and Juntheikki, 1999; Hätälä and Kauppila, 1999). Thus, the calculations of direct income and employment effects shown in the table represent only a part of the total effects of tourism in the regional context and only a limited use of the Nordic model.

The rather significant contrast in the indirect effects as compared to the direct effects between the municipalities is based on the difference in the regions' economic structures and their relative location in a core–periphery system. Inari clearly represents a peripheral region with a narrow economic structure which leads local tourism businesses (the first-cycle companies) to purchase outwith the region.

The major differences between the direct economic effects on a regional scale are related to the income structure. For example, in the municipalities of Kuusamo and Inari, the majority of the income is based on hotels and restaurants (Kuusamo 38%; Inari 56%) and general retailing (Kuusamo 13%; Inari 22%) (Alakiuttu and Juntheikki, 1999; Hätälä and Kauppila, 1999). One important difference, which is closely related to the amount of employment and its local connections, lies in nature-based tourism or other outdoor tourism activities.

In the Nordic Model nature-based tourism as an activity is indicated mainly within the branch of the economy labelled 'recreation and other services'. These refer to activities such as snowmobiling, reindeer safaris and other products of experience economy. In Kuusamo about 20% of the direct income came from recreation and other services in 1997, while in Inari only 7% was derived from that source in the same year (Table 3.2).

The recreation services are much more employment-oriented than are restaurant and accommodation services or general retailing (Kauppila, 1999). There is also a need for local and often traditional knowledge of the business environment in nature-based tourism services, which encourages the tourism industry to employ local people. At the general level, this is evident in the municipality level employment figures. The tourist companies in the municipality of Kuusamo employed a total of 465 persons during the year 1997, of whom 428 were registered as residents there. Thus, only 8% of the employees were resident outwith the municipality. In Inari, the industry employed 95 persons (23%) from outwith the municipality, and in Pelkosenniemi the industry provided jobs for 42 persons from outwith the municipality, which can be regarded as quite a high ratio (41%).

Concluding Remarks: Integration on Tourism Planning and Regional Development

In general, the high seasonality and the quite low ratio of recreational and other services both indicate low local (municipality) employment, which emphasizes the sustainability issues and related problems in the relationship between the tourism industry, localities and other regional economies (Butler, 1994; Nyberg, 1995). According to Poon (1993, p. 205) 'the boundaries within the tourism industry and between this industry and others' are already becoming increasingly blurred. In addition, a paucity of such linkages has been noted as being one of the major factors limiting local benefits from tourism development (Walpole and Goodwin, 2000, p. 572).

Therefore, one fruitful perspective on the regionally and locally beneficial – and perhaps sustainable – use of local resources in tourism could be a development of links between the tourism industry and other livelihoods using the same resources and locations.

In order to develop deeper linkages between the tourism industry and traditional local and regional economies and production sectors, tourism should be placed in the regional socio-economic context. This represents an alternative approach to tourism-centred planning. The regional development and well-being and sustainable use of resources and environment are the areas in which tourism could and should contribute in synergy with other economies and functions.

Burns (1999) refers to these approaches by the terms 'tourism first' and 'development first'. In tourism first the development of the industry is in the focus of planning. In the development first approach a planning process, which (potentially) includes the tourism industry, is placed in the context of regional or national development needs.

This 'replacement' or 'decentralization' of tourism in a regional and local context and development is demonstrated in Fig. 3.1. The traditional scheme in tourism planning and development ideology is to place tourism in the centre, with potential links to other sectors (Burns, 1999, p. 330). However, by locating the region, its social and physical environment and

(a)   (b)

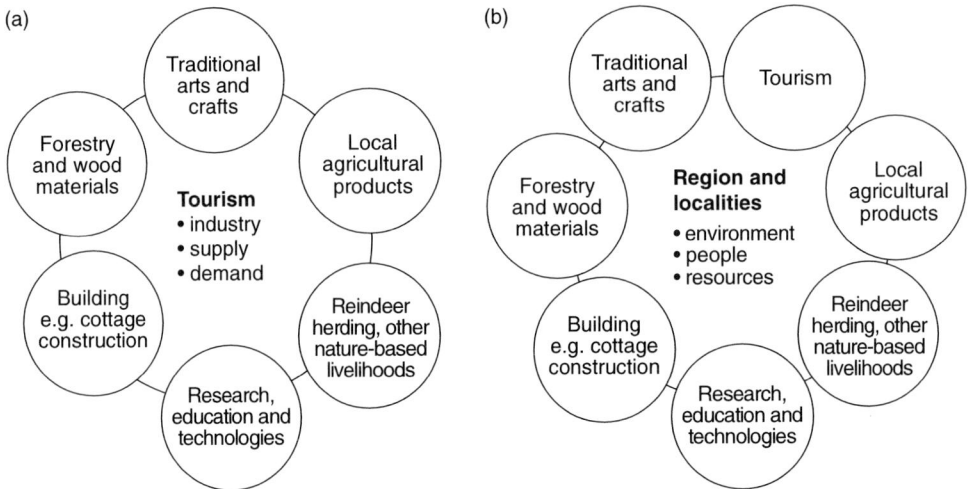

Fig. 3.1. Conventional tourism-centred (a) and development-centred (b) approaches in regional planning. In (a) other regional and local activities are integrated with the tourism industry and its development needs; in (b) tourism represents 'only' one potential activity among others in regional development.

local needs at the centre, the role of tourism as a potential tool – not as a goal – for regional and local development becomes highlighted.

The problematic placement of tourism in the centre is not only visible in conventional tourism planning: it is also evident in the basic logics of sustainable tourism development in regional settings. In order to exist, sustainable tourism requires tourism. Thus, tourism and the tourism industry are the starting points and conditions for the conceptual basis for sustainable tourism; the objective and driving force of sustainable tourism seems often to be to sustain tourism. Therefore, the question of whether there should be tourism or not is an irrelevant and impossible one in the context of sustainable tourism planning.

The decentralization of tourism with an emphasis on strong integration within a region and its development goals, economies and communities creates a basis for the networks, use and accumulation of social capital at the local level. At the same time, the negative impacts of seasonal changes of tourism to local tourism-based or other communities can be assumed to be lower than in the situation of 'monoculturing' tourism. By using, maintaining and even creating the social capital of a destination region, tourism could more effectively benefit both regional development and its own economic growth purposes.

The usage of regional and local social capital requires not only an increasing interaction and networking between the tourism industry and other sectors of the regional economy and communities, but also mutual benefits and agreement on practices, related norms and trust between the actors and organizations (Portes, 1998; Hall and Page, 1999, p. 253). The role of trust and related politics in tourism and land use decision processes in general is often a neglected subject in planning and academic studies, but in the context of social capital its role can be seen as being crucial. In a positive situation tourism development may encourage the growth, i.e. production and use of social capital, in host communities and organizations.

In the current situation and context in northern Finland and on the basis of the regional structure and employment effects of tourism, the present challenge is to link tourism development more strongly with the local and regional traditional knowledge, economies and production of goods and services. In both practice and theory, tourism is an interrelated system where demand and supply factors are highly dependent on each other. Therefore, from the perspective of the region and the industry, it is important that future tourism planning in northern Finland aims for integrated development of all the various parts and partners (stakeholders), including host regions, communities and infrastructure such as transportation system and public services.

The goal of such an integrated approach to tourism development is to analyse tourism from the regional scale down to individual projects in the industry within the region, and also regional development and planning perspectives (Hall, 2000). The integrated strategy of tourism planning may, for example, resolve potential conflicts over the use of certain resources and locations and assist in the distribution of the benefits and costs more equitably (Inskeep, 1994; Hall and Page, 1999, p. 253).

Without the emphasis of integrated approach, the current development of tourism in many parts of northern Finland is partly – or in some cases mainly – using regional resources solely for its own economic purposes. From the industry's perspective that may be logical, but it may also marginalize and perhaps present the local way of life for tourism purposes only, which has been evident in the relation between the industry and the Sami culture, for example (Saarinen, 2001, pp. 41–45, 75–78). This may lead, as Mitchell and Reid (2001, p. 114) have stated, to a situation where 'local people and their communities have become the objects of development but not the subjects'. In that particular case, tourism is not used as a vehicle but rather as an end in itself, without any active integration towards regional or local development goals.

This kind of tourism planning does not create trust in the regional context and it may discourage the accumulation of social capital and lead to the loss of traditions and knowledge by increasing regional insecurity and differentiation. The seasonality of tourism is already problematic not only for the industry itself, but its consequences in the long term for peripheral places can be dramatic. In tourism-driven communities and regions the seasonality of tourism will be reflected more strongly in everyday living, communities, employment and the changing scale of services, i.e. between the peak seasons there is no employment and no services. Therefore, the industry itself and regional tourism planning strategies should really aim for integrated strategies and local participation in tourism development and product design.

The current trend in tourism production, however, is not moving towards the greater use of local knowledge and traditional uses of resources: there are also other obstacles. For example, local attitudes may be negative towards service work, and there is a lack of capital in peripheral communities to permit entry to the industry as an outdoor recreation, heritage-based or other such entrepreneur. From the perspective of 'traditional' branches of the local economy in northern Finland, such as forestry or reindeer husbandry, tourism development can also represent a competing and conflicting land-use activity.

However, there are also positive trends and possibilities for integration of the growing and changing tourism planning with regional and local long-term well-being. One of the main trends is the increasing use of second homes and seasonal cottages: destinations are used increasingly as seasonal living places and for distant working, which supports local private and public services and provides employment opportunities outside the traditional tourism services (e.g. construction work, material production) and also outside the main tourism seasons (Hall and Müller, 2004).

Second homes may also provide opportunities for creation of new products and events for seasonal inhabitants and tourists to consume (Baum and Hagen, 1999; Williams and Hall, 2000). This second-home development phenomenon also generates significant new employment opportunities in the construction phase and afterwards in the support of those houses and other related infrastructure. However, the use of local resources, labour and knowledge should be actively stressed in the planning processes and integrated development strategies (Simmons, 1994; Müller, 2002).

The other positive trend in this context is the growing segment of nature-based tourism in northern Finland. For example, the average number of visits to national parks has approximately tripled during the 1990s in this region. Nature-based tourism and related activities are, in many cases, based on the usage of the skills and knowledge of people in traditional local economies. As noted, nature-based tourism and other recreation services are also work-intensive sectors that do not always require long or special training compared to that in many other fields of tourism service work. Therefore, nature-based tourism development in peripheries has the potential to provide employment opportunities and well-being to local inhabitants in tourism and related economic sectors such as reindeer herding, forestry and other nature-based careers.

References

Alakiuttu, K. and Juntheikki, R. (1999) Matkailun aluetaloudelliset vaikutukset Inarin kunnassa. *Nordia Tiedonantoja*, April 1999.

Archer, B.H. (1982) The value of multipliers and their policy implications. *Tourism Management* 3, 236–241.

Baum, T. and Hagen, L. (1999) Responses to seasonality: the experiences of peripheral destinations. *International Journal of Tourism Research* 1, 299–312.

Burns, P. (1999) Paradoxes in planning: tourism elitism or brutalism? *Annals of Tourism Research* 26, 329–348.

Butler, R. (1994) Seasonality in tourism: issues and problems. In: Seaton, A.V. (ed.) *Tourism: the State of Art*. John Wiley and Sons, Chichester, UK.

Butler, R. (1999) Sustainable tourism: a state-of-the-art review. *Tourism Geographies* 1, 7–25.

Hall, C.M. (2000) *Tourism Planning: Policies, Processes and Relationships*. Prentice Hall, Harlow, UK.

Hall, C.M. and Müller, D.K. (2004) *Tourism, Mobility and Second Homes: Between Elite Landscape and Common Ground*. Channel View Publications, Clevedon, UK.

Hall, C.M. and Page, S.J. (1999) *The Geography of Tourism: Environment, Place and Space*. Routledge, London and New York.

Hätälä, E. and Kauppila, P. (1999) Koillismaan seutukunnan matkailututkimus: matkailun aluetaloudelliset vaikutukset ja kehittämisen lähtökohdat. *Nordia Tiedonantoja* 2, 37–114.

Inskeep, E. (1994) *National and Regional Tourism Planning: Methodologies and Case Studies*. Routledge, London and New York.

Kauppila, P. (1999) Matkailu ja aluetalous: työkaluja matkailun taloudellisten vaikutusten arviointiin ja mittaamiseen. *Nordia Tiedonantoja* 2, 115–163.

Milne, S. and Ateljevic, I. (2001) Tourism, economic development and the global–local nexus: theory embracing complexity. *Tourism Geographies* 3, 369–393.

Mitchell, R.E. and Reid, D.G. (2001) Community integration: island tourism in Peru. *Annals of Tourism Research* 28, 113–139.

Montanari, A. and Williams, A.M. (1995) *European Tourism: Regions, Spaces and Restructuring*. John Wiley and Sons, Chichester, UK.

Müller, D.K. (2002) Second home ownership and sustainable development in northern Sweden. *Tourism and Hospitality Research* 3, 343–355.

Murphy, P. (1985) *Tourism: a Community Approach*. Methuen, London.

Nyberg, L. (1995) Scandinavia: tourism in Europe's northern periphery. In: Montanari, A. and Williams, A.M. (eds) *European Tourism: Regions, Spaces and Restructuring*. John Wiley and Sons, Chichester, UK, pp. 87–107.

Poon, A. (1993) *Tourism, Technology and Competitive Strategies*. CAB International, Wallingford, UK.

Portes, A. (1998) Social capital: its origins and applications in modern sociology. *Annual Review of Sociology* 24, 1–24.

Putnam, R.D. (1995) Bowling alone: America's declining social capital. *Journal of Democracy* 6, 65–78.

Roehl, W. (1998) The tourism production system: the logic of industrial classification. In: Ioannides, D. and Debbage, K.G. (eds) *The Economic Geography of the Tourism Industry*. Routledge, London, pp. 53–76.

Saarinen, J. (2001) The transformation of a tourist destination – theory and case studies on the production of local geographies in tourism in Finnish Lapland. *Nordia Geographical Publications* 30.

Saarinen, J. and Kauppila, P. (2002) Matkailun aluetaloudellisten vaikutusten arviointi: matkailun tulo- ja työllisyysvaikutukset Pelkosenniemellä. *Terra* 114, 25–36.

Shapley, R. and Telfer, D.J. (2002) *Tourism and Development: Concepts and Issues*. Channel View Publications, Clevedon, UK.

Simmons, D. (1994) Community participation in tourism planning. *Tourism Management* 15, 98–108.

Telfer, D.J. (2002) Tourism and regional development issues. In: Sharpley, R. and Telfer, D.J. (eds) *Tourism and Development: Concepts and Issues*. Channel View Publications, Clevedon, UK, pp. 112–148.

Toivonen, T. (2002) Regional development of Finnish tourism at the end of the 1990s: some considerations. *Tourism and Hospitality Research* 3, 331–342.

Tourism Statistics (1996–2004) SVT/*Transportation and Tourism* 2004: 11. Statistics Finland, Helsinki.

Valtioneuvoston periaatepäätös (2001) *Suomen matkailupoliittiset linjaukset. Valtioneuvoston periaatepäätös Suomen matkailupolitiikasta 13 June 2001.* Valtioneuvosto, Finland.

Vuoristo, K.-V. and Arajärvi, T. (1990) Methodological problems of studying local income and employment effects of tourism. *Fennia* 168, 153–177.

Walpole, M.J. and Goodwin, H. (2000) Local economic impacts of dragon tourism in Indonesia. *Annals of Tourism Research* 27, 559–576.

Williams, A.M. and Hall, C.M. (2000) Tourism and migration: new relationships between production and consumption. *Tourism Geographies* 2, 5–27.

4 Organizing Tourism Development in Peripheral Areas: the Case of the Subarctic Project in Northern Sweden

Malin Zillinger

ETOUR, Mid-Sweden University, Östersund, Sweden and Department of Social and Economic Geography, Umeå University, Sweden

Introduction

The title of the project presented in this chapter already indicates that peripheral areas are involved: with the mention of the word Subarctic, many people think of snow, ice, darkness and the northern lights, and this image is partly what the Subarctic project works with in trying to present the region to information providers within tourism from abroad, such as journalists or those working within television.

Due to an increase in journeys being undertaken, tourists are becoming more experienced and sophisticated, as regards both travel destinations and expectations on the chosen destination. This development, together with increasing competition in the marketplace, requires new and better approaches from the supply side. One possible way of reaching this goal is to increase cooperation in the tourist region. Targets of this work mode are, among others, to enhance the attractiveness of the region and to be able to offer a greater variety of attractions without conflicts between them. This novel approach can be particularly interesting and rewarding for peripheral tourist destinations, as the time and money spent by the tourist on travelling from one attraction to another are remarkably higher than in more densely populated areas.

The project Subarctic, which aims at a more intensive cooperation than has recently existed in the region, has been running for more than a year now. It is the intention of this chapter to evaluate this activity. Questions to be asked include: (i) what has been going on until now?; (ii) who has joined the project?; and (iii) is it successful enough to continue in existence after the first year of sponsorship from the county administrative board?

Tourism in Peripheral Areas

The Subarctic project has been conducted in Norrbotten, the northernmost county in Sweden (Fig. 4.1), since 2002. In 2001, about 250,000 people lived there, between the 65th and the 69th latitude – with a falling population. Seventy-two thousand of these residents lived in the capital of the county, Luleå, 930 km north of Stockholm. The county is in itself a peripheral area and, as indicated, the larger part of the population is concentrated in the capital and in other towns along the coast. Today, 1.7 million tourist overnight stays are registered per year. This figure corresponds to 4% of overnight stays in the whole of Sweden.

The study of tourism in rural and peripheral areas must be combined with the study of the socio-economic development in rural areas in general. Particularly since the 1950s, rural societies and economies have been restructured intensely. However, the lack of effortless accessibility and requirements of substantial wealth and time have rendered the number of visitors rather limited (Butler *et al.*, 1998, p. 4).

Changes have taken place due to both endogenous (e.g. population loss of younger and skilled people, policies supporting multiculturalism and exogenous (e.g. transnational corporations, technological innovations) forces (Jenkins *et al.*, 1998, p. 43)). Tourism development in the County of Norrbotten is, as in most other peripheral areas in developed countries, partly a result of a comprehensive range of other transformations. One example of this change in Norrbotten is in migration, either to central places within the county or to even larger towns in the middle and south of Sweden. Another example is the transformation in both political and

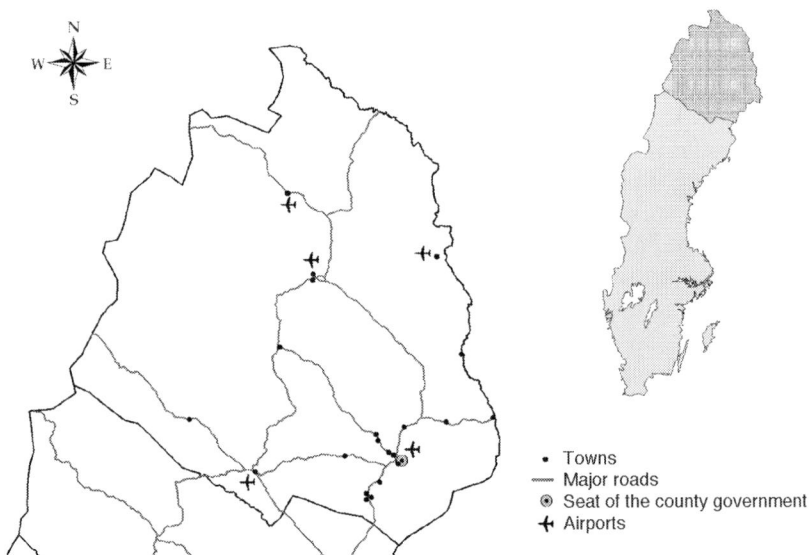

Fig. 4.1. County of Norrbotten, northern Sweden.

trading organizations at a global level, which has made parts of Norrbotten's industry obsolete.

One can think of, for example, the exploitation of iron ore in Kiruna, where the number of employees has been reduced drastically over several years. Other changes have directly reinforced tourism to this peripheral area, of which only two are mentioned here. Generally, the demand for recreation has risen, and the accessibility to peripheral areas has improved. Today, there are five airports with regular traffic in Norrbotten, which makes it easier for tourists to reach the area within an acceptable amount of time (Länsstyrelsen i Norrbottens län, 2002b, p. 39).

Economic, political, social and technological developments have in many cases led to the restructuring of peripheral areas. Instead of focusing on the primary economy, tourism is often understood as part of a natural procedure towards a service economy (Hudson and Townsend, 1992, p. 64) and is today considered an instrument for economic development. Due to links to developments at both global and local levels, many rural and peripheral areas are becoming increasingly urban-like. Within this progress, tourism has emerged as a central means by which rural areas are modified in an economic, social and political way.

None the less, not every region is suitably located or outstandingly attractive to make tourism and recreation a substitute for the decline of industry. According to Jenkins, the periphery characterizes a district in which a long-established rural economy has failed and restructuring in economically feasible terms has not been viable. It should not be forgotten that peripheral areas frequently remain regions that require transfers of public funds and where alternatives in rural development have not been successful (Jenkins *et al.*, 1998, p. 43).

Governments that control and serve rural and peripheral areas have realized the economic benefits that can accrue from tourism development. According to Sorensen, governments have two responsibilities, which are interrelated and inseparable. First, they have a backward-looking and caring function. This implies taking responsibility for the well-being of the weakest members of society who are unable to adapt to the changes taking place. Secondly, governments have a forward-looking role. This involves assistance in economic and social change in order to reflect the emerging order (Sorensen, 1993, p. 278).

A change has also appeared at other levels: during the 1990s, tourism became part of EU planning and policies. Since Sweden joined the EU in 1995, the County of Norrbotten has received economic support from the EU structural funds, which were established in order to lessen both economic and social differences between regions. Within the period 2001–2006, the EU has deposited 3.3 billion Swedish kronor (SEK) for the programme 'Objective 1 Norrbotten and Västerbotten' (the county south of Norrbotten). As the different parts of Objective 1 are co-financed by public and private funds, the projects in total comprise 9 billion SEK. Further support is provided by Objective 3 (competence development) and Interreg IIIA North (cooperation across the borders) (Länsstyrelsen i Norrbottens län, 2002b, pp. 18–19).

According to SOU (1990), the tourism industry is crucial for survival in large parts of peripheral Sweden, and especially for the County of Norrbotten. Since the 1960s, the employment rate in the primary sector has been decreasing rapidly in Norrbotten, with the loss in this sector being counteracted by the employment of people in the public sector. As this strategy is no longer possible due to financial bottlenecks in the municipal and national economies, tourism is therefore seen as a possibility for compensating the weakened employment rate with vacant jobs in long-term, profitable tourist projects. To be able to achieve this goal, however, a concentration of capital expenditures is needed (SOU, 1990, pp. 13, 54).

But what are the touristic advantages and disadvantages of Norrbotten? What can the county offer from a touristic view? It is firstly the nature, scenery and environment that attract tourists to the region (cf. Table 4.1). These factors can be said to be recognized as the most important competitive advantages, especially considering that many regions in Europe must deal with increasing environmental problems. This fact has led to more people appreciating unharmed and undisturbed nature. Of course, the midnight sun is a great benefit to the region, not least because other regions with midnight sun cannot, at the same time, provide the same infrastructure. Another advantage is the county's central location in the Nordic arctic and subarctic areas, which in itself is a great attraction. Many tourists combine a journey to Norrbotten with a trip to the North Cape in Norway or to ski resorts in Finland (SOU, 1990, p. 64).

There are two characteristics that can be seen in both a positive and negative way: climate and infrastructure. Especially in the winter, the climate prevents a number of tourists from visiting the region. On the other hand, the cold, the snow and the winter contribute to the exotic image , and this is what tourism organizations in Norrbotten work with when trying to attract visitors from other parts of Europe. Although the infrastructure in the region is not as well developed as in other, more densely settled areas in Sweden and elsewhere, it is more developed than in other regions offering similar natural resources.

Still, infrastructure in Norrbotten is a problem. The huge distances, both within the region and to important markets in Sweden and Europe, place heavy demands on the transport system. Two obstacles arise from this fact. First, travel costs become a problem. Most tourists want to visit Norrbotten with their own car. This means that many must stop over on the way to their destination. Another solution is to fly, but this means that travel costs will increase even more, especially for families. Another alternative, namely using a car train from the middle of Sweden, is often impossible due to the trains' capacity being too small.

Secondly, it can generally be said that greater distances from a tourist's home to the destination lead to higher demands on unique experiences and attractions. Tourist organizations must offer attractions of a high quality in order to make tourists feel that the long journey will be worthwhile. In order to improve the situation, almost 1.8 billion SEK will be spent on infrastructure during the period 1998–2007. Compared to the expenditure in this field in the whole of Sweden, this accounts for only 1% of the total expenditure. With this investment accessibility, travel time and negative influences on the environment are expected to be reduced (Länsstyrelsen i Norrbottens Län, 1998, p. 5).

In relation to the long distances, it can be viewed as negative that while Norrbotten indeed offers great nature, there are few other extraordinary attractions or special objects of touristic interest. Another problem is that potential visitors simply know too little about Norrbotten. This is an even larger dilemma abroad. Sweden in general and Norrbotten in particular are hardly perceived as tourist destinations in Europe. When different people are asked what they think of Norrbotten, they say that there are too many mosquitoes, that it is too cold or that there are other regions they would rather visit than this peripheral region in the north of Sweden.

The last disadvantage mentioned here is the lack of daylight in the region during the winter. Tourists simply cannot perform as many activities as they might want to – not to mention the cold, which possibly keeps them from many outdoor activities (SOU, 1990, p. 65). Table 4.1 gives an overview of the pros and cons presented in this text.

The most urgent obstacles to tourism development in Norrbotten can thus be identified as follows: First, it is the large distances to areas with high population density, both within Sweden and on the European continent. The current infrastructural and institutional prerequisites are another point. Thirdly, to date, efforts have been rather uncoordinated. Tourism development requires a strategic point of view with both short-term and long-term goals, and thus far there has been a lack of a coordinated view.

In 2001, there were 1.7 million overnight stays in hotels, holiday villages, youth hostels and campsites in Norrbotten. This figure corresponds to 4% of overnight stays in the whole of Sweden. Seventy-eight per cent of the tourists come from Sweden, 12% from the EU and 18% from the remainder of Europe – a large number of Norwegian tourists are responsible for this latter figure. The corresponding figures for the whole of Sweden are as follows: 68% of all tourists come from Sweden, 12% from the

Table 4.1. Tourism advantages and disadvantages in the County of Norrbotten, northern Sweden.

Positive features	Features both positive and negative	Negative features
Nature	Climate	Distance to population centres
Scenery	Infrastructure	Travel costs
Environment		Few extraordinary attractions
Midnight sun		Tourists' lack of knowledge about the region
Light during the summer		Darkness during the winter

EU and 7% from the remainder of Europe. Important countries of origin for the County of Norrbotten are Germany (17%), Finland (6.6%) and Denmark (3.5%). Fifty-five per cent of all overnight tourists travel here due to work (Länsstyrelsen i Norrbottens län, 2002b, p. 32).

Until around 25 years ago, activities conducted by tourists in peripheral areas were relaxing, traditional and passive. Activities like walking, picnicking or horseback riding were preferred. These features have changed since the 1970s. Today, activities are characterized as individual, active, modern and fast. Favoured leisure pursuits include survival games, parasailing, in general: adventure tourism.

Naturally, this development has strongly influenced tourism facilities and establishments. It is not only structural changes that have occurred, however, as mentioned above, but also a greater range of uses. Thus, the conflicts that have aroused cannot be related solely to those between recreation/tourist uses and other forms of land use. They also concern conflicts between various forms of tourism, such as motorized and non-motorized tourists staying in the same area (Butler *et al.*, 1998, p. 9).

As has been shown in this chapter, the countryside not only provides tranquillity, a beautiful landscape and passive enjoyment, but also increasing opportunities to discover a previously ignored heritage, and to participate in cultural and active tourism (Dewailly, 1998, p. 123). In Norrbotten, there are a great number of purpose-built facilities, including Sami centres or the ice hotel, which will be mentioned later. Special attention has been given to a varied and event-filled programme for tourists. This also entails visitors seldom staying at one place for a longer period of time, with the possibility instead to travel around the county in a relatively short period of time and thus to experience manifold attractions in both sparsely and densely populated areas in the mountains and at the coast. In this way, the region has adapted to current tourism trends.

In harmony with this touristic supply, the image of Norrbotten that is disseminated in Sweden and abroad is multifaceted. For people living in densely populated areas in Europe, a peripheral area is a place both spatially and temporally – but also psychologically – distanced from everyday life. This view is usually enhanced by distance (Hopkins, 1998, p. 139) – a quality that makes the County of Norrbotten even more exotic. The marketing of this county both promotes and emphasizes urban–rural differences by suggesting images that evoke and enlarge images of rural areas. The way Norrbotten markets itself to those who have never been to the region is of great importance. Through the dissemination of impressions, mental images are transferred, and form the basis for an evaluation and selection of the individual's choice of destination (Butler and Hall, 1998).

None the less, the disseminated image of the region must be supported by cultural authenticity. While both identity and authenticity can be promoted by duplications, this will not satisfy everyone – one could consider reactions by purists or ethnologists here. However, these tactics will probably satisfy local desire for education as well as encourage tourist visits (Dewailly, 1998, p. 128).

The Subarctic Network in Northern Sweden

Subarctic, an EU-funded 3-year project, started in the County of Norrbotten in July 2002. The aim was to increase the number of foreign tourists, with a vision of positioning the County of Norrbotten as a strong, attractive and safe destination within global competition. The project is based on a cooperation between Scandinavian Airlines, the Swedish Tourism Authority, different incoming operators, tourist entrepreneurs and the county administrative board in Norrbotten. Within the network there is a board of directors, which includes the project leader and representatives from the tourist administrative board, the county administration board, Scandinavian Airlines and the incoming operator Norrbotten/Lappland (see Fig. 4.2).

The expenditure was calculated at 7.3 million SEK during the period between July 2002 and December 2003. In this context, the county administrative board has granted support of approximately 3.1 million SEK (Länsstyrelsen i Norrbottens län, 2002a).

In the investigation of the Subarctic project, a qualitative approach was chosen. As a first step, a large part of the analysis consisted of determining how different individuals with distinct backgrounds would evaluate the project, something that cannot be quantitatively measured. Two modes of procedures were chosen for the exploration. First, persons who had already been made familiar with the project were interviewed. This involved both entrepreneurs and members of the board of directors of Subarctic, as well as officials on the county administrative board. The interviews were carried out in Luleå in April 2003.

Additionally, a guided tour for the mentioned information providers was arranged, and conducted with German broadcast producers. The

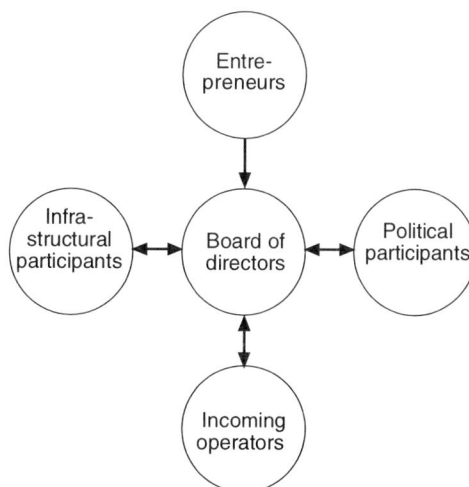

Fig. 4.2. The structure of the Subarctic network; the arrows indicate the direction of information flows.

journey took place in February 2003. For 3 days, the group travelled from Luleå to Arvidsjaur and Arjeplog. Thus, there was a possibility not only to observe the entire journey, but also to interview the German information providers about their opinions on the project. Magazine articles about guided tours conducted by Subarctic were also analysed. In future, a more quantitative approach will be adopted, comparing figures on foreign arrivals over the years before and after the project.

The project can be seen as a reaction to the great success of northern Finland in international tourism. The current problem with tourism in northern Sweden is that the number of tourists in both lodging and activity companies is too low to be profitable. In Finland, an attractive destination for international travellers has been created, with places like Rovaniemi, Kemi and Levi. The focus is on winter tourism and a great product variation, from skiing to scooter safaris and adventure trips, is offered.

Due to Finnish Lappland having begun to be over-exploited, tourist entrepreneurs in the County of Norrbotten jointly want to create a destination that benefits from the attention northern Finland has attracted and from the profits from an expected spill-over. It is most important to the Swedish entrepreneurs that they present the region as a genuine destination, where the products are authentic and nature has remained untouched. Building tourist regions, where attractions have been created and built for tourists only, will be avoided.

However, there is another advantage of intensifying tourism, as has been done in Finland. More than one in three tourists who visited Norrbotten in 2001 declared that they had also visited the north of Norway or Finland. The tendency to combine destinations over the nations' borders increases with the distance the tourists have travelled to Norrbotten. Regarding tourists from Sweden, 44% of those who came from the south of the country combined two or more countries, while this figure was one in three regarding tourists from northern Sweden (Länsstyrelsen i Norrbottens län, 2002b, p. 37).

For travellers from the European continent, such studies have not yet been carried out, but one can assume that the tendency is even stronger in this case, and not simply because one strong attraction in the northern hemisphere – namely the North Cape – lies outside the Swedish border.

The Subarctic project fits well with the current intentions of the Swedish Tourism Authority. As described in the 'Innovation Programme', the Swedish State has invested 40.5 million SEK in order to increase the innovativeness of the Swedish tourism economy, as well as to promote research on the topic. The predominant aim of the programme is to stimulate growth in the tourism industry. In order to be able to achieve this goal, the Swedish Tourism Authority is of the opinion that the tourism industry, together with both the entire industrial sector and public participants, has to follow a conscious and mutual strategy (Turistdelegationen, 2003, pp. 1, 5).

For a long time, governmental actions in regional policy were almost exclusively aimed at physical investments, e.g. roads or new accommodation.

Other sorts of expenditure were fairly rare (SOU 1990, p. 82). The realization of the Subarctic project is special, because it is an investment in a project that seeks to create a basis for international tourism in Norrbotten. No money is spent on objects that can actually be seen or touched. Instead, the aim is to address new target groups and to establish both Sweden in general and Norrbotten in particular in the mental maps of tourists.

The goal of becoming a strong and attractive destination is to be achieved through active marketing and intensified cooperation. Marketing activities have targeted the European market, especially France, Italy and Germany. One of these activities involves offering guided tours to foreign media. This method aims at informing possible visitors about the attractions Norrbotten has to offer. In many cases, the intent is to illustrate where Norrbotten is located on the Swedish and European map and to demonstrate that there actually exists a place in Europe which has all these sights and natural resources.

To contact foreign media, initial steps have been taken by making use of contacts with information providers in the applicable countries. The board of directors has travelled to, e.g. France and Italy and presented the County of Norrbotten. In this area, the Subarctic project has gained much advantage in the circle of contacts that the project leadership has established. Two members of the Subarctic project group have long experience within international marketing; knowledge about which information providers should focus on is naturally a substantial and decisive factor in the success of the project.

The attraction and character of a tourist destination usually demand a multitude of complementing suppliers. Thus, dependencies usually exist between the providers responsible for the range of supply (Elbe, 2002, p. 28). It is not only the suppliers at the tourist destination itself who are dependent on each other, however; the state of dependence is also noticeable at other levels (Fig. 4.3).

As seen in Fig. 4.3, the quality of the tourist's experience depends not only on the core service, i.e. the (main) attractions, but also on both the quality and competence of supporting and assisting services. Since the participants are dependent on each other, 'good performance by one can boost the success of the others' (Porter, 1998, p. 77).

As mentioned, the collaboration in the Subarctic project is based on working with both national and international partners. In the County of Norrbotten, the cooperation is based on local counterparts. The companies work as complements, with similar requirements and possibilities. The final goal is to gain a greater profit through an intensified cooperation than if each of the entrepreneurs had worked alone. What the entrepreneurs have in common is that all activities are to be commercial and that they focus on customers' benefits and accessibility as well as on competent and motivated partners. Within the project, common working forms are established to secure cooperation on a long-term basis (newsletters and interviews with the county administrative board in Norrbotten and with Subarctic's board of directors in September/October 2002).

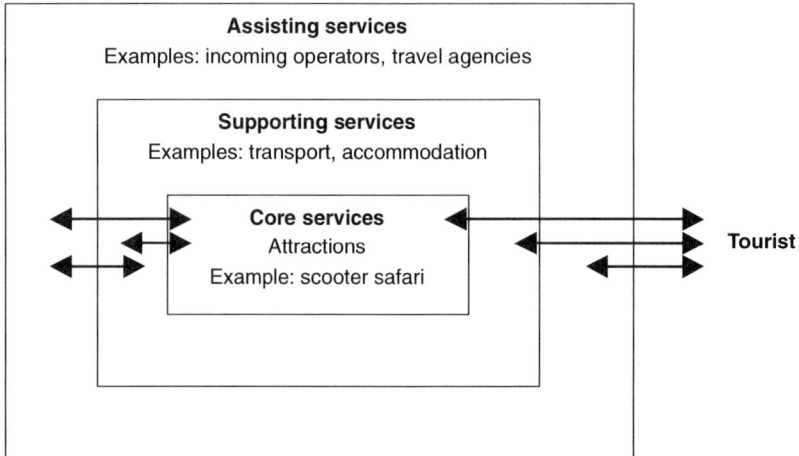

Fig. 4.3. The structure of dependence within tourism; the arrows indicate states of dependence between the various services (remodelled from Elbe, 2002).

Subarctic can be seen as a project that tries to increase tourism income by addressing not only leisure tourists, but also the population in general. The project focuses partly on the MICE segment (meetings, incentives, conferences/congresses and events/exhibitions). It is clear that holidays for foreign tourists in northern Sweden are fairly expensive, thus a great number of tourists can hardly be expected.

Of course, it is impossible to create new markets within a short period of time. Especially in the case of business trips, this sector can be further improved with a long-term construction of economic activities that promote this type of travelling. Thus, efforts must not aim only at tourist goals, but should also be targeted at a general economic growth. Developing a new destination for international tourism is a long process, requiring both endurance over many years and a high level of investment.

Tourism does not differ from other export trade. In both cases a determined, systematic and long-term treatment of the foreign market is needed, in addition to a good product (SOU, 1990, pp. 70, 75). In the Norrbotten case, this was made possible by a large amount of public spending. An important tactic within Subarctic is being proactive from the beginning. Instead of waiting, analysing and evaluating, swift action is preferred. The decision making is unbureaucratic, which strengthens the project. One risk associated with this procedure, however, is that some participants feel disregarded.

A great number of entrepreneurs from different backgrounds are included in the project, for example hotel owners, leaders of activity companies and employees at tourist companies. This results in many different experiences, viewpoints and valuations being consolidated within the network, which promotes many business opportunities. Monetary profit is a strong reason for the cooperation, but within the group it is not foremost money, but instead personal effort, that is considered essential.

A great monetary effort cannot be made by many of the participants, as some have only recently become entrepreneurs and are not able to afford such an input. Instead, they contribute to the prosperity of the project by welcoming media to their hotels or by including these groups in their tours through the County of Norrbotten. For these measures, they receive a designated amount of money from the Subarctic management. The amount of this support is rather small, but it helps the entrepreneurs limit their deficit in this early period of their long-term investment. To provide an example, a restaurant owner receives 150 SEK per guest and dinner. This amount does not cover the actual expenditure, but is considered a great help by the entrepreneurs.

In Norrbotten, with so many individual operators, it has been difficult to coordinate efforts for a long period of time. In addition to this, the separate operators often had – and still have – different ideas on and goals for activities and enterprises (SOU, 1990, pp. 38, 45). The founder of Subarctic noted over a longer period of time that foreign tourists who visit Norrbotten actually prefer a varied stay at their destination. Visitors want to discover the sea, the forest and the Sami culture as well as different accommodation and food, ranging from top of the range to genuine local regional standards.

This desire could not be granted, as there was no collaboration between the different tourism operators. The plan to accumulate knowledge is innovative in the county. Until last year, individual operators worked almost exclusively alone, and as was discovered in the interviews conducted in April 2003, most entrepreneurs in Norrbotten are now satisfied with the current development that binds them more closely together.

Networks are characterized by a high degree of creativity. Partners with different backgrounds work together and thereby diverse ideas and conceptions are combined into new information. In the analysis of the Subarctic network it was found that the foundation of the network itself is advanced in comparison to tourism organizations on a regional as well as on a national scale. It is of great importance that the individual entrepreneurs work together to serve the tourist with a positive total impression. The entire experience must be of high quality, as a tourist estimates general and overall impressions. It is also of substantial importance that the collected supply of activities, experiences, sights, etc. is large and inviting enough to attract a sufficiently high number of tourists every year.

It was also found, however, that there is only a small amount of creativity within Subarctic. A variety of ideas naturally exists within the project but, as it would seem, these are in no way combined. The project leader depends on the international contacts of the incoming operators. These incoming operators (two persons) are part of the board of directors. Thus far, this cooperation has worked well. However, instead of passing the knowledge on to the entrepreneurs or discussing current trends with them, the project leader makes plans partly on his own and partly with the board of directors – naturally, only his own thoughts, assessments and estimations are taken into account.

Together with the incoming operators he arranges where and when foreign media will be invited. A few weeks before these groups arrive, he informs the entrepreneurs. The entrepreneurs are creative, but this creativity remains mostly within their own respective companies. With little knowledge of the (international) market, they make plans as best they can. This problem – that knowledge and creativity exist but are not combined – should be solved within the Subarctic network.

As has been demonstrated, knowledge and diversity exist but are not connected. Knowledge about the international tourism market combined with knowledge about the region is of utmost importance. Communication is not lacking everywhere, however. Within the network theory, interaction can be divided into inner and outer communication channels. Research results indicate that the ability of an enterprise to innovate and learn is evidently improved in the interaction between manifold actors in a region in which there is a diversity that guarantees a rich and varied proficiency (Porter, 1998).

Relating to this statement, flows of information and knowledge are in many cases more important than flows of products and money. In this context, both inner and outer communication channels are of importance. Consequently, development and competitiveness can be best understood when individual activity is regarded as part of a greater system consisting of the entire network, in which the company plays an active part. In the end, competitiveness is determined by the power and capacity for innovation, readiness for continuous learning, production of new knowledge and investment in better products and/or more effective processes (Malmberg, 2000, p. 224).

Connections from the network succeed remarkably well: the incoming operators stand in close contact with the European tourism market, and meetings are arranged both in Sweden and abroad. The group of entrepreneurs is dependent on the incoming operators, who invite foreign media to the County of Norrbotten. The persons working in the incoming firms have long been building up a network of contacts – in a larger context, these connections can also be seen as a network. Without these persons the region could not be promoted as intensively as is now the case.

Within the Subarctic network, it is the inner communication channels that are in need of improvement. In the interviews, the entrepreneurs were asked what they knew about the project. It is astonishing that no interviewee knew which companies were participating in the project. In the 11 months of Subarctic's existence, there had been only one meeting, which might be called an 'inauguration meeting'. At this convention, entrepreneurs were to be informed on the meaning and goals of Subarctic. The imparting of information obviously did not work very well: none of the interviewees could say what the content of the meeting had been. One respondent was of the opinion that all participants who had gone to the meeting went home just as uninformed as they had been four hours earlier.

Certain entrepreneurs were invited to the inauguration meeting, while others were never notified of it; the board of directors had decided who would be allowed to come. This procedure causes problems, as the project is actually sponsored by the EU and the county administrative board, with the aim that everyone be allowed and able to join.

As a great share of the money spent on the Subarctic project is public, it is important that there be a coordinated approach to the development and structure of the economy. This implies that the project must also be judged according to how it affects the economy around it. One aim is to generate supportive and complementary units instead of groups that compete with each other on the tourism market.

When the entrepreneurs were asked how much money Subarctic had at its disposal, no-one could answer. Additionally, no-one knew for how long the project would be sponsored. The entrepreneurs are not able to take part in decision processes, as there are no meetings or the like. They do not even know why they belong to the 'chosen ones' – but hope that they will remain in the group, as everyone interviewed is of the opinion that cooperation in the region is of great importance if they are to survive in the competitive international market.

To summarize, the flow of information in the project can be seen as nothing short of disastrous. Many researchers consider the bottom-up principle, combined with a horizontally determined cooperation, as crucial to the success of regionally based learning. In addition, the process ought to be supported by an extensive social recruitment as well as by the participation of a broad spectrum of organizations. Such an arrangement is likely to initiate economic growth and social solidarity (Ennals and Gustavsen, 1999, p. 3).

From the outside, Subarctic looks like a bottom-up project. It brings together regional entrepreneurs, with persons taking decisions on national and international levels. In this way, knowledge and creativity can be spread throughout the region. But, within the project, a top-down way of working is predominant. Decisions are made at the top of this pyramid, where the board of directors stands at the peak and the entrepreneurs at the bottom; there is a clear hierarchy in the network.

For the success of this project, it is absolutely necessary that the leadership understands the importance of informing the participants and allowing them to participate to a considerably higher degree. For this modification, a change in the project leader's view must take place. The leadership needs to recognize that the entire project rests on the entrepreneurs, as they possess the knowledge about the region that is needed to satisfy both national and international tourists.

Conclusions

What conclusions can be drawn from the information presented above? A project has been started to motivate new markets on the international level and to place the County of Norrbotten on tourists' mental maps. The participating entrepreneurs are dedicated to the activities of the project. Appreciation of the importance of cooperation is beginning to manifest itself in the county.

None the less, problems within the network are evident. In a cooperation project like this, information flow is a central, fundamental feature. The entrepreneurs want to know – and have a right to know – why they are authorized to take part in the project, what is expected from them and what the intermediate goals are? The project leadership must pay more attention to the dissemination of information, and this holds true for several levels. It is important to inform entrepreneurs in the county that Subarctic actually exists, as many have not heard about it yet. Indeed, it is also important to jointly set up goals and express how these goals can be reached – namely through broad cooperation in the county.

Through a broader spread of information, the project leadership can be sure that as few resources and social competences as possible are disregarded and ignored. Regular meetings aim not only at communicating information from the project leadership to the entrepreneurs, but also at disseminating facts in the opposite direction. In this way, the many forms of knowledge that exist in the region can be combined. Accordingly, the meetings can be seen as knowledge transfers, and this again can only be positive for the project in the long term. If this recommendation is to be carried out, it is important that those within the project agree upon the question concerning which entrepreneurs should take an active part.

Other questions that are still open are: is the collaboration time-limited? Is long-term cooperation intended? Naturally, no one can see exactly what the future holds, but the entrepreneurs have a right to know how positive or negative tourism development in the county affects them, individually and in their cooperation with Subarctic.

Another problem is that many possibilities and opportunities depend on personal contacts between members of the board of directors and important information providers in other countries. If the success of the project hinges on these few individuals, what happens if they decide to stop working within Subarctic? The fact that Subarctic operates in a peripheral area can be seen as both an advantage and a disadvantage. Because of the great distances to most tourists' home areas, this region is not likely to expect a huge number of tourists. Again, this means that there is a good chance of keeping the exotic nature of the region alive.

In order for the tourism economy to improve its profitability, this author is of the opinion that it is necessary to concentrate efforts, both financially and geographically. One example of this is the mental maps of potential tourists, on which Norrbotten hardly exists. It is of great importance to make these people recognize what northern Sweden has to offer. To achieve this, it would be a good idea to establish a number of main attractions that stand out in the international tourism market and that occupy a place in consumers' minds. If this is to be made possible, the available resources cannot be spread evenly over the entire county but must be centred in a few, albeit crucial, projects. Subarctic stands as an example for such a concentration of efforts.

Another example of a significant tourist attraction is the ice hotel in Jukkasjärvi. Subsequently, this initiative ought to lead to a situation in which the areas not given priority can also take advantage of a higher number of tourists in the region (SOU, 1990, p. 91).

A first step in the right direction has been taken, however. A change in train of thought is a significant factor within the networks. After 1 year's existence of Subarctic, many entrepreneurs are aware of the importance of working together. They see themselves more as cooperating partners aiming at the same goal than as competing rivals, fighting for shares of incoming tourists.

References

Butler, R. and Hall, C.M. (1998) Image and reimaging of rural areas. In: Butler, R., Hall, C.M. and Jenkins, J. (eds) *Tourism and Recreation in Rural Areas*. Wiley, Chichester, UK, pp. 115–122.

Butler, R., Hall, C.M. and Jenkins, J. (1998) Introduction. In: Butler, R., Hall, C.M. and Jenkins, J. (eds) *Tourism and Recreation in Rural Areas*. Wiley, Chichester, UK, pp. 3–16.

Dewailly, J.M. (1998) Images of heritage in rural regions. In: Butler, R., Hall, C.M. and Jenkins, J. (eds) *Tourism and Recreation in Rural Areas*. Wiley, Chichester, UK, pp. 123–138.

Elbe, J. (2002) *Utveckling av turistdestinationer genom samarbete*. Department of Business Economics, Uppsala University, Uppsala, Sweden.

Ennals, J.R. and Gustavsen, B. (1999) *Work Organisation and Europe as a Development Coalition*. John Benjamin, Amsterdam.

Hopkins, J. (1998) Commodifying the countryside: marketing myths of rurality. In: Butler, R., Hall, C.M. and Jenkins, J. (eds) *Tourism and Recreation in Rural Areas*. Wiley, Chichester, UK, pp. 139–158.

Hudson, R. and Townsend, A. (1992) Tourism employment and policy choices for local government. In: Johnson, P. and Thomas, P. (eds) *Perspectives in Tourism Policy*. Mansell, London, pp. 49–68.

Jenkins, J.-M., Hall, C.M. and Troughton, M.J. (1998) The restructuring of rural economies: rural tourism and recreation as a government response. In: Butler, R., Hall, C.M. and Jenkins, J. (eds) *Tourism and Recreation in Rural Areas*. Wiley, Chichester, UK, pp. 43–68.

Länsstyrelsen i Norrbottens län (1998) *Infrastruktur för 2000-talet*. Luleå, Finland.

Länsstyrelsen i Norrbottens län (2002a) *Resolution about Project Funds for the Project Norrbotten – Subarctic*. Luleå, Finland.

Länsstyrelsen i Norrbottens län (2002b) *Fakta om Norrbottens Län 2002*. Luleå, Finland.

Malmberg, A. (2000) Lokal miljö, agglomeration och industriell konkurrenskraft. In: Berger, S. (ed.) *Det Nya Samhällets Geografi*. Uppsala Publishing House, Uppsala, Sweden, pp. 221–246.

Porter, M. (1998) Clusters and the new economics of competition. *Harvard Business Review* 76 (6), 77–90.

Sorensen, A.D. (1993) Approaches to policy. In: Sorensen, A.D. and Epps, R. (eds) *Prospects and Policies for Rural Australia*. Longman Cheshire, Melbourne, Australia.

SOU 1990:103 (1990) *Turism i Norrbotten – att Utveckla Affärs- och Privatresandet i Landet*. Stockholm.

Turistdelegationen (2003) *Innovationsprogrammet för Utveckling av Innovationskraft i Turistnäringen*. Swedish Tourism, Stockholm.

5

The Impact of Tourism on the Local Supply Structure of Goods and Services in Peripheral Areas: the Example of Northern Sweden

GÜNTER LÖFFLER

Department of Geography, University of Würzburg, Germany

Introduction

The direct and indirect socio-economic impacts of tourism in the regions of destination are widely discussed in literature. One aspect within this context concerns the effects of purchase and consumption of goods of non-permanent residents. Especially in rural and sparsely populated areas, the share of tourism purchases can be relatively high and thus an important factor for the local retail trade. In this context we have to define who is a tourist and to analyse which kinds of goods tourists buy and consume.

From a more theoretical point of view a tourist is a person who leaves his home to spend his leisure time at other places. Then we can differentiate between the activities or the activity pattern, the duration of staying outside their home or the travelling distance. One of these activities might be buying goods. Thus, on one hand a German who flies to New York for Christmas shopping or goes to Milan to buy designer clothes is normally seen as a tourist. Here, distance as well as the event itself leads to this definition. Also, mobile home owners or second-home owners who do their daily shopping at their destination are seen in literature as tourists as well.

On the other hand, someone who drives a couple of kilometres from home to buy convenience goods in a shopping centre is not to be seen as a tourist. But what about a person who, for one day only, drives by car to a distant factory outlet or crosses the border between countries to buy petrol, tobacco or alcohol products which are cheaper in the other state because of a different tax system?

In these few examples the inaccuracy or imperfection of all definitions in the context of tourism and retail trade can be seen. Here, neither the motivation of purchasing (event- or price-orientated) nor the kind of goods nor aspects of duration or distance can help to undo this Gordian knot. Thus, for this study, we define all persons as tourists who stay one night or more at their destination or who leave their local or regional environment for shopping purposes.

In this wider sense the turnover in retail trade can be distinguished between a share which comes from the inhabitants of the market area of the local shops and the influx from tourism. In rural or sparsely populated areas the latter share can be very important in conserving the local supply structure in retailing as well as in other services.

By using the example of Sweden and some Swedish municipalities we have tried to estimate the impact of tourism and/or cross-border shopping. Thus, first, we have to show that there is such an impact in general. Then, secondly, we have to estimate the shares of turnover from tourism and/or cross-border shopping in selected rural municipalities in order to assess the impact on the local retail trade.

Research Data and Methods

In this study the figures for annual turnover in retail trade for the Swedish municipalities are used, as they have been published since the end of the 1980s by the Swedish Handelns Utredningsinstitut (HPI, 1991–1997; HUI, 1998–2002). These figures distinguish between the turnover for convenience goods (dagligvaror) and durables (sällanköpsvaror). In the definition of HUI, convenience goods cover food, perfume, tobacco, newspapers, magazines and flowers, while durables cover all other kinds of goods.

With the assistance of the inhabitants in a municipality the local consumer buying power in retailing can be estimated. Using the turnover for this small area per capita and defining a greater region as a closed market area, a quota is calculated which gives us the first approximation of consumer buying power or of its in- or out-flux, respectively. This form of estimation is used by the HUI, calculating the so-called HUI-köp-index (see equation 1, Box 5.1).

In this kind of calculation the variation in the disposable income per capita or per household is not taken into account. The disposable income of a private household is used for savings and consumption. Within consumption a larger part of the spending power is used for housing, travelling, holidays, services and so on and a smaller part for consumption of goods. This smaller part – the consumer buying power in retailing – corresponds to the turnover in retailing in closed economic or spatial systems, e.g. there is no in- or out-flux across the border. From there we use this variation in the disposable income in the aggregated figures of the municipalities to calculate weighting factors. The indices to describe this variation are calculated in equation 2.

After we have estimated the consumer buying power per capita (equation 3) we can compute the quota Q (Bindungsquota) as in equation 4. This Bindungsquota Q gives us the share of the in- or out-flux of consumer buying power for the municipalities in Sweden. The difference between turnover per capita and consumer buying power per capita shows us the in- or out-flux in SEK per inhabitant (equation 5), multiplied by the number of inhabitants (in million SEK at current prices, equation 6) or weighted by the consumer price indices at 2000 prices (equation 7) (Löffler and Schrödl, 2002, p. 7).

Finally, reported guest-nights for the years 1990, 1995 and 2000 and the number of second homes in 1991 and 1996 were utilized. The figures on reported guest-nights are published only at the macro level for the 21 Swedish counties, but here the figures for municipalities from Statistics Sweden (Stockholm, http://www.scb.se) are used. The quality of these data depends on the reporting discipline in the municipalities. Thus there are also missing values in the data file. The number of second homes in the municipalities is derived from the UMCOBase (Umeå cottage base, Sweden), produced by Statistics Sweden and located in the Department of Social und Economic Geography, Umeå University, Sweden (Müller, 1999, p. 17).

Box 5.1. Equations 1–7.

(1) HUI-köp-index (based on the Swedish HUI estimation):

$$Q(HPI)_{Sw,m_i} = \frac{TC_{m_i}}{TC_{Sw}} \times 100$$

(2) Regional index of spending power (Sweden = 1.00):

$$ISP_{Sw,m_i} = \frac{DIC_{m_i}}{DIC_{c...}}$$

(3) Consumer buying power per capita:

$$CBPC_{Sw,m_i} = TC_{Sw} \times ISP_{Sw,m_i}$$

(4) Bindungsquote Q (based on the Swedish HUI estimation):

$$Q_{Sw,m_i} = \frac{TC_{m_i}}{CBPC_{Sw,m_i}}$$

(5) Flow of consumer buying power at current prices:

$$FCCP_{Sw,m_i} = (TC_{m_i} - CBPC_{Sw,m_i})$$

(6) Total flow of consumer buying power at current prices:

$$FCP_{Sw,m_i} = (TC_{m_i} - CBPC_{Sw,m_i}) \times P_{m_i}$$

(7) Total flow of consumer buying power at 2000 prices:

$$F2P_{Sw,t,m_i} = (TC_{t,m_i} - CBPC_{Sw,t,m_i}) \times P_{t,m_i} \times CPI_t$$

Sw = Sweden
m = municipality
TC = turnover per capita in retailing
DIC = average disposable income per capita in 1995
P = number of inhabitants
CPI = consumer price index, year t

Data

The following data were included in our work:

- Data on the turnover in retail business at the municipality level, separated for durable and convenience goods, published by HPI/HUI (Handelns Planinstitut/Handelns Utredningsinstitut) annually since 1991. Data are available for the years 1988 to 2000.
- Data on the population for the municipalities are from the same source.
- Data on people's disposable income at the municipality level for the year 1995. These were extracted from the data base at the Department of Social and Economic, Geography, Umeå University, Sweden and calculated as the average disposable income per capita in SEK.
- Consumer price indices (CPI) for different groups of goods and services since 1980, published by SCB, were recalculated for convenience goods, durables and both (index for the year 2000 = 100).
- Data on reported guest-nights for the years 1990, 1995 and 2000 (from Statistics Sweden).
- Number of second homes within municipalities in 1991 and 1996 (from UMCOBase).
- Data on food retailing in Västerbotten 1997 for all shops including, among other things, floor space, classes of turnover, theoretical market areas with their number of inhabitants (from Konsumentverket Stockholm/Länsstyrelsen Västerbotten, GBV and KO, 1997).

The impact of tourism and cross-border shopping on retail trade in Sweden

For separating intra-regional flows of consumer buying power from inter-regional flows it is useful to reflect on the ranges of flows or the range of regular shopping trips, respectively. From Christaller (1980) we have learnt that the range and orientation of normal shopping trips depend on the kind of goods. Concerning the range, longer shopping trips can be assumed for durables and shorter ones for convenience goods. Concerning the orientation from a rational point of view all shopping trips are oriented upwards in the hierarchy of central places (Löffler and Klein, 1989, p. 406; Löffler, 1998, p. 269).

If we assume that in the Swedish case virtually every municipality outside the main urban agglomerations contains only one central place, then central places in municipalities with a small number of inhabitants have a lower hierarchy level in the Swedish urban system than those in municipalities with a large number of inhabitants. Using the number of inhabitants as a measure for the central character of a municipality and the average turnover per capita as an expression for in- or outflows of consumer buying power, the following two hypotheses can be established:

(H1) Turnover per capita in durables is related to the number of inhabitants.
(H2) Turnover in convenience goods is related to the number of inhabitants.

Looking at the correlation coefficients, concerning H1 there are significant coefficients for durable goods in all analysed years (1990, 1995, 2000). For H2, the turnover per capita in convenience goods related to the number of inhabitants, no correlation having been found (see Table 5.1). Thus, greater inflows of consumer buying power for convenience goods into municipalities, especially those with small numbers of inhabitants, cannot be caused by rational shopping trips, but flow in from tourism or cross-border shopping.

To get a first insight into the impact of tourism on the turnover in retailing in general and for different kinds of goods we can correlate the turnover per capita for convenience goods and durables and the reported number of guest-nights per inhabitant as well as the number of second homes per inhabitant. Both variables describe the relative importance of tourism in a municipality. Thus, the following hypotheses are established:

(H3) Turnover per capita in durables is related to the number of guest-nights per inhabitant.
(H4) Turnover per capita in durables is related to the number of second homes per inhabitant.
(H5) Turnover per capita in convenience goods is related to the number of guest-nights per inhabitant.
(H6) Turnover per capita in convenience goods is related to the number of second homes per inhabitant.

The hypotheses H3 and H4 can be rejected. While there are no significant correlation coefficients concerning the turnover per capita in durables and the number of guest-nights per inhabitant at all, significant negative correlations are found for the number of second homes per inhabitant. This means that there is no significant inflow of consumer buying power for durables from tourism or, respectively, the share of inflows from tourism is very small.

On the other hand, hypotheses H5 and H6 cannot be rejected: both positive correlation coefficients are significant in all analysed years (see Table 5.1). These results show that there are inflows of consumer buying power for convenience goods in less populated municipalities, which have a higher share of tourism, as the negative correlation coefficients between population density and the tourism variables show. For the variable second homes per inhabitant in 1991 and 1996 the negative coefficients are to be regarded as significant.

Finally, the influence of cross-border shopping has to be analysed. For this purpose, the geographical positions of the municipalities are used. A first hint on the impact of cross-border shopping is given, comparing the average turnover per capita between the two groups of municipalities bordering on Norway/Finland and non-bordering on Norway/Finland. In addition, it may be of value to regard the municipalities with or without a frontier crossing to Norway. Thus, the following hypotheses are established:

(H7.1) Turnover per capita in durables is related to the geographical position (bordering on Norway/Finland or non-bordering on Norway/Finland) of the municipalities.

(H7.2) There is a difference in the average turnover per capita in durables between the groups of municipality bordering on or non-bordering on Norway/Finland.

(H8.1) Turnover per capita in durables is related to the existence of a frontier crossing to Norway.

(H8.2) There is a difference in the average turnover per capita in durables between the groups of municipalities with or without a frontier crossing to Norway.

(H9.1) Turnover per capita in convenience goods is related to the geographical position (bordering on Norway/Finland or non-bordering on Norway/Finland) of the municipalities.

(H9.2) There is a difference in the average turnover per capita in convenience goods between the groups of municipalities bordering on or non-bordering on Norway/Finland.

(H10.1) The turnover per capita in convenience goods is related to the existence of a frontier crossing to Norway.

(H10.2) There is a difference in the average turnover per capita in convenience goods between the groups of municipalities with or without a frontier crossing to Norway.

On one hand, from Table 5.1 it can be seen that there are no significant correlations for durable goods at all. On the other, there are significant correlations between the turnover per capita in convenience goods and the geographical position, as well as the existence of a frontier crossing to Norway in all years (Table 5.1).

Concerning the differences in the average turnover between the defined groups of municipalities, significant results are only to be seen for convenience goods. For both groups the average turnover in each year is higher for the municipalities near to the border. Mainly in the municipalities with a frontier crossing, the average turnover in convenience goods is significantly higher and has increased from 1990 to 2000 (see Table 5.2).

The reasons for cross-border shopping to Norway and Finland result from price differentials between the countries. Thus, in a comparison of border-close stores in 1996 for Norway an average of 25% higher prices for food was noticed (HUI, 1997, p. 36). Therefore, the accession of Sweden and Finland to the EU in 1992 is one important factor. While the lag in prices for convenience goods between Norway and Sweden increased over the 1990s, the differentials between Sweden and Finland were decreasing.

HUI (1998–2002, p. 12) has worked out the changes in the Binding quotas for selected Norwegian and Finnish municipalities for 1990 and 2000, and these are shown in Table 5.3.

All these results show that there are greater inflows of consumer buying power for convenience goods into less populated municipalities,

Table 5.1. Hypotheses H1 to H 10.1.

Hypotheses	Parameter	1990	1995	2000
H1 Turnover per capita in durables is related to the number of inhabitants	r	0.433	0.435	0.416
	α	0.000	0.000	0.000
	n	284	284	284
H2 Turnover in convenience goods is related to the number of inhabitants	r	0.050	0.036	0.033
	α	0.405	0.546	0.577
	n	284	284	284
H3 Turnover per capita in durables is related to the number of guest-nights per inhabitant	r	−0.129	−0.108	−0.109
	α	0.096	0.154	0.151
	n	168	177	174
H4 Turnover per capita in durables is related to the number of second homes per inhabitant (1991/1996)	r	−0.229	−0.242	
	α	0.000	0.000	
	n	283	283	
H5 Turnover per capita in convenience goods is related to the number of guest-nights per inhabitant	r	−0.499	−0.322	0.206
	α	0.000	0.000	0.000
	n	168	177	174
H6 Turnover per capita in convenience goods is related to the number of second homes per inhabitant	r	0.371	0.238	
	α	0.000	0.000	
	n	283	283	
H7.1 Turnover per capita in durables is related to the geographical position (bordering on Norway/Finland or non-bordering on Norway/Finland) of the municipalities	eta	−0.057	−0.073	0.067
	α	0.339	0.222	0.264
	n	284	284	284
H8.1 Turnover per capita in durables is related to the existence of a frontier crossing to Norway	eta	−0.031	−0.035	0.029
	α	0.597	0.557	0.621
	n	284	284	284
H9.1 Turnover per capita in convenience goods is related to the geographical position (bordering on Norway/Finland or non-bordering on Norway/Finland) of the municipalities	eta	0.386	0.295	0.299
	α	0.000	0.000	0.000
	n	284	284	284
H10.1 Turnover per capita in convenience goods is related to the existence of a frontier crossing to Norway	eta	0.353	0.338	0.384
	α	0.000	0.000	0.000
	n	284	284	284

r, correlation of coefficients; α, level of significance; n, number of cases; eta, effect size.

which cannot be caused by rational shopping trips, but flow in from tourism or cross-border shopping. Because of some missing data for the number of guest-nights per inhabitant it is not possible to classify the municipalities from the variables describing tourism and to compare the average turnover per capita between these classes afterwards. Instead, we have moved the perspective and established a classification according to population density, the number of inhabitants and the turnover in convenience goods.

Table 5.2. Hypotheses H 7.2 to H 10.2.

Hypotheses	Parameter	1990	1995	2000
H7.2 There is a difference in the average turnover per capita in durables between the groups of municipalities bordering on or non-bordering on Norway or Finland	D (SEK) t α	−1,218 −1.257 0.217	−1,647 −1.653 0.107	−2,040 −1.273 0.213
H8.2 There is a difference in the average turnover per capita in durables between the groups of municipalities bordering on or non-bordering on Norway or Finland	D (SEK) t α	−882 −0.605 0.554	−1,038 −0.659 0.520	−1,183 −0.445 0.663
H9.2 There is a difference in the average turnover per capita in convenience goods between the groups of municipalities bordering on or non-bordering on Norway or Finland	D (SEK) t α	4,328 7.029 0.000	4,666 5.193 0.000	8,476 5.261 0.000
H10.2 There is a difference in the average turnover per capita in convenience goods between the groups of municipalities with or without a frontier crossing to Norway	D (SEK) t α	5.179 6.337 0.000	6.982 6.027 0.000	14,266 6.993 0.000

D, differences of means; t, t-values; α, level of significance.

Table 5.3. Binding quotas (HUI-köp-index) for 1990 and 2000 in retail trade for convenience goods and durables in selected Swedish municipalities on the Norwegian/Finnish border (from HUI, 1998–2002, P. 12).

Municipality	Convenience goods (dagligvaror)		Durable goods (sällansköpsvaror)	
	1990	2000	1990	2000
Haparanda	190	110	71	61
Övertorneå	148	112	96	58
Pajala	128	99	23	24
Överkalix	137	103	62	51
Strömsund	117	111	46	45
Åre	123	161	49	43
Östersund	103	106	152	147
Eda	152	149	69	48
Arjäng	136	214	101	69
Strömstad	195	660	148	225

Figure 5.1 shows municipalities in Sweden where an above-average turnover in convenience goods was seen (> [mean + 0.5 standard × deviation]) and which have a below-average population density (< median) and below-average number of inhabitants (< median). Twenty-five municipalities were thus classified in 1990, 22 in 1995 and 14 in the year 2000. The average guest-nights per capita and the number of second homes per capita in this class are significantly higher than in the rest of Sweden in each of the three years. Over the period 1990 to 2000 in total 33

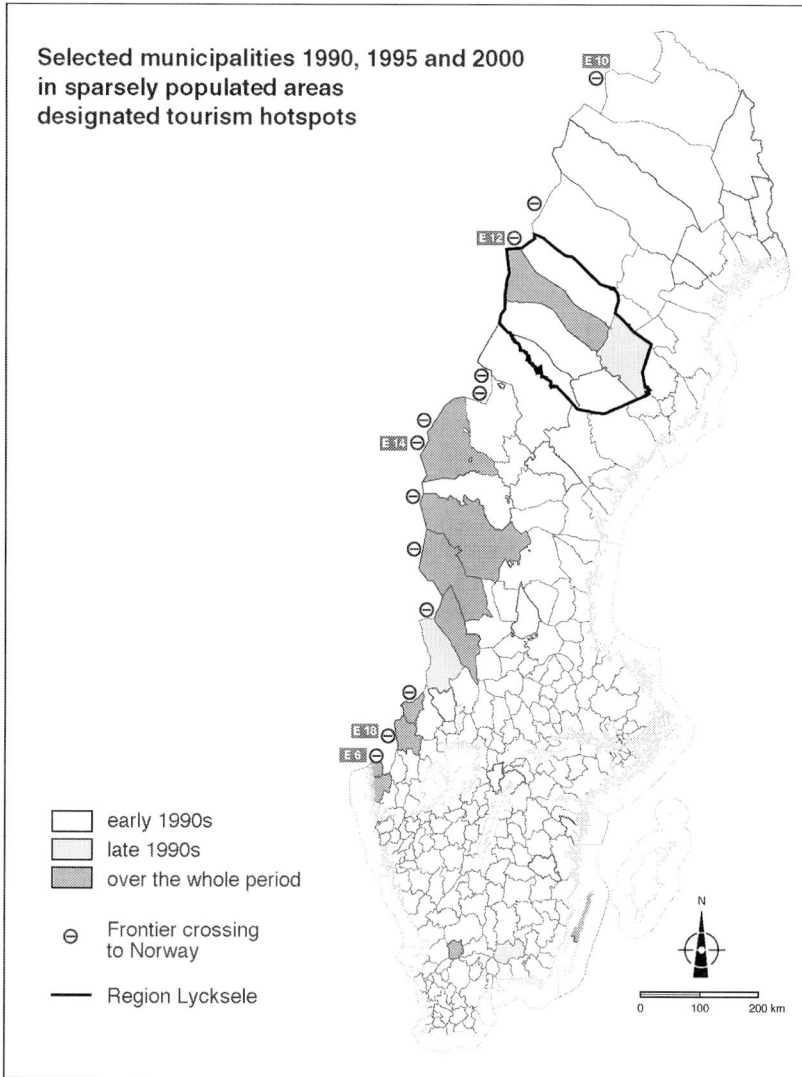

Selected municipalities 1990, 1995 and 2000 in sparsely populated areas designated tourism hotspots

Legend:
- early 1990s
- late 1990s
- over the whole period
- ⊖ Frontier crossing to Norway
- —— Region Lycksele

N

0   100   200 km

Fig. 5.1. Selected municipalities with high retail turnover and low population density.

municipalities were classified thus. Except in a very few cases – e.g. Markaryd – they are all engaged in tourism. Most of them are tourism hotspots, such as Borgholm, Mörbylånga, Vimmerby and Jokkmok, while others are or were important destinations in cross-border shopping (e.g. Strömstad, Haparanda).

Unfortunately, nearly all of the municipalities along the borderlines of Norway and Finland serve both purposes (e.g. Älvdalen, Åre, Storuman). Thus, it is difficult to separate both functions. As there are large and significant correlations between the variables guest-night or second homes per capita and the variables on the geographical positions of the municipalities, there is no possibility of quantifying the difference between the influences.

Finally, the total inflows of consumer buying power for convenience goods in these 33 municipalities were estimated for each year. In 1990 approximately 1680 million SEK of consumer buying power flowed into the 25 municipalities. This corresponds to an average share of 33.11% for these municipalities. Related to Sweden in total these inflows in the 25 municipalities had a share of 1.19%. In 1995 the same figures for 22 municipalities are 2017 million SEK, 34.48% and 1.27% respectively. For 14 municipalities in 2000 the following figures were calculated: 2634 million SEK, 50.45% and 1.53%, respectively.

However, it is impossible to calculate which share came from abroad and which from Swedish tourists. This differentiation can be calculated only by empirical studies. For instance, in 1997 Müller (1999, p. 166) estimated that, in a second home area in Småland, German owners of second homes on average spent 7667 SEK per year and household for everyday commodities.

The impact of tourism and cross-border shopping on the functional region of Lycksele, Västerbotten

The functional region of Lycksele covers six municipalities of Västerbotten, a län (county) in northern Sweden (Figs 5.1 and 5.2). Two of the municipalities, Åsele and Lycksele, with the central place of the region being Lycksele, belong to the so-called inland communes; the other four – Dorotea, Vilhelmina, Sorsele and Storuman – belong to the Fjäll communes. The latter three border on Norway, but only Storuman has a larger frontier crossing to Norway (E 12). Not far away from this frontier crossing are situated the well-known tourist places Hemavan and Tärnaby (see Fig. 5.2). Both are famous for downhill skiing and other winter sports activities. Besides Storuman, which has nearly one-third of the guest-nights of the region, the other municipalities are also engaged in tourism. Table 5.4 shows selected data for the municipalities from the year 2000.

Comparing these data with those of 1990 (1990 = 100), a decrease in both population (91.03%) and guest-nights (78.67%) is obvious. Also, the turnover in durables decreased by 77.52% (at current prices), while the turnover in convenience goods increased during the same period by 109.45% (at current prices). Figure 5.2 (a) shows the locations of convenience stores with their classes of turnover for the year 1997; in total, 90 outlets existed in the region at that time.

As a preliminary step in measuring the impact of tourism and cross-border shopping, the inflows have to be estimated in the Lycksele Region. For this purpose the consumer buying power per capita in the six municipalities was estimated, using the regional index of spending power, calculated for Västerbotten instead of for Sweden (see Box 5.1). Thus, the

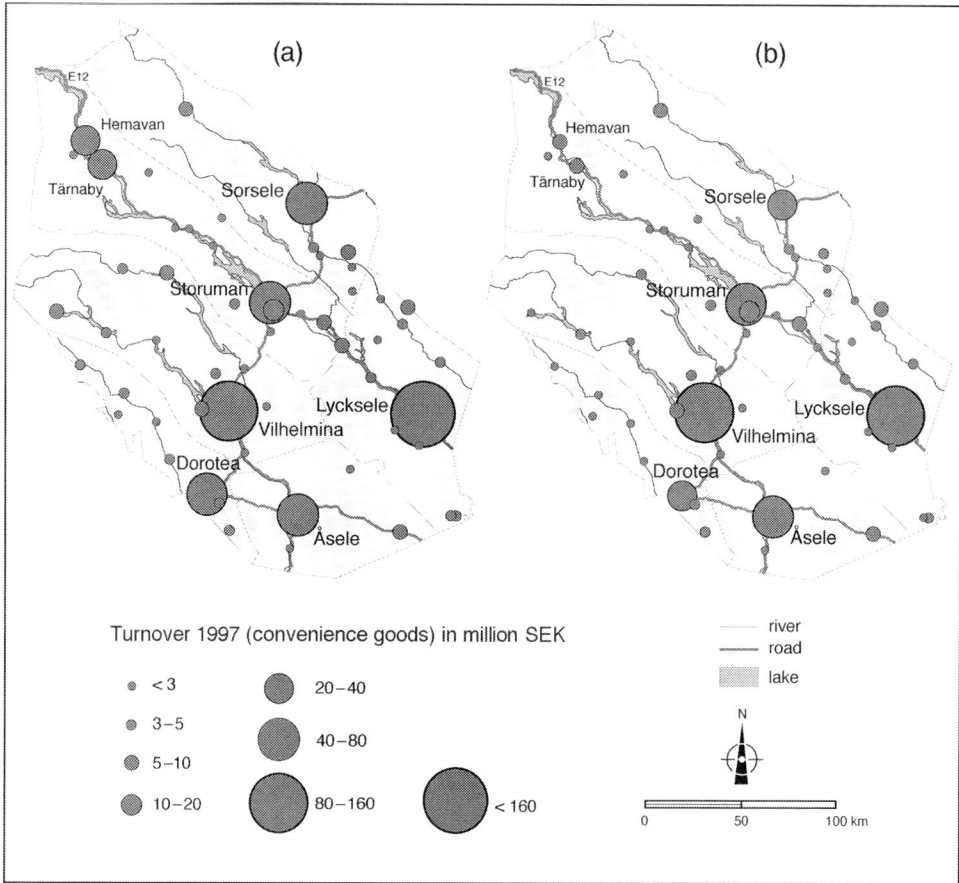

Fig. 5.2. Retail turnover in the Lycksele region by location, 1997, for convenience goods; (a) in total, (b) after deduction of inflows from tourism.

Binding quota and the inflows can be estimated more exactly for every municipality using an iterative algorithm.

After the first calculation the inflows are subtracted for further calculations, so the turnover in convenience goods for Västerbotten län in total was recalculated without the inflows into these six municipalities. Then the estimation was repeated. After four to five iterations no significant inflows in the six municipalities could be calculated. By carrying out this procedure for every year, a time series for 1990 to 2000 for the inflows from tourism and cross-border shopping can be established, as shown in Fig. 5.3.

Comparing the inflows with the guest-nights over the period 1990 to 2000 in selected municipalities, some differences are obvious (Fig. 5.4). On the one hand, in the two Fjäll municipalities – Vilhelmina and Sorsele – where no large border crossings exist, both curves are quite similar; on the other hand, for Storuman and Lycksele, which are within relatively easy

Table 5.4. Selected data for the functional region of Lycksele, 2000.

Municipality	Area (km²)	Inhabitants (n)	Population density (n/km²)	Guest-nights	No. of second homes (1996)	Turnover (Million SEK) Conven-ience goods	Durable goods
Storuman	7,485	6,934	0.926	73,067	2,699	177	73
Sorsele	7,493	3,195	0.426	17,963	666	51	23
Dorotea	2,803	3,353	1.196	24,914	636	72	16
Vilhelmina	8,120	7,918	0.975	62,496	2,023	147	76
Åsele	4,315	3,624	0.840	*no data*	405	59	25
Lycksele	5,639	13,058	2.316	53,050	1,156	305	218
Region	35,855	38,082	1.062	231,490	7,585	811	431

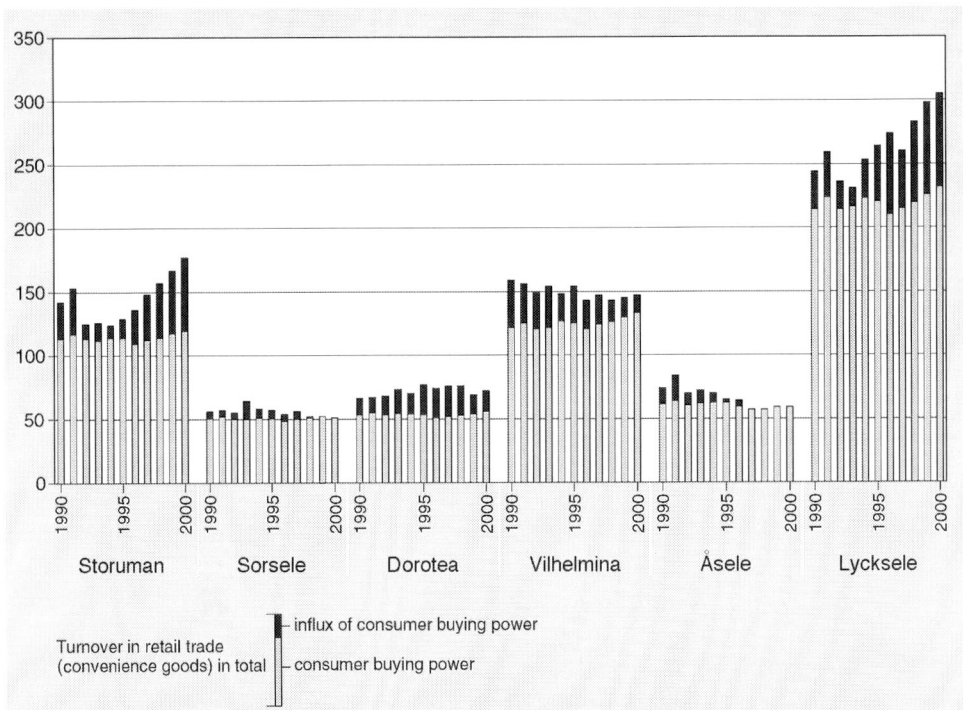

Fig. 5.3. Retail turnover and estimated shares of inflows (convenience goods, million SEK) for six municipalities in Lycksele, 1990–2000.

reach of Norway, no similarity can be seen. For the year 2000 in Sorsele no inflows could be estimated, in Vilhelmina only a share of 9.5%, while in Storuman and Lycksele the shares are much higher, at 33 and 24%, respectively. However, the most famous tourist villages, located within the municipality of Storuman, showed larger shares, which resulted from cross-border shopping.

Lycksele

Storuman

Sorsele

Vilhelmina

—●— Guest-nights per 1000
—■— Estimated inflows of consumer buying power

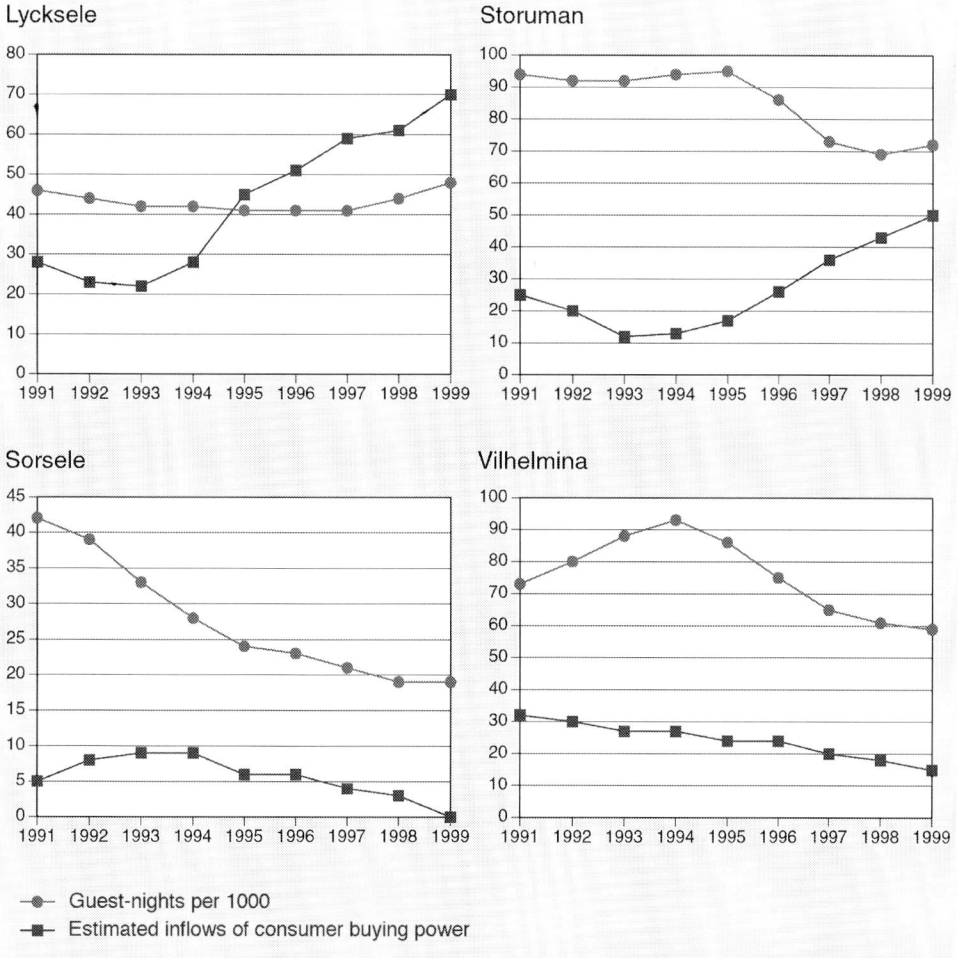

Fig. 5.4. Estimated consumer purchasing power inflows (convenience goods, million SEK) and guest-nights per 1000 nights spent between 1990 and 2000 for selected municipalities in Lycksele (3-year rolling average).

Looking for the impact of all these inflows from tourism and cross-border shopping for the local retail trade, we get an estimation from the 1997 data from Konsumentverket at the local level. In Table 5.5 the number of shops, the floor space and the turnover are given for the central place and for the remainder of each municipality in 1997. Thirty-five of the 90 shops reported a turnover of less than three million SEK, 23 of them being the only shop in the village. Most of the 35 shops received subsidies from the government in 1997 (Löffler, 2002, pp. 233–234; see also Konsumentverket, 1996 or Wiberg, 1983, pp. 171–172.).

In the mid-1990s, from business economics aspects, a shop required a turnover of three million SEK or more to survive in the long term (HPI,

Table 5.5. Retail trade 1997 (convenience goods) data for the functional region of Lycksele.

Municipalities, central place (CP) selected settlements and rural area	Shops[a] (n)	Floor space (km²)		Turnover for the three classes of size (million SEK)			Turnover in convenience goods (million SEK)	
		in total	per shop	< 3	3–20	> 20	in total	influx
Storuman (CP)	4	1,510	378	2	0	2	148	37
Hemavan	2	480	240	0	2	0		
Tärneby	3	735	245	1	2	0		
Rural area	14	1,455	104	9	5	0		
Sorsele (CP)	4	950	238	1	3	0	56	6
Rural area	6	676	113	3	3			
Dorotea (CP)	4	1,187	297	1	2	1	76	24
Rural area	7	937	134	4	3	0		
Vilhelmina (CP)	5	2,970	594	0	3	2	147	23
Rural area	12	999	83	5	7	0		
Åsele (CP)	5	1,415	283	2	2	1	57	−3
Rural area	3	255	85	3	0	0		
Lycksele (CP)	11	3,075	280	0	7	4	260	46
Rural area	10	1,200	120	4	6	0		
Region	90	17,844	198	35	45	10	744	133

1997, p. 16). If we now estimate the inflows at the local level, using the population within the theoretical market areas, it is possible to create a scenario of what would happen without the inflows from tourism. In 1997 the turnover in the functional region of Lycksele was 744 million SEK. Of that total, 611 million remained after the reduction by the inflows from tourism of 133. The distribution of this residual amount is shown for the local level in Fig. 5.2(b). On the whole, in this scenario 29 locations had only one store and a turnover of less than 3 million SEK. One location will lose its shop. In the central places and in the tourist villages the turnover decreased dramatically, e.g. in Hemavan and Tärneby.

Without tourism a turnover of more than 3 million SEK could be expected at only 26 locations. If, in addition, the public subsidies for the shops were to be dropped and, instead, the transportation costs of the households were supported – as discussed in recent years (see Löffler, 2002, p. 239) – in the longer term in only 26 of these villages would one or more shops survive.

Conclusions

This study has shown the obvious impact of tourism on the local supply structure of convenience goods in peripheral and sparsely populated regions in Sweden. Regarding the Swedish municipality level we have worked out the influence of tourism and cross-border shopping for a special type of municipality, as shown in Fig. 5.1, and have quantified the inflows of consumer buying power. Unfortunately, it is not possible to distinguish between different types of tourism and to quantify the inflows from each type.

For six municipalities in the functional region of Lycksele we have further shown the impact of tourism at the local level in more detail. Although it was not possible to quantify the different inflows of consumer buying power from cross-border shopping and other types of tourism, they were estimated at the local level to assess the impact for the supply structure and to establish a possible scenario. This scenario shows what would happen if the functional region of Lycksele ceased to be a tourist destination. In addition, if the public subsidies for the shops were dropped, only 26 villages instead of 56 would keep their stores.

Thus, the actual supply structure in the functional region of Lycksele depends on the following factors: (i) price differences for convenience goods between Norway and Sweden; (ii) the attractiveness as a tourist destination; and (iii) further public subsidies for small shops.

References

Christaller, W. (1980) *Die zentralen Orte in Süddeutschland: Eine ökonomisch-geographische Untersuchung über Gesetzmäßigkeiten der Verbreitung und Entwicklung der Siedlungen mit städtischen Funktionen*. 3rd edn, Reprografischer Nachdruck der 1. Auflage Jena 1933. Wissenschaftliche Buchgesellschaft, Darmstadt, Germany.

GBV and KO (1997) *Service i gles- och landsbygd – Analys och förslag till åtgärder*. Konsumentverket and Glesbygdverket, Stockholm and Östersund, Sweden.

HPI (1991–1997) *Handeln i Sverige – Siffror och Kommentarer till Detaljhandelns Omsättning i Kommuner och Län*. Handelns Utredningsinstitut AB, Halmstad, Sweden.

HUI (1997) *Prisspridningen i Dagligvaruhandeln*. Forskingsrapport S30. Handelns Utredningsinstitut, Stockholm.

HUI (1998–2002) *Handeln i Sverige – Siffror och Kommentarer till Detaljhandelns Omsättning i Kommuner och Län*. Handelns Utredningsinstitut, Stockholm.

Konsumentverket (1996) *Stöd till Kommersiell Service – Budgetåret 1995/96*. Konsumentverket, Stockholm.

Löffler, G. (1998) Market areas: a methodological reflection on their boundaries. *Geojournal* 45 (4), 273–287.

Löffler, G. (2002) Wer kann künftig noch wo Lebensmittel einkaufen? Strategien und Maßnahmen zur Sicherung der Grundversorgung der Bevölkerung dünnbesiedelter Räume in Schweden. In: Löffler, G. and Voßmerbäumer, H. (eds) *Mit unserer Erde leben*. Verlag Königshausen & Neumann, Würzburg, Germany, pp. 225–243.

Löffler, G. and Klein, R. (1989) Raumfunktionale Modellansätze zur Bestimmung von Standorten und Kaufkraftströmen im Lebensmitteleinzelhandel. *Kurzberichte aus der Bauforschung* 6, 405–410.

Löffler, G. and Schrödl, D. (2002) *Retail Business in the Functional Region of Umeå 1985–2000. Analysis of Structural Changes, Impacts of Shopping Centres and Consumer Behaviour*. CERUM *Working Paper* 56. CERUM, Umeå, Sweden.

Müller, D.K. (1999) *German Second Home Owners in the Swedish Countryside.* Department of Social and Economic Geography, Umeå, Sweden.

Wiberg, U. (1983) *Service i Glesbygd – Trender och Planeringsmöjligheter.* Department of Social and Economic Geography, Umeå, Sweden.

6   Tourism Development and the Rural Labour Market in Sweden, 1960–1999

DIETER K. MÜLLER AND PHILIP ULRICH

Department of Social and Economic Geography, Umeå University, Sweden

Introduction

The recent internationalization and restructuring of the economy has caused a redistribution of labour away from European peripheries and has thus entailed a renewed interest in tourism development (Townsend, 1997). The main impetus for this interest is the need for new jobs that can substitute for recent losses in not only agriculture, forestry and industry but also the public sector. Tourism development has been identified as a tool for achieving this goal and has been consistently supported by governments and regional developers (Hall and Jenkins, 1998; Jenkins *et al.*, 1998; Sharpley, 2002).

This is also true for northern European peripheries that lack the touristic assets associated with the Mediterranean area. Nevertheless, the lack of alternative development options entails the tourism option being transferred even to these European peripheries. It seems to be expected that tourism development will occur successfully in all peripheries, even in regions not currently involved in tourism.

In this context it is at least indirectly assumed that almost all places and regions have the possibility of developing into tourism destinations. To achieve this, a focus is usually placed on promotion of and cooperation in the destination area. Moreover, packaging offers for an international market have been tested for competition on the international charter market. Hence, development strategies usually look at the demand market rather than at the geographical location. Instead of focusing on the domestic market, success is expected on the international market and from high-yield tourism. Destinations with extraordinary amenities, such as Kiruna/ Jukkasjärvi which features top attractions like the Icehotel, have shown how peripheral destinations can compete on the international tourism market despite a peripheral location (Prideaux, 2002).

For a rather long time, rural and peripheral areas have been considered tourist destinations. In an attempt to define the place of tourism, the geographer Walter Christaller (1963) identified the European peripheries as places for pleasure and recreation for the citizens of the urban centres. Indeed, in Europe, Mediterranean peripheries have attracted considerable numbers of tourists, particularly since transportation and increased welfare have opened the periphery to a greater share of society.

The emergence of these *pleasure peripheries* (Turner and Ash, 1975) has also implied a considerable transfer of capital from the centres to the peripheries, creating employment and welfare (Williams and Shaw, 1991; Shaw and Williams, 1994; Williams and Montanari, 1995). Christaller's work (1963) is an early theory that tourism forms a system that connects origins and destinations. Accordingly, population centres are the main tourism-generating areas. Peripheral areas are important receivers of tourists.

Current knowledge and empirical evidence indicate that Christaller's original notion cannot be taken for granted. Most tourism only connects urban centres and does not involve rural or peripheral areas at all. Additionally, early tourism development in, for example, the Mediterranean area itself created urban centres that now attract mainly mass tourism. However, rural and peripheral areas still attract tourists and, particularly from their perspective, tourism forms an important industry and a significant source of income and employment.

Hence, it is reasonable to ask whether rural or peripheral areas are typically or naturally the places where tourism takes place (see Hall, this volume, Chapter 2). This also refers to a more social problem. Rural areas in Sweden have faced the same economic and social problems as have rural areas in other European countries. In search of perspective on the future of the countryside, politicians placed their hopes on tourism as early as the 1980s. But has tourism truly been a prospect for rural areas since then, and will it continue to be in the future? And can it be a prospect for all types of rural areas?

Thus, the purpose of this chapter is to analyse the spatial development of tourism in Sweden during the period 1960–1999. Within Sweden, rural areas are of particular interest. In this context the focus is on the labour market, illuminating tourism development from a local perspective. This is achieved using five cross-sections representing 1960, 1970, 1980, 1990 and 1999.

Time-geography and the Tourism System

Basically, tourism is about people's movement over space, linking an individual's place of origin to a destination. Potential destinations thus must be within a distance that can be reached within the individual's leisure time. Consequently, the selection of potential destinations depends on (i) available leisure time; (ii) the destination's distance from the origin;

and (iii) available means of transportation. For example, Ljungdahl (1938) showed that for the Stockholm area around 1930, second homes were located along the steamboat routes in the archipelago. Hence, the second-home locations could be reached using the available infrastructure and within a reasonable time. Time, space, and technology thus form important constraints for individuals' possibilities of moving through space.

Hägerstrand (1970, 1991) conceptualized this notion in his time-geography. Accordingly, individual agency is framed by individual constraints that can be characterized as capacity constraints, coupling constraints and authority constraints. Capacity constraints refer mainly to the individual's physical ability to do things, for example to move over space. Coupling constraints arise owing to the fact that individuals are tightly bound in a number of social contracts. For example, tourists often travel in the company of their family. Hence, individual time plans must be synchronized and bundled.

Authority constraints are the result of societal contracts creating certain common rules applicable to (at least) large groups of individuals. For instance, a tourist must apply for a vacation from his job and for a visa to travel to certain countries. However, most of these constraints are not stable but dynamic. Technical developments in transportation have caused the number of destinations that can be reached within a fixed time to increase dramatically. Today, a 2-week vacation allows for visiting almost any spot on Earth. This phenomenon is sometimes referred to as space-time-compression (Harvey, 1989).

Accordingly, tourism volumes are dependent on authority and coupling constraints. The emergence of paid holidays entailed an increase in the numbers of those with enough leisure time to travel. An increase in welfare – for example, financial holiday benefits – has allowed an increasing segment of society to participate in tourism (Shaw and Williams, 1994). The direction of tourism is, however, dependent on various factors. First, the residential distribution of population is of major importance. It forms the patterns of origins from which all tourism departs.

Secondly, the spatial distribution of friends and relatives causes the most important tourist flows. Thirdly, the available means of transportation contributes to defining a set of potential destinations. Fourthly, individual preferences constructed with regard to available information sources and negotiated with family and friends allow the tourist to choose between those potential destinations. In conclusion, tourism does not occur randomly. It is a function of individual agency embedded in a complex set of constraints and opportunities.

Tourism Patterns

Major cities are main sources of travel flows. Traditional concepts of spatial interaction can be utilized with this abstraction. The distance decay function is one of these concepts (Taylor, 1971). The volume of tourist travel is expected to decline with growing distance due to the time and monetary budgets of travellers. The demand for recreation decreases with growing distance. There are three types of demand: day use, weekend and vacation. Each type of demand has a different inverse distance curve because of the different time and monetary budgets involved.

The day use demand curve has the steepest slope, with an intersection (distance limit) very near to the city. Greer and Wall (1979) showed these and other relationships in a general model. They suggested that a particular supply for tourism should increase with growing distance, 'as each successive unit of distance [from the city] gives access to increasingly larger areas of land' (Greer and Wall, 1979; Pearce, 1995). This intersection of supply and demand, they argue, would theoretically produce a 'cone of visitation', peaking some distance from the generating centre with the exact form of the cone depending on the nature of the activity and its sensitivity to distance (Pearce, 1995). Figure 6.1 shows a simplified view of these general relationships.

Hall (2005) developed the conceptual base of distance decay further to show important relationships between a city and its recreational hinterlands. In its original form, the distance decay function does not give the periphery an important role for tourism and recreation in relation to all travel flows. In fact, it rejects assumptions such as that of Christaller (1963): 'It is typical for places of tourism to be on the periphery.'

Hall concentrates on tourism, often defined in terms of overnight stay(s) rather than by demand for recreation or number of travellers. He argues that long-distance trips usually associated with tourism form only a small share of all journeys. However, they account for a higher amount of distance travelled, higher commercial value and greater pollution (see Hall, this volume, Chapter 2).

Tourism is thus a function of time distance away from a point of origin. The number of overnight stays increases with growing distance from the

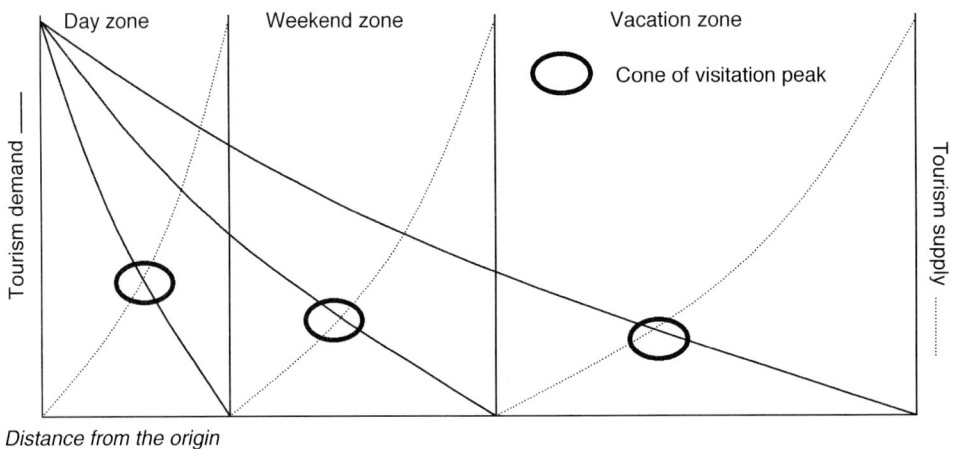

Distance from the origin

Fig. 6.1. Distance decay of demand and supply increase (after Greer and Wall, 1979).

origin and decreases again as one goes beyond the weekend limit. Hence, overnight stays are expected to cluster in a belt around the origin, assuming there is a uniform plane and an isolated central tourism generating point. It is assumed that individuals and households have perfect knowledge of the distance cost and select a tourism location that maximizes their utility subject to their time/distance constraints. The uniform plane assumption can be partly resolved. Travel distances are highly affected by transport networks. Hall (this volume, Chapter 2) describes a deformation of the belt by the transport system, which offers faster and farther-reaching travel along certain axes.

It is, however, important to note that tourism is not about simple distance decay functions such as those applied to define the range of goods, as the traveller's perception and preferences, among other things, play an important role as well (Pearce, 1995). Considering the overwhelming importance of VFR (visiting friends and relatives) tourism, it is obvious that cities in particular are themselves important destinations. Lundgren (1982) concentrates on towns as both origin and destination for travel flows. With his hierarchy of tourist destinations, he shows the role that destinations, as central places, have for tourist flows and how important or dominant tourism is for them. Towns as destinations have different functions according to their attributes, which are:

- Position in space.
- Degree of mutual travel interaction (generation *versus* inflow of tourists).
- Relative economic geographical centrality within the system.
- Geographic place attributes (attractions).
- Ability to supply tourist demand services from within its own local or regional economy.

Accordingly, Lundgren (1982) mentioned the following four broad destination types, which are thought to build a hierarchical system:

- Centrally located metropolitan destinations.
- Peripheral destinations of urban type.
- Peripheral countryside destinations.
- Natural environment/wilderness destinations.

These categories also represent a hierarchy of accessibility. Centrally located metropolitan areas are easily accessible areas that often serve as transportation hubs as well. In contrast, wilderness areas are difficult and/or expensive to reach. This condition should also be mirrored in the geographical patterns of tourism labour. Moreover, changes in transportation should lead to a relocation of these patterns. Lundgren's hierarchy can be combined with Hall's notion of distance decay (Fig. 6.2).

In a time–space environment, cities are located close to each other because of train and flight connections, and hence form parts of the belt of overnight stays. Zones of recreation used mainly for 1-day visits surround these metropolitan areas. Destinations in the origin's periphery constitute a part of the belt of overnight stays as well. Peripheral countryside destinations and wilderness destinations are indeed destinations owing to a greater extent of amenities. Hence, visits to these destinations can be expected to last longer.

The resulting system is subject to change, owing to technical development and the consecutive ability to overcome distance. In an initial phase without access to leisure and transport technology, tourism is limited in scope and space. Technological development increases the number of destinations that can be reached within an increasing leisure time. Today, wide areas can be reached within a day. Thus, the geography of amenities gains more influence regarding the distribution of tourists.

The tourist labour market should be a function of these processes as well. Accordingly, tourism employment should first occur in the metropolitan regions. This is due to two reasons. First, the metropolitan areas themselves are the main tourism-generating areas. Limited mobility therefore favours areas in the close vicinity of the metropolitan area. Secondly, other cities connected to transportation systems such as railway lines are other areas favoured by early tourism development.

The growth of individual transportation caused by greater access to cars has led to the emergence of belts of overnight stays around the major metropolitan areas representing the distances that can be travelled during the space of a day. Naturally, the geography of amenities influences the resulting shapes of the belts. Improvements in the road and rail networks

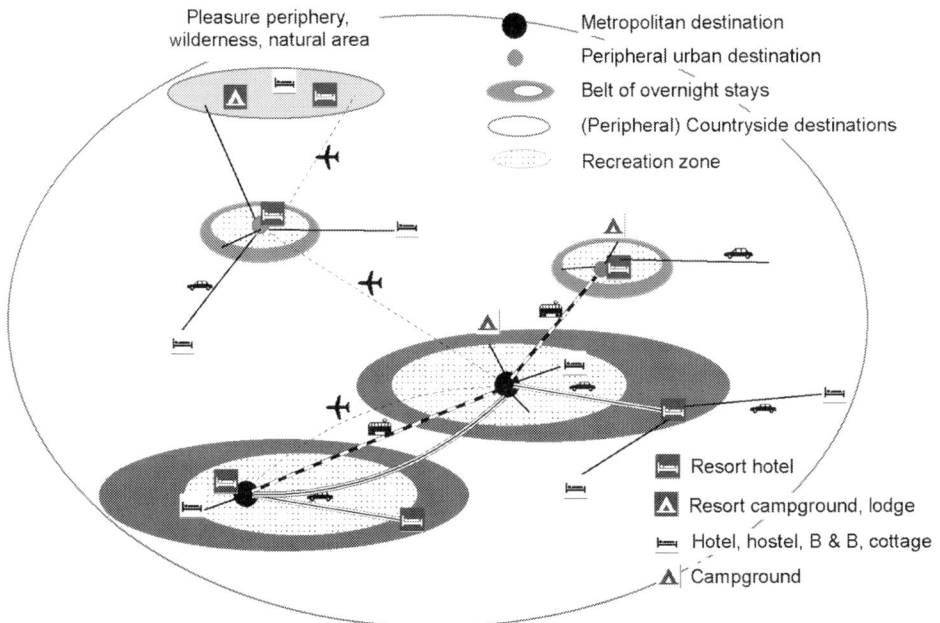

Fig. 6.2. Destination hierarchy and belts of overnight stays.

and the democratization of air transportation has finally allowed access to even more remote places. Moreover, this also leads to a relocation of the belt of overnight stays away from the metropolitan areas. This also means an increase in tourism-related labour in more remote areas.

In summary, tourism is not a random phenomenon. It is, instead, dependent on the amount of available leisure and economic resources, the availability of transportation and, finally, the geography of amenities. The tourism labour market is a blueprint of tourism patterns, and hence its development can be used to reconstruct the development of tourism.

Methodology and Data

Studying the labour market requires a definition of tourism. Composing the tourist sector in a database requires an operational definition of tourism. Tourism, recreation and leisure can be defined in different ways. In research concerned with these issues, these concepts are often not defined clearly and tend to be interchangeable (Butler *et al.*, 1998). Hence, even the definition used here is not absolute but is a result of the available data.

This study is based on a comprehensive database produced by Statistics Sweden and located at the Department of Social and Economic Geography, Umeå University, Sweden. The purpose of the database is to facilitate micro-simulation experiments based on longitudinal and spatial data representing the entire population of Sweden (Holm *et al.*, 2002). This project contributes with knowledge regarding the tourism labour market. For this project, five cross-sections were extracted from the database representing 1960, 1970, 1980, 1990 and 1999.

The data contained in the database are micro-data collected for the 1960, 1970 and 1980 censuses. Since then, data have been collected annually. Each individual in the database is characterized with a large number of indicators representing factors such as demography, labour, income, housing and property ownership. For this study, only indicators representing economic activity were chosen. Various employees are either identified by the type of industry and branch they work in or by their profession. In the data, these branches were already aggregated to the traditional sectors, and a special sector containing the tourism branches was created.

For each year, every individual is also characterized with a pair of coordinates representing place of residence, allowing for spatial analysis. Until 1975, the coordinates represent the parish where an individual was registered and, from 1980, they have also indicated the place of residence within 100 m. To achieve comparable cross-sections in this study, the parish level was used for all. There were approximately 2500 parishes in Sweden in 1980.

The long-term perspective and the small spatial units entail a number of complications. The first concerns the identification of the employment sectors. For 1990 the SE-SIC69 was used and adopted to the codes used for 1999, the SE-SIC 92. For the years 1960 to 1980 the employees are identified by their profession, not by the branch they worked in. The comparability between the two time periods can therefore be questioned. The second problem occurs through the many changes the parishes had undergone. During the 40-year span of the study, new units have appeared and others disappeared. It was therefore necessary to adapt the data to the one administrative order (1990).

Additional problems were caused by the lack of data regarding localization of workplaces. The seasonal labour force living far away from their actual workplaces is represented by places of residence. This gives a correct picture for taxation purposes but fails to represent the true patterns of tourism employment. However, data for workplaces were not available until 1980 and hence, for reasons of comparability, we chose to use place of residence to represent tourism labour for the entire research period. A similar problem occurs owing to the fact that some tourism labour in the transportation sector have mobile workplaces, such as trains or aircraft. Hence, results must be treated with care.

The number of people employed in the tourist sector should represent a grade of tourism and recreation activities. The advantage of this indicator is the presence of data over a long period of time and its easy handling. This indicator also has its weaknesses, however, as it includes only a view from the supply side of tourism. Within the wide range of jobs involved in meeting tourist demand for commodities and services, it includes only jobs in the 'tourism industry'. The branches included are listed in Tables 6.1 and 6.2.

A broader definition of tourist jobs is not appropriate, because other branches may be involved in tourism and recreation at one place/point in time and not involved at another. The broad time and space perspective makes the simple indicator a good alternative.

After preparing the data for analysis, the data were aggregated for parish level and finally integrated into a GIS where pairs of coordinates represent the parishes. To achieve greater clarity, the data were summarized for a neighbourhood defined as a circle with the radius of 50 km around each parish. This is intended to account for commuting labour as well.

Table 6.1. Tourism employment – data from 1960, 1970 and 1980.

Code	Description
293	Tourist office civil servant
621	Pilot
631	Train driver
632	Railway worker
912	Cook, cold buffet manager
913	Catering assistant
916	Hotel porter
917	Waiter
921	Head waiter

Table 6.2. Tourism employment – data from 1990 and 1999.

SE-SIC 92 Key (1999)		SE-SIC 69 Key (1990)	
55111	Hotels with restaurants, except conference centres	63201	Hotels and motels
55112	Conference centres, with lodging	63201	Hotels and motels
55120	Hotels and motels without restaurant	63201	Hotels and motels
55210	Youth hostels, etc.	63202	Lodging/camping sites
55220	Camping sites, etc., including caravan sites	63202	Lodging/camping sites
55230	Other short-stay lodging facilities	63202	Lodging/camping sites
55300	Restaurants	63100	Restaurants and cafés
55400	Bars	63100	Restaurants and cafés
55521	Catering for the transport sector	63100	Restaurants and cafés
61200	Inland water transport	71220	Inland water transport
62100	Scheduled air transport	71310	Air transport (including space travel)
62200	Non-scheduled air transport	71310	Air transport (including space travel)
63210	Other supporting land transport activities		
63301	Activities of tour operators	71911	Activities of travel agencies
63302	Activities of travel agencies	71911	Activities of travel agencies
63303	Tourist assistance	71911	Activities of travel agencies
92320	Operation of arts facilities	94141	Theatre and opera
92330	Fair and amusement park activities	94903	Fair, zoo, etc.
		94142	Concert activities
92340	Other entertainment activities	94909	Dance and other amusement activities
92520	Museum activities and preservation of historical sites and buildings	94202	Museum activities, art exhibits and botanical gardens
92530	Botanical and zoological gardens and nature reserve activities	94903	Fair, zoo, etc.
92611	Operation of ski facilities	94901	Competitive sporting activities, running of sporting and gym establishments
92612	Operation of golf courses	94901	Competitive sporting activities, running of sporting and gym establishments
92722	Operation of recreational fishing waters	94901	Competitive sporting activities, running of sporting and gym establishments
92729	Various other recreational activities	94901	Competitive sporting activities, running of sporting and gym establishments
52485	Retail sale of sports and leisure goods	13020	Various fishing-related activities

Afterwards, the relative importance of tourism for the local labour market became visible. For this, values were interpolated with regard to the 12 closest parishes using the inverse distance-weighted model with a power of 2. A mainly descriptive analysis was then conducted.

Changes in Tourism Constraints in Sweden

As mentioned earlier, tourism is embedded in a complex set of constraints that influence the amount of tourism as well as the resulting patterns. A first important factor is size of population. Between 1960 and 2000, the Swedish population increased by more than 18% (Table 6.3). This should, therefore, also increase the amount of tourism and tourism labour.

Very important is the population's distribution over time. Sweden's population is urbanized, and already was so by 1960. The level of urbanization has increased over the past four decades, according to the definition applied in Sweden. Accordingly, urban places have more than 200 residents. The proportion of the population living in those urban places increased from 72.8% in 1960 to 83.9% in 1995. The number of urban places increased from 1814 to 1938 during the same period. Even if we regard only urban places with more than 5000 inhabitants, the same trend can be observed, with figures of 146 in 1960 and 226 in 1995 (Statistics Sweden).

Even increasing car ownership has had a strong impact on tourism and consequently on the tourism labour market. In 1960, the number of personal cars per 1000 inhabitants was 159.6. By the 1990s, around 420 per 1000 inhabitants had a car (Statistics Sweden). Moreover, even the public transportation network has been expanded significantly (see Table 6.4).

Lundgren (1995) mentions the importance of improved accessibility for destinations in the periphery. Throughout the country, the improvement and construction of roads has contributed to the establishment of new destinations, for example, in the Swedish mountains. According to Statistics Sweden, the total length of roads in Sweden was 95,211 km in 1963, of which 15,485 were surfaced (16%). For 1999, the total length is given at 98,093 km and the share of surfaced roads is approximately 77% (75,890 km). This also emphasizes the major factor of mobility increase in Sweden in general.

Another constraint for the development of tourism is the amount of available leisure. In almost all industrialized countries, leisure time has increased since 1960 (Shaw and Williams, 1994). A review of leisure time

Table 6.3. Population growth in Sweden, 1960–1999 (from Statistics Sweden).

Year	1960	1970	1980	1990	2000
Total population	7,497,967	8,081,229	8,317,937	8,590,630	8,882,792

Table 6.4. Increase in public transportation, 1976–1995 (from Statistics Sweden).

	1976	1986	1995
Route length (km)	22,249	20,800	46,300
Bus seats available (n)	91,720	118,300	196,620
Vehicle-km	73,395	114,600	196,300

and monetary budgets of the Swedish households between 1950 and 1980 showed significant growth (see Table 6.5). The same is true for average travelled distance and access to second homes.

Second-home tourism in particular has increased since 1960, when second-home construction was supported by governmental schemes. Second homes were constructed mainly on the outskirts of major metropolitan areas and around regional centres. Additionally, in amenity-rich areas former permanent residences were converted into second homes. However, second-home tourism mainly favours businesses not necessarily connected with tourism (Jansson and Müller, 2003).

In addition, the nature of tourism has changed in most industrialized countries, with outdoor activities in attractive landscapes in particular becoming more popular (Butler, 1998). According to the Swedish Environmental Protection Agency (1974), the population's recreation behaviour showed that outdoor activities as recreation increased by around 20% from 1963 to 1973. For all other activities, the share decreased by 10% during the same time period.

Important for the development of 'Outdoor Sweden' were the efforts and investments of the public sector in the middle of the 1970s. The Swedish Environmental Protection Agency established standards and recommendations for outdoor activity facilities and the state created facilities such as hiking and ski trails. In the mid-1980s the state, after huge investments over the space of a decade, handed responsibility over to the municipalities (Ahlström, 2000).

Today, in nearly every municipality in Sweden, a ski trail is obligatory. One important issue for the development over the past decades is the breakthrough of downhill skiing in Sweden. From 1965 to 1980, also with the financial help of the state, the capacity of ski lifts was doubled. While in 1940 there was only one facility of this kind, in 1990 there were 1000. (Ahlström, 2000) As regards summer activities as well, strongly increasing demand has led to important investments. In 1962 there were 17 guest yacht harbours and in 1990 there were around 500 (Ahlström, 2000).

These new activities not only made outdoor activities the predominant way of spending leisure time, but they also caused people to travel farther within their own country. The distance travelled for ski trips (weekend or holiday trips) is longer than for other outdoor activities. There are also other activities for which people must travel long distances. The possibilities and facilities for fishing and hunting in the hinterland of northern

Table 6.5. Leisure and consumption (from SOU 1983).

	1950	1980
Working time per week (h)	48	40
Working time per week (days)	6	5
Holiday time per year (weeks)	2	5
Distance travelled per inhabitant-year (km)	100,000	500,000
Second homes per 1000 inhabitants	20	80

Sweden attract tourists from the entire country. These new forms of tourism and the increasing mobility, especially in the 1980s, have resulted in the development of 'nature destinations' and the idea of a 'tourist frontier' moving out into the wilderness (Lundgren, 1982).

Rural Restructuring and the Changing Interest in Tourism

The constraints above enable individuals to participate in tourism to a greater extent. Other constraints influence individuals' motivation to participate in the tourism labour market as well. Considering labour markets in rural areas, the process of rural restructuring cannot be ignored.

In the rural areas of all industrialized countries, agriculture dominated up to the middle of the 20th century. Since then, rural depopulation and other factors such as changes in agricultural production methods, mechanization and agribusiness practices have weakened the economic and social viability of rural areas and associated services, and have changed the physical appearance of the countryside (Butler, 1998).

One effect is that the importance of agriculture for employment and the local economy has been reduced dramatically. In the rural areas of northern Sweden forestry has been very important, but it too lost its importance for employment through mechanization (Pettersson, 2002). Instead, manufacturing and service industries have increased in relative importance, especially during the past decades (Pettersson, 2002). Thus, tourism plays an increasing role. In fact, by 1980 the number of people employed in tourism was as great as those employed in agriculture, forestry and fishery combined (Fig. 6.3).

Nevertheless, rural restructuring also facilitated a growing leisure use of rural areas (Butler, 1998). Buildings previously used for agriculture and forestry were often adapted for tourism, e.g. accommodation or second homes (Müller, 1999). Furthermore, abandoned farmland can become a golf course, or stock breeding buildings can be transformed into equine facilities with commercially let boxes. This process is also referred to as the commodification of rural areas (Cloke and Godwin, 1992). The population earlier employed in these sectors could sometimes generate incidental earnings or obtain a new job in tourism service industries. However, tourism does not necessarily supply labour to those formerly employed in agriculture and manufacturing. Instead, tourism labour is recruited from in-migrants and young people (Jussila and Järviluoma, 1998).

Tourism employment is therefore sometimes featured as the employment of the future (Riley et al., 2002). In this context, the worth of tourism employment for regional development is rarely contested. Townsend (1997), however, indicated that tourism development also implies an 'Americanization' of the labour market. Accordingly, tourism development introduces a new labour market regime featuring flexibilization, tertiarization and feminization. Consecutively, seasonal and part-time employment substitute for full-time employment; low-paid service jobs taken by women replace well-paid industrial jobs traditionally taken

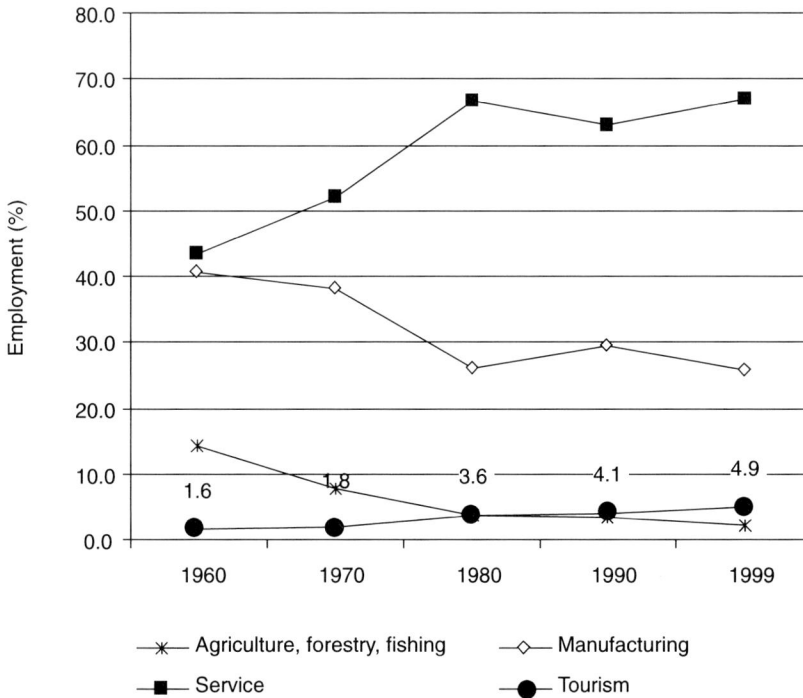

Fig. 6.3. Employment in Sweden by category, 1960–1999.

by men. Hence, tourism development is not only about creating jobs, it also introduces new societal structures probably affecting not only the labour market but also gender relations and societal life in the periphery.

Surprisingly, there is a lack of comprehensive knowledge about tourism development from a labour market perspective. Against this background, it is of interest to review the development of tourism-related employment from a long-term perspective.

Tourism Labour Patterns in Sweden

Tourism employment can be measured in absolute numbers representing the number of people employed in tourism, and in relative numbers representing the share of tourism labour in the local labour market. Here, focus is placed on both.

Absolute changes

The total number of persons working within the tourism sector increased from 93,300 in 1960 to about 121,700 in 1999. In 1960, tourism was mainly concentrated in the three metropolitan areas and the areas between them (Fig. 6.4). Although these general patterns were maintained until 1999, it is obvious that there has been diffusion to the hinterland and more remote parts of the country as well.

Most areas experienced an increase in tourism labour during the period of the research period (Fig. 6.5). However, it will also be noted that tourism employment in fact has decreased in parts of northern Sweden. Patterns of tourism employment changed particularly during the 1980s. Since then, tourism employment has increased in the northern parts of the country, while it has decreased in areas adjacent to the metropolitan areas. During the 1980s, tourism employment in the southern mountain regions grew significantly, while the 1990s saw an increase in the coastal areas of northern Sweden.

Absolute and significant growth in tourism employment can be charted, mainly for the metropolitan areas. This is expected, considering the small scope of the total labour market in peripheral areas in Sweden. Outside the metropolitan areas and their hinterland, tourism increased first in the south of the country between the metropolitan areas.

Relative changes

Naturally, the above patterns mainly mirror the population distribution within the country and do not tell us anything about the importance of the

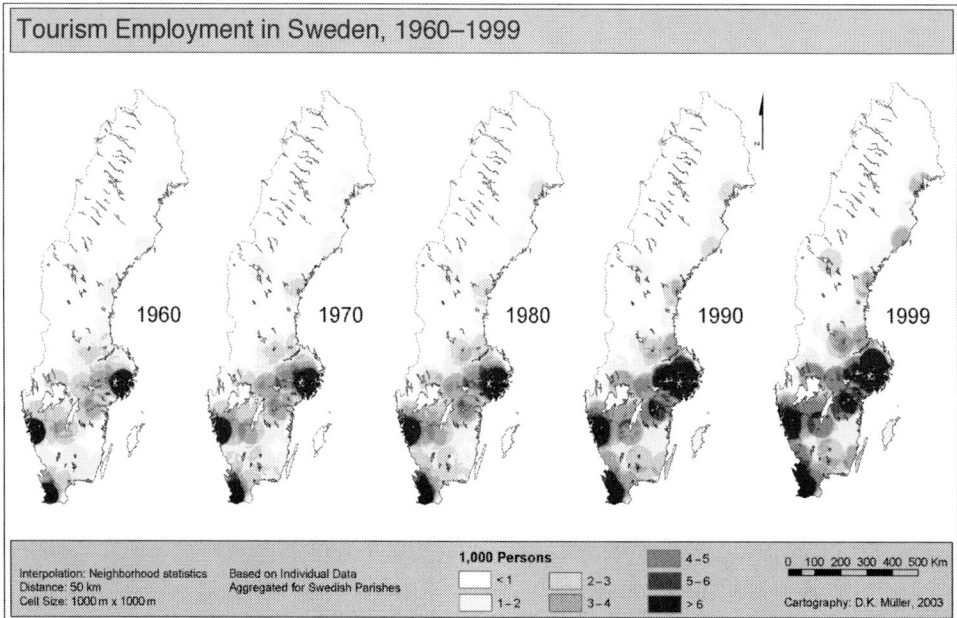

Fig. 6.4. Tourism employment in Sweden, 1960–1999 (from Statistics Sweden).

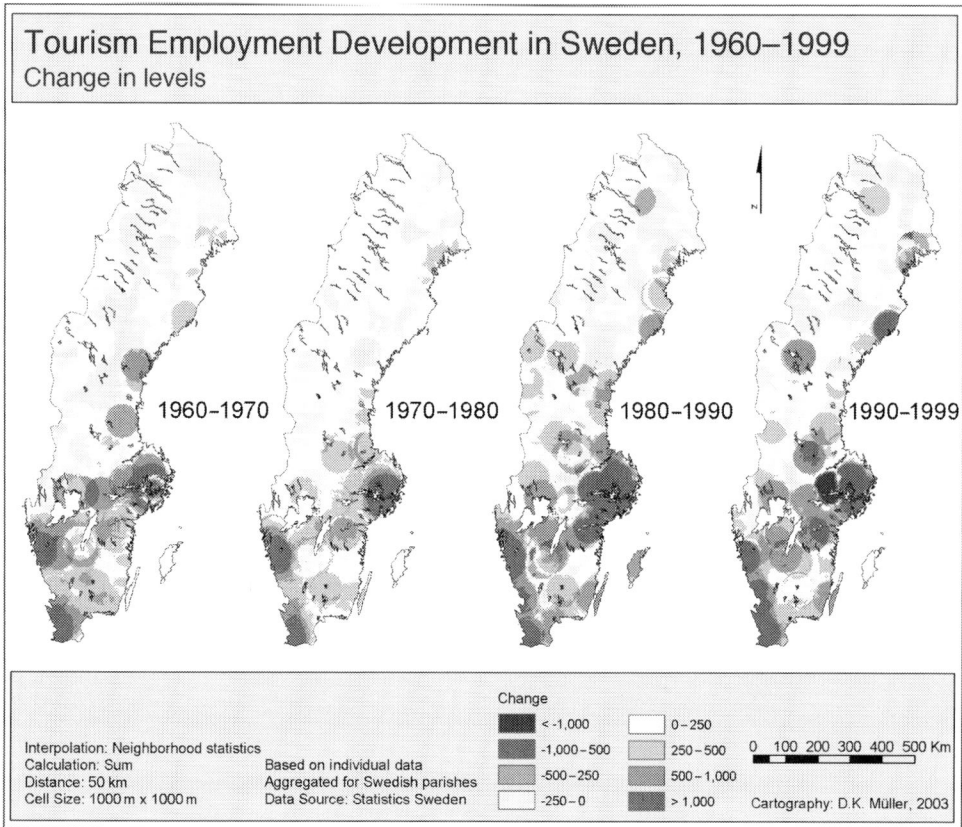

Fig. 6.5. Tourism employment development in Sweden, 1960–1999 (from Statistics Sweden).

tourism sector for the local labour market. Hence, it is imperative to review this development as well.

In 1960, tourism represented a share of more than 2.5% of the total labour market in only a few parishes. Besides the Åre and Kiruna areas, the nodes of the railway networks were other parishes in which tourism had increased beyond the 2.5% level (Fig. 6.6). These patterns were maintained until 1970. During the 1970s, however, tourism-related employment increased almost everywhere in the country. Besides the metropolitan areas, the Jämtland mountains in particular became more dependent on tourism, which represented more than 5% of all employment. Even in the railway nodes, tourism employment reached a level of more than 10% of all employment.

During the 1980s the patterns became more polarized, with a further increase of tourism in the mountain areas and city regions. A further diffusion took place during the 1990s. In 1999 in many areas of the mountain range, the tourism sector represented more than 15% of all employment, in some locales surpassing 30%.

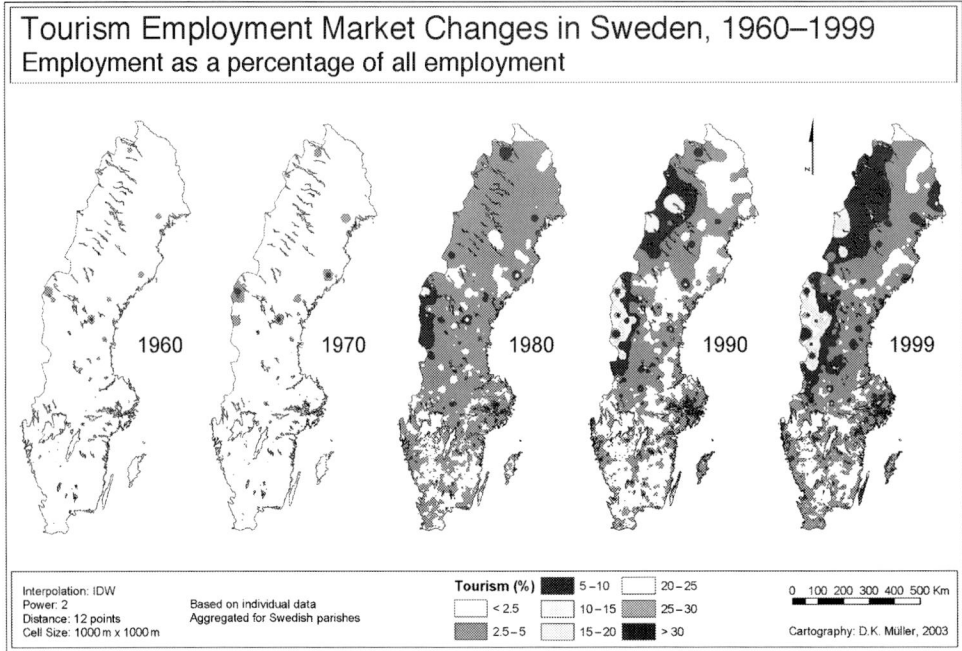

Fig. 6.6. Tourism employment market changes in Sweden, 1960–1999 (from Statistics Sweden).

More emphasis in the importance of tourism has occurred mainly in the mountain areas, where tourism has increased in importance rather dramatically and consistently (Fig. 6.7). During the 1980s, the method of recording employment changed and hence the patterns are difficult to interpret. However, the 1990s showed a more varied picture, with areas losing employment in tourism and others gaining. It can be said that positive changes occurred mainly in areas known as typical tourist destinations such as the mountain resorts in Dalarna, Jämtland and Västerbotten. However, the island of Öland and the border region near Finland also showed the increasing importance of tourism for the labour market.

Regions with expanding labour markets

Depending on whether absolute or relative changes are assessed, various popular regions can be identified. The greatest absolute change as regards tourism employment occurred in the densely populated areas in the south of Sweden, showing significant increases (250 persons per decade) during virtually the entire research period (Fig. 6.8). A positive change can also be spotted during the 1970s in the adjacent regions in the south. During the

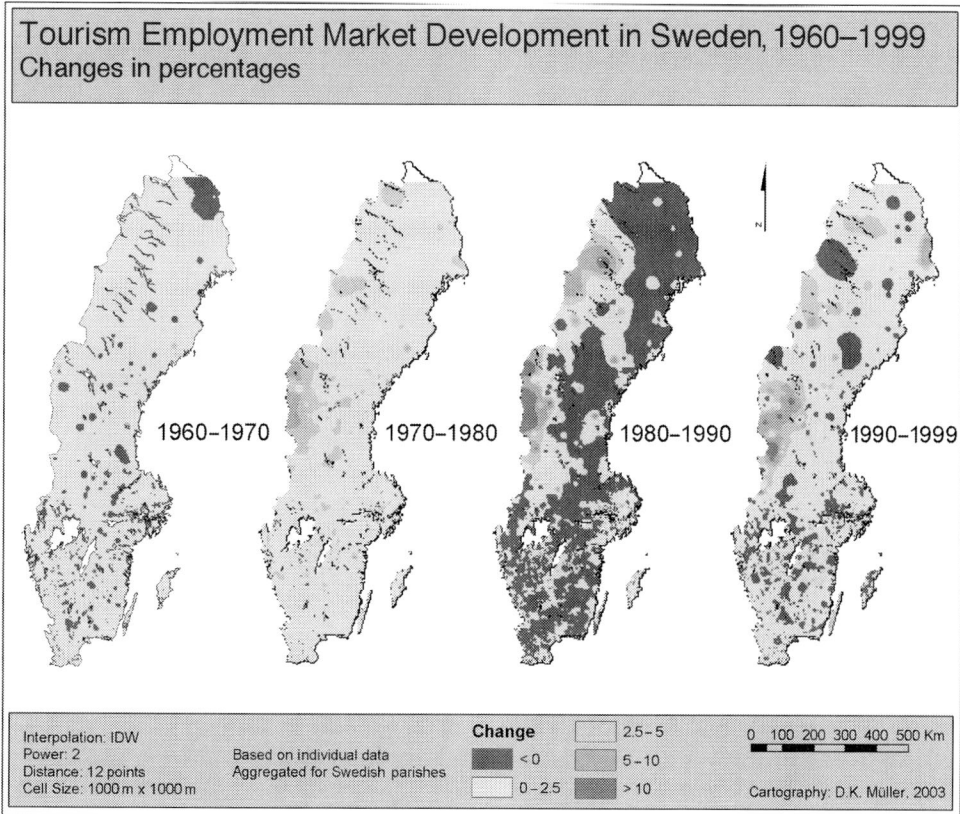

Fig. 6.7. Tourism employment market development in Sweden, 1960–1999 (from Statistics Sweden).

1980s and 1990s, increases took place in the north of the country and even in more remote regions. This is remarkable, not least with regard to the small scope of the labour markets. Thus, it indicates that tourism has, in fact, become an important sector of the labour market.

Additionally, in terms of relative importance of tourism for the labour market, the largest changes will be noted in the north of the country (Fig. 6.8). Here, tourism represented an essential share of employment, particularly in the southern mountain range and the Tärnaby/Hemavan area. Moreover, tourism employment has grown over several decades. The tourism sector has expanded even in southern Sweden; however in most parishes this development took place before 1980. Exceptions to this are some west coast parishes and the islands of Gotland and Öland.

Hence, although the most significant changes in numbers took place in the densely populated areas, tourism gained importance for the local labour markets in more remote areas and particularly in the mountain range.

(a)

Tourism Employment Growth
in Sweden, 1960–1999
Growth > 250 persons per decade

Growth

■ 1990–1999

□ 1980–1990

□ 1970–1980

■ 1960–1970

0   100   200   300   400   500 Km

Interpolation: Neighborhood statistics
Calculation: Sum   Based on individual data
Distance: 50 km   Aggregated for Swedish parishes
Cell Size: 1000 m x 1000 m   Cartography: D.K. Müller, 2003

(b)

Tourism Employment Market Growth
in Sweden, 1960–1999
Growth > 2.5 per cent per decade

Growth

■ 1990–1999

□ 1980–1990

□ 1970–1980

■ 1960–1970

0   100   200   300   400   500 Km

Interpolation: IDW
Power: 2   Based on individual data
Distance: 12 points   Aggregated for Swedish parishes
Cell Size: 1000 m x 1000 m   Cartography: D.K. Müller, 2003

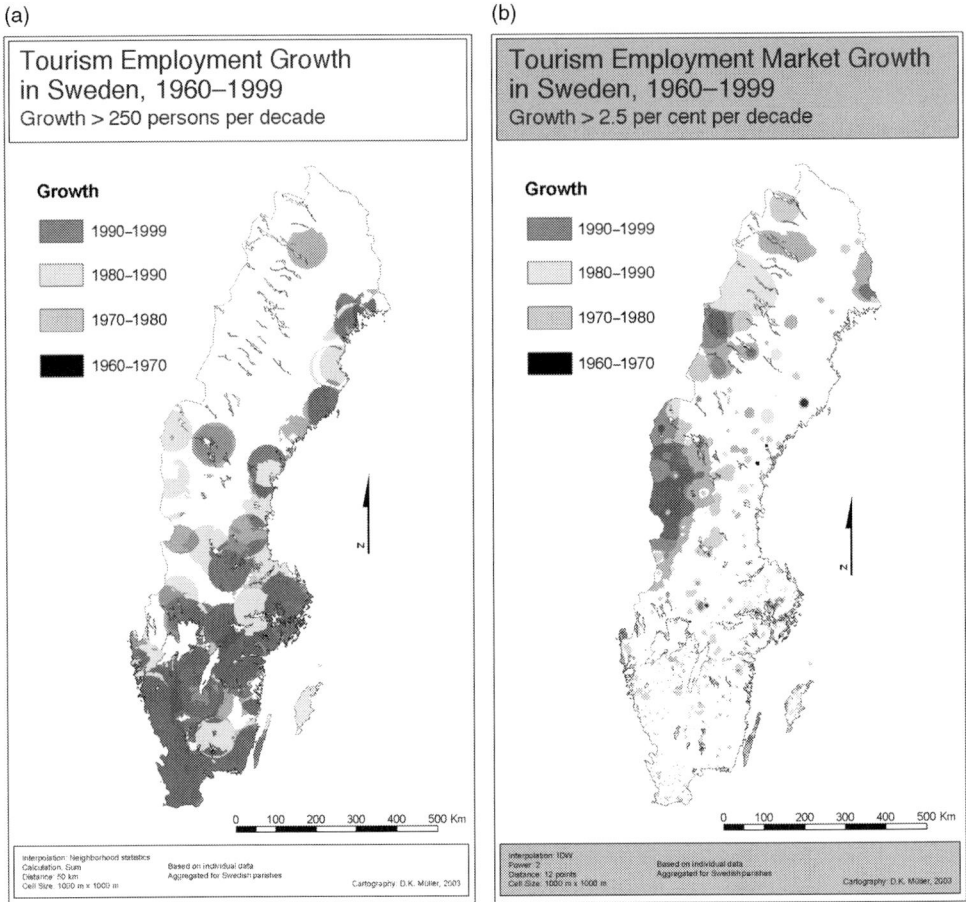

Fig. 6.8. Regions of expanding tourism employment in Sweden, 1960–1999 (from Statistics Sweden).

Conclusions

Obviously, tourism plays an important role on the Swedish labour market. Even though the majority of tourism employment occurs mainly in the metropolitan areas, it is the rural labour markets that are mainly dependent on tourism employment and development. However, seen from a 40-year perspective, tourism has gained importance in the entire country and since 1980 has surpassed the primary sector of the labour market, at least regarding the creation of employment.

In this chapter, tourism development was approached from a time-geographical perspective. It was argued that tourism should occur mainly in the metropolitan regions, which was also demonstrated empirically. However, it was also demonstrated that tourism employment initially occurred in areas in the metropolitan hinterland as well, before it spread to the northern parts of the country. This becomes particularly clear considering the increasing car ownership that has boosted tourism further away from the metropolitan areas.

Hence, it can be argued that tourism development indeed follows in the footsteps of technological achievements, pushing the belts of overnight stays further away from the metropolitan areas. Moreover, the figures indicate that tourism has become increasingly commodified. In the periphery, growth can be observed in areas commonly known as alpine ski resorts.

Looking at data from the 1980s and 1990s, it becomes clear that tourism comprises the entire country. Even north of the Arctic Circle, far from major population centres, considerable increases in tourism employment can be seen. Since then, it can be argued, tourism development and employment mirrors the geography of amenity-rich areas comprising areas in the mountains as well as islands like Öland and Gotland.

Considering absolute figures, the periphery is not an ideal place for tourism or tourism employment. Tourism occurs where people interact, and urban areas are hence mostly favoured by tourism development. However, a perspective from the periphery throws a different light on the situation. Here, society is considerably involved in tourism. In some cases, more than 30% of the total labour force works in tourism. The extent to which this is a deliberate engagement can be contested, however. Rural restructuring has undermined the peripheral labour markets and tourism has hence remained one of few options for making a living in the periphery.

Thus, tourism development and tourism employment must be taken seriously. The number of people engaged in tourism in these peripheral areas should make it a core point of rural planning and development strategy. Technological advances and political changes imply that tourism is becoming an international phenomenon to a greater extent. Thus, peripheral destinations are contested on an international market and must acquire new meaning for international customers.

However, a subject for further research should be the assessment of the consequences of tourism development for local society. In this study, every job has been treated on an equal footing. It is clear, however, that seasonality and other factors imply that tourism jobs are often part-time, poorly paid and are thus merely a complement to other employment. An assessment of these issues must be addressed elsewhere.

References

Ahlström, I. (2000) Utomhus i konsumtionssamhället. In: Sandell, K. and Sörlin, S. (eds) *Friluftshistoria: från »härdande Friluftslif« till Ekoturism och Miljöpedagogik.* Carlssons. Stockholm, pp. 168–184.

Butler, R. (1998) Rural recreation and tourism. In: Ilbery, B. (ed.) *The Geography of Rural Change.* Longman, Harlow, UK, pp. 211–232.

Butler, R., Hall, C.M. and Jenkins, J. (1998) Introduction. In: Butler, R., Hall, C.M. and Jenkins, J. (eds) *Tourism and Recreation in Rural Areas.* Wiley, Chichester, UK, pp. 3–16.

Christaller, W. (1963) Some considerations of tourism location in Europe: the peripheral regions – underdeveloped countries – recreation areas. *Regional Science Association Papers* 12, 95–105.

Cloke, P. and Godwin, M. (1992) Conceptualizing countryside change: from post-Fordism to rural structured coherence. *Transactions of the Institute of British Geographer* 17, 321–336.

Greer, T. and Wall, G. (1979) Recreational hinterlands: a theoretical and empirical analysis. In: Wall, G. (ed.) *Recreational Land Use in Southern Ontario*. Department of Geography, Waterloo, Ontario, Canada, pp. 227–245.

Hägerstrand, T. (1970) What about people in regional science? *Regional Science Association Papers* 24, 7–21.

Hägerstrand, T. (1991) Tidsgeografi. In: Carlestam, G. and Sollbe, B. (eds) *Om Tidens vidd och Tingens Ordning: Texter av Torsten Hägerstrand*. Byggforskningsrådet, Stockholm, pp. 133–142.

Hall, C.M. (2005) *Tourism: Rethinking the Social Science of Mobility*. Pearson Education, Harlow, UK.

Hall, C.M. and Jenkins, J. (1998) The policy dimensions of rural tourism and recreation. In: Butler, R., Hall, C.M. and Jenkins, J. (eds) *Tourism and Recreation in Rural Areas*. Wiley, Chichester, UK, pp. 19–42.

Harvey, D. (1989) *The Condition of Postmodernity: an Inquiry into the Origins of Cultural Change*. Blackwell, Oxford, UK.

Holm, E., Holme, K., Mäkilä, K. Mattsson-Kauppi, M. and Mörtvik, G. (2002) *The SVERIGE Spatial Microsimulation Model: Content, Validation, and Example Applications*. Kulturgeografiska Institutionen, Umeå, Sweden.

Jansson, B. and Müller, D.K. (2003) *Fritidsboende i Kvarken*. Kvarkenrådet, Umeå, Sweden.

Jenkins, J.M., Hall, C.M. and Troughton, M. (1998) The restructuring of rural economies: rural tourism and recreation as government response. In: Butler, R., Hall, C.M., and Jenkins, J. (eds) *Tourism and Recreation in Rural Areas*. Wiley, Chichester, UK, pp. 43–67.

Jussila, H. and Järviluoma, J. (1998) Extracting local resources: the tourism route to development in Kolari, Lapland, Finland. In: Neil, C. and Tykkyläinen, M. (eds) *Local Economic Development: a Geographical Comparison of Rural Community Restructuring*. UN University Press, Tokyo, pp. 269–289.

Ljungdahl, S.G. (1938) Sommar-Stockholm. *Ymer* 58, 218–242.

Lundgren, J.O.J. (1982) The tourist frontier of Nouveau Quebec: functions and regional linkages. *Tourist Review* 37 (2), 10–16.

Lundgren, J.O.J. (1995) The tourism space penetration processes in Northern Canada and Scandinavia: a comparison. In: Hall, C.M. and Johnston, M.E. (eds) *Polar Tourism: Tourism in the Arctic and Antarctic Regions*. Wiley, Chichester, UK, pp. 43–62.

Müller, D.K. (1999) *German Second Home Owners in the Swedish Countryside: on the Internationalization of the Leisure Space*. Department of Social and Economic Geography, Umeå University, Sweden.

Pearce, D. (1995) *Tourism Today: a Geographical Analysis*. Routledge, London.

Pettersson, Ö. (2002) *Socio-economic Dynamics in Sparse Regional Structures*. Department of Social and Economic Geography, Umeå University, Sweden.

Prideaux, B. (2002) Building visitor attractions in peripheral areas: can uniqueness overcome isolation to produce viability? *International Journal of Tourism Research* 4, 379–389.

Riley, M., Ladkin, A. and Szivas, E. (2002) *Tourism Employment: Analysis and Planning*. Channel View, Clevedon, UK.

Sharpley, R. (2002) Tourism: a vehicle for development? In: Sharpley, R. and Telfer, D.J. (eds) *Tourism and Development: Concepts and Issues*. Channel View, Clevedon, UK, pp. 11–34.

Shaw, G. and Williams, A.M. (1994) *Critical Issues in Tourism: a Geographical Perspective*. Blackwell, Oxford, UK.

SOU (1983) *Områden för Turism och Rekreation*. Jordbruksdepartementet 1983:43. Fritzes, Stockholm.

Statistics Sweden: Databases (http://www.scb.se).

Swedish Environmental Protection Agency (1974) *Fritid – Friluftsliv: en Undersökning av Vanor och Önskemål hos den Vuxna Tätortsbefolkningen 1973*. Stockholm.

Taylor, P.J. (1971) Distance transformation and distance decay function. *Geographical Analysis* 3, 221–238.

Townsend, A.R. (1997) *Making a Living in Europe: Human Geographies of Economic Change*. Routledge, London.

Turner, L. and Ash, J. (1975) *The Golden Hordes: International Tourism and the Pleasure Peripheries*. Constable, London.

Williams, A.M. and Montanari, A. (1995) Introduction: tourism and economic restructuring in Europe. In: Montanari, A. and Williams, A.M. (eds) *European Tourism: Regions, Spaces and Restructuring*. Wiley, Chichester, UK, pp. 1–15.

Williams, A.M. and Shaw, G. (eds) (1991) *Tourism and Economic Development: Western European Experiences*. Belhaven, London.

Part III
Challenges to Peripheral Area Tourism

7

The Vulnerability of Peripheral Tourism: the Rapid Disenchantment of Peripheral Attraction

WILSON IRVINE AND ALISTAIR R. ANDERSON

Aberdeen Business School, Robert Gordon University, Aberdeen, UK

Introduction

The purpose of this chapter is to explore the impacts of foot-and-mouth disease on peripheral tourist destinations. Our theoretical orientation is that tourists are attracted to the 'otherness' of peripheral places; that whilst such places stand as different, this conception of difference can rapidly shift from attraction to repulsion. Hence peripheral tourism is vulnerable. We first outline our conceptual framework, then report on the role of tourism in the periphery of Scotland, Grampian region, and in the northern periphery of England, the Cumbria region.

To develop our understanding we studied two different areas; Grampian, which was only indirectly affected, and Cumbria, which was directly affected by the presence of the disease. Our empirical data, collected by survey, show a very uneven effect: by region as we had expected, but also by type of tourist establishment. Finally we discuss our findings in the light of our theoretical model.

The Attractions of Places

Whilst Mathieson and Wall (1982) notes that there is little agreement about the importance of any specific factor that motivates people to visit particular places (Tiefenbacher *et al.*, 2000), Galloway (2002) proposes two types of motivation, push and pull factors (Crompton, 1979; Goossens, 2000). Push factors are broadly associated with demographic attributes and psychological variables such as need and personal values. Pull factors are seen as those external to the individual and are aroused by the destination.

Dann (1981) points out many researchers focus on the pull factors since they represent the specific attractions of place. Goossens (2000) suggests that both sets of factors should be considered, since each is one side of the motivational coin. Emotion is seen to be the connecting link, because tourists are pushed by their emotional needs and pulled by the emotional benefits. Leisure is thus seen as a positive and subjective experience; in particular, that emotion plays a major role in hedonistic consumption.

In terms of destination pull factors, there is broad agreement on the influence of tourism image on the behaviour of individuals (Mansfield, 1982; Ashworth and Goodall, 1988). There is now considerable evidence (Crompton and Ankomah, 1993; Kent, 1996; Gartner, 2000) of the influence of tourism image on the choice of holiday destination. Places with stronger positive images will have a higher probability of being included and chosen in the process of decision making (Alhemoud and Armstrong, 1996; Bigne *et al.*, 2001).

Pike (2002) recently reviewed 142 academic papers about image. One key element of his review was that images were either favourable or not. Tiefenbacher *et al.* (2000) argue that such perceptions are generated by advertisements, movies and word of mouth. Amongst the range of proposed factors they suggest that 'keeping up with the Jones's' is important. Thus group perceptions of a place are an influence. Reid and Reid (1993) make a similar point, that positive images are shared and also lead others to visit the location.

Image will therefore influence a tourist in the process of choosing a place to stay (Bigne *et al.*, 2001) and image – and its influence – is likely to be constructed prior to the actual experience of the place. So influence begins at the stage of choosing the holiday destination, and consequently destination choice cannot be explained exclusively in terms of the objective environment (Johnson and Thomas, 1995).

As Gallanti-Moutafi (1999) notes, tourists embark on their journeys with images already formed, largely the product of popular cultural representations. Places are transformed into a tourist site through the system of symbolic and structural processes. Tourists 'read' these signs and judge their aesthetic appropriateness. Stewart *et al.* (1998) stress how interpretation of place provides a better framework for understanding perceptions of place than merely asking visitors to recount 'facts'. Moscardo and Pearce (1996) suggest this is because people cannot process all the available information.

Conversely, Owen *et al.* (1999) suggest that, because of a lack of detailed information, prospective tourists will place greater reliance on long-established impressions and possibly stereotypical impressions. Mathieson and Wall (1982) suggest, in terms of push factors, that the motivation to visit a place may hinge upon the perception of the value in visiting that destination.

Thus, images of place are broad conceptions, loosely formed and probably based on the assimilation of diverse and incomplete information.

For example, Dann (1996, p. 79) shows how representations of destinations rely on cultural stereotypes and received images, 'which remain to be confirmed or invalidated by experience'. Images of place and the consequent choice of destination are therefore an individual subjective interpretation, but formed from social and shared representations selected from our economy of space and sign (Lash and Urry, 1994).

So tourism consists of a demarcation of both space and time. For time, as Baudrillard (1998) points out, it is a leisure time, differentiated from work time and caught up in the consumption of signs and experiences. For space, tourism is about created leisure space, places that are first signed as appropriate (Urry, 1995) and then consumed. 'A new or renewed importance attaches to place [...] even when these are imagined or invented' (Kumar, 1995, p. 123).

Tourism thus creates specific social space (Meethan, 2001). Yet this specificity of place is also caught up in the headlong dash of space–time compression, what Harvey calls the 'annihilation of space through time'. As Harvey (1989, p. 293) puts it so well:

> Mass television ownership coupled with satellite communication make it possible to experience a rush of images almost simultaneously, collapsing the world's spaces into a series of images on a television screen […] mass tourism, films made in spectacular locations, make a wide range of simulated or vicarious experiences of what the world contains available to many people.

What is paradoxically in this fission and fusion of the local and the global? The global spread of tourism depends upon the specificity of place, but the processes of globalization bring about such a greater range of wider couplings, demonstrating that globalism pulls two ways. One specific arena of this global local acting out is the periphery, where the otherness of image places a vital role in attracting tourists.

Peripheral Places

Peripherality is also a matter of perception; Brown and Hall (1999, p. 9) argue that a place that is remote and difficult to reach may be perceived by tourists to have certain qualities symptomatic of its situation, such as natural beauty, quaintness and *otherness*. Such places are seen as authentics, (Urry, 1990) rich in symbolic representations of the unspoilt, the pristine and the traditional. Urry (1995) also makes a powerful case for showing that it is this otherness that creates attraction. Thus, as Blomgren and Sørensen (1998) propose, the attractiveness of a periphery relies on the subjective interpretation of such symbols.

Anderson (2000) argues that peripheral spaces have moved from outlying production zones to become areas that are consumed in their own right. He also argues that it is their very otherness, non-industrialization, distance and an absence of core activities that create value in the consumer's eye. Moreover, it is those very qualities of otherness that are consumed (Anderson, 2000, p. 102): 'the periphery is the ideal zone for the production of aestheticised cultural goods.' Brown and Hall (1999) describe a peripheral area as one that suffers geographic isolation, being distant from core spheres of activity and having poor access to and from markets. Such areas, they claim, are characterized as economically marginalized with much of the business activity confined to micro-business.

But, as Wanhill (1997) notes, the European Union's Maastricht Treaty acknowledged that tourism could reduce regional disparities. Taken together we see the importance of tourism for the peripheral place, highly dependent on the 'difference' of image from the core, but equally we see how it appears to depend on a positive image.

The Vulnerability of Subjective Interpretations

One problem with image and motivation to visit is the fragility of symbolic otherness. Pearce (1982) considers appropriate images as transitory, but insulated from danger. Meethan (2001) talks of trust in a destination; trust in it measuring up to its image. He makes the salient point that the elimination of risk and issues of safety appear as prime factors in choice of destination.

Cavlek (2002) points out that peace, safety and security are the primary conditions for the tourism development of a destination. He also notes (2002, p. 479) how 'nothing can force them to spend a holiday in a place they perceive as insecure'. Indeed, Sonmez and Graefe (1998, p. 120) argue that if the destination choice is narrowed down to two alternatives which promise similar benefits, the 'one that is safe from threat is likely to be chosen'.

Pearce (1999) suggests that concern with personal security is a major factor in the decision-making process through which individuals make their travel choices (Sonmez, 1998). Although Galloway's (2002) paper explores sensation seeking as an explanatory factor in motivation and Elsrud (1999) discusses 'risk taking' as an attraction in backpacking holidays, these are special instances where risk appears to enhance image. So, different groups may have different perceptions or even different social constructs of thrills and danger (Carter, 1998).

In any case we know that images are incomplete. For example, Cavlek (2002) reports that, during the Indonesian crisis, tourism to Bali was not affected. This was because of the general lack of awareness that Bali was part of Indonesia. Similarly, the Greek island of Kos was badly affected by the misinformed association of it with Kosovo! Drabek (2000) notes how the effects of crisis ripple out to areas where no such problem exists (Cavlek, 2002).

Crises have become integral to business activity and tourism, in particular, suffers more than any other. Faulkner and Vikuluv (2001) propose that all destinations face the prospect of either a natural or a human-induced disaster. In particular, Cavlek (2002) suggests that government warnings to potential tourists always have strong psychological effects, thus creating a major impediment to the selling of holidays, even to parts of the country still entirely safe.

Thus far we have explored the importance of image in motivating tourism. We have demonstrated that the otherness of peripherality is a key mechanism for attracting tourists. This otherness, we have argued, is an incomplete social construction, driven by globalization but dependent upon a positive impression of local place. We have also noted how perceptions of risk, real or imagined, like the images themselves, can act in reversing the attraction and turn it into a repelling force. We now continue to explore the vulnerability of a peripheral tourist place

Tourism in Scotland

Tourism is Scotland's most important industry, injecting £2.5 billion into the economy annually (http://www.scotexchange.net, 2003). It is the 4th biggest employer, employing 193,000, some 8% of the workforce. In 1995 the UK ranked 4th in the top ten tourist destinations in Europe, with 23.7 million arrivals (De Vaal, 1997). However, inbound tourist statistics show that only 1.9 million of these UK visitors came to Scotland (http://www.staruk.com, 2003), with that figure dropping to 1.5 million in 2001 (Tourism Attitudes Survey, 2002). This decrease is blamed on the effects of both the 11 September terrorist attack and on foot-and-mouth disease. 2002 did, however, experience increased visits to Scotland by UK residents, with visits being up by 10% on those of 2001 (McKay, 2003).

Tourism in Grampian

Grampian is the north-east shoulder of Scotland with a tourist product primarily focused on scenery and castles. Heritage and history play a major part in tourist attraction; seeing historic house and castles is important for eight out of ten visitors. Grampian's attractions currently range from outdoor activities, natural and built heritage to adventure and theme parks. However, Aberdeen and Grampian visitor numbers fell by 13.1%, from 140,743 in 2001 to 122,255 during the same period in 2002 (http://www.scotexchange.net, 2003). The local tourist board confirmed the drop at −12.8%, which was the second largest decline in numbers in Scotland.

Tourism in peripheral Grampian

Researchers have spent much time debating Grampian's problems of seasonality and peripherality and analysing what disadvantage, if any, is placed on the area because of these factors. Peripherality has been viewed as the biggest problem, being held responsible for the increasing amount of difficulties being experienced within the industry (Baum, 1996) and is most often viewed as the most consistent policy issue within cold-climate areas.

A peripheral area is seen as an area of remote geographical isolation that is far away from central areas of activity; with poor infrastructure meaning access is difficult (Brown *et al.*, 1999).

This problem is especially evident in Grampian where the majority of the region is isolated from major cities. It is an area of mainly peripheral structure, with poor roads and a large rural community not dissimilar to that of Cumbria. It also contains some unique tourist attractions and wonderful scenic beauty comparable to the north-east of England.

Tourism in Cumbria

Cumbria was an area directly affected by foot-and-mouth disease and is devoted to tourism. Cumbria includes the Lake District National Park and the Hadrian's Wall World Heritage Site and has recently been awarded, after a rigorous assessment, Green Globe Destination Status (Cumbrian Tourist Board, 2003, http://www.golakes.co.uk). It is a relatively remote area composed of sparsely populated sectors with some minor concentrations of population.

Foot-and-Mouth Disease

Foot-and-mouth disease is one of the most contagious animal diseases. Although most affected adult animals will recover within two weeks, the drop in yields could have enormous economic impact. It has few effects on humans. None the less, the UK government policy of slaughtering affected or at-risk herds had an enormous impact on Britain's countryside. The first cases of foot-and-mouth disease (since 1967) were confirmed on 10 February 2001. Within 2 weeks the disease had spread widely, creating a large number of cases. After peaking in April/May numbers tailed off to October 2001.

As Anderson (2003, p. 5) noted, a total of 2026 cases of the disease were identified and a total of over 4 million animals were culled during the crisis. Media attention during the crisis focused dramatically on the agricultural community, showing the destruction of livestock and the closure of farms across the country, the major part of which was brought about without confirmation of the disease in that area.

Ireland and Vetier (2002, p. 5) detail the steps taken when farms were not directly affected, but which were unfortunate to be in the cull area or to have links with foot-and-mouth cases: 'A quarantine ban was established on farms with traced former connections to the confirmed case and animals killed under the classification of "slaughter on suspicion".'

However, there were also direct effects felt in some way or other by most other industries. In particular, tourism that is dependent on access to accommodation and associated tourist facilities in core and peripheral areas was badly affected.

The two study areas affected by the disease were Cumbria and Grampian, both peripheral in the sense that they do not contain any major population areas, and the associated activity and tourism attractions are principally in the countryside, e.g. The Lakes, landscapes and associated activities in Cumbria and the castle and whisky trails and golf in Grampian. Cumbria was affected directly, with a large number of affected cases, but Grampian only indirectly, as it did not have one case during the outbreak and was more than 150 miles from the nearest case (in the south-west of Scotland).

Foot-and-mouth in Cumbria

Cumbria's main industries are agriculture and tourism, and tourism was affected just as badly as agriculture. As Ireland and Vetier (2002, p. 6) put it: 'it is … evident that demand failure among tourists has a severe impact on the British tourism industry.' The BBC News web site (April 2001) dramatically described the devastation and fear of the unknown future for the farmers of Cumbria saying: 'Cumbria is holding its breath. Not just in dread of future outbreaks, but also because of the smell of the burial sites.' Television dramatized the extreme actions taken by the government and the effect on peoples' lives. Tourism in Cumbria suffered particularly when the Government closed the countryside down.

The Anderson report (Anderson 2003, p. 3) noted the closure of many footpaths: 'The instrument to close footpaths and bridleways was necessary not only in infected areas but also outside them.' But many of the tourism businesses within Cumbria rely on the footpaths and surrounding areas to be open for their survival. One consequence was the difficulty in gaining access to many of the small villages within Cumbria when these roadways were closed.

Television coverage of the foot-and-mouth epidemic detailed every case and scare within Cumbria. The television coverage scared many potential tourists away from the countryside; many areas that had no contact with the outbreak suffered because of the media messages given. Ireland and Vetier (2002, p. 1) identified that: 'Exaggerated media reporting of a crisis can be as damaging as inept Government policy.' Many of the tourism businesses within Cumbria closed because of the dramatic reduction in visitors within the area. After the epidemic was over tourism organizations within Cumbria began to try and rebuild the businesses by extra advertising and property upgrading. Although considerable efforts were made, tourism numbers were still poor relative to those of previous years.

Table 7.1 shows the drop in numbers experienced by tourism businesses, partly due to the foot-and-mouth epidemic, for both Cumbria and other parts of England. The trips refer to the summer months of June to September, 2000–2002.

Table 7.1 demonstrates that of the four representative locations Cumbria was the worst effected, with the largest drop in visitor numbers and no obvious signs of recovery. Anderson (2003, p. 3) argues that numbers were kept low by the unnecessarily prolonged closure of footpaths and woodland areas.

Table 7.1. Tourism trips in England, June–September 2000–2002 (from International Passenger Survey, 2003).

	2000 (million)	2001 (million)	2002 (million)
England	64.9	55.5	63.0
Cumbria	2.3	1.8	1.8
Yorkshire	6.0	5.4	5.8
London	9.1	7.7	8.0

The effects within Cumbria were devastating, with both tourism and agricultural businesses affected. Many of the businesses exist in remote towns and villages spread out within the district and many directly rely on tourists drawn to their areas by the impressive wildlife. Thus, the closure of footpaths and roads connecting the tourists with the remote areas of Cumbria meant that most of this wildlife could not be reached. This reliance on footpaths and road connections for the remote tourism businesses caused many of the problems when the foot-and-mouth epidemic struck. It caused a decrease in tourists so dramatic that all tourism businesses within the area were affected.

A large number of the Cumbrian attractions were shut down for at least 3 months, and many of these never reopened. As well as the closure of businesses, the loss in tourism numbers reduced turnover within the area; many people lost their jobs because businesses couldn't afford to support themselves, let alone pay wages; nearly all business investment stopped.

Foot-and-mouth directly affected Cumbria and had indirect effects upon Grampian. Are there lessons to be learned by comparing these effects and trying to analyse the reason for any differences or similarities encountered in these two mainly peripheral tourism-focused areas?

Methodology

Our sample frames were drawn from tourist businesses in Grampian and Cumbria. The Grampian sample of 180 businesses was drawn from a sample frame provided by Dunn and Bradstreet. The Cumbrian sample, 170 businesses, was selected by choosing one in five from a list taken from the official Cumbrian Tourist Board Guide (2002).

The Grampian sample, the main locus of our study, was surveyed twice. The first survey, A, was carried out in April 2001 at the height of the outbreak and received 85 responses (47%). The second survey, B, was carried out in March 2003 and received 60 responses (33%); 18 others were returned uncompleted. Either the businesses were no longer operating from the address given or were under new ownership. These surveys were intended to provide data to allow us to gauge and compare the anticipated with the real effects.

The Cumbrian survey, C, was carried out in February 2003 and contained a number of identical or similar questions. This survey had a response from 70, giving a 39% response rate. Questions were asked about both the expected and the actual effects of the disease. In all of the surveys many of the questions were open-ended to allow respondents to enlarge on the data.

Data Analysis

The data were analysed using descriptive statistics to analyse single variables, and simple non-parametric tests were used to compare variables and significance of normally distributed results. The tests included frequency analysis and cross-tabs analysis. The cross-tabs analysis (Pearson chi-square test) was used to check significance within the normally distributed results. A number of variables were recoded where results were considered important and significant. Significance was tested at a 90% confidence level (the majority of tests proved significant and are all represented).

All of the tests were carried out after the variables were coded onto SPSS (Statistical Package for Social Sciences) and entered and run in order to test the confidence of the data. A large number of the variables had open-ended responses, which were grouped using a Pragmatic Content Analysis in order to collate the similar responses and include them as part of the descriptive analysis. A number of tables were constructed at appropriate stages to describe the results.

To provide a comparative framework, tourism providers were recoded into two types of business organization: (i) Type 1: hotel, guest house (GH) and bed and breakfast (B&B) providers; and (ii) Type 2: 'other' providers, which covered a diversity of organizations from caravan sites and golf courses to speciality equipment or other service providers in both areas. The data retrieved from the different surveys are shown in Table 7.2.

The Grampian surveys, data and discussion

Survey A took place in Grampian at the height of the disease and could be expected to reflect the worst expectations of the impact. We also expected these prognoses to reflect the general gloom created by the vivid and dramatic media portrayal. The results shown in Table 7.3 below confirm our expectations and show the extent of business reduction anticipated.

The overall view was very pessimistic; more than half our respondents anticipated cancellations and large decreases in the business volume and profits. Some 25% expected to have to lose staff and a significant number anticipated closure of their business. Most appeared to expect the impact to last for a considerable time. Taken by type of business, Type 1, i.e. those most likely to be dependent on visitors, we see a very large impact on volume and the duration of the adverse effects.

Table 7.2. General characteristics of all the samples.

Survey	Business type	n	% of total	Professional body membership (%)	Customer type: tourist (%)
A, Grampian, April 2001 (n, 180)	1	58	69	65	36
	2	27	31	34 (0.066)[a]	50 (0.065)[a]
B, Grampian, April 2003 (n, 180)	1	42	70	64	34
	2	18	30	67 (0.3)[a]	17 (0.042)[a]
C, Cumbria, February 2003 (n, 170)	1	46	66	66	93
	2	24	34	58 (0.031)[a]	75 (0.1)[a]

1, Type 1, accommodation providers; 2, Type 2, 'other' providers; [a] level of significance.

Table 7.3. Survey A: the impacts of foot-and-mouth disease.

Business type	Cancellations anticipated (%)	Decrease in volume (%)	Decrease in profits (%)	Staff cuts (%)	Total closure (%)	Impact duration >2 weeks/ 1 year (%)
1	56	70	67	28	14	86/36
2	55	56	59	22	26	48/18
	(0.3)[a]	(0.1)[a]	(0.3)[a]	(0.1)[a]	(0.1)[a]	(0.003)[a]

[a] level of significance.

Survey B (Table 7.4) was able to measure the real impact and shows that, whilst the impact was large, it was not as bad as had been anticipated. It is worth noting that 10% of our original sample had gone away. This could be partially attributed to the impact or simply business churn. Table 7.4 demonstrates that cancellations were worse than anticipated for Type 1 businesses and, with a 64% drop in bookings, reflects a major loss of business.

None the less, we note that actual volume decrease was 'only' 53%, suggesting that some replacement visitors were found. Again, the worst impact was on accommodation types of business, with 47% lasting for more than weeks and 26% being affected for more than a year.

The Cumbria survey, data and discussion

The Cumbrian survey (Table 7.5) is a snapshot of data collected 2 years after the epidemic. Since Cumbria was physically affected as an area where the disease was present, the data provide us with some comparisons of perceptions and impacts. Table 7.5 shows a dramatic reduction in visitor

Table 7.4. Survey B: the impacts of foot-and-mouth disease.

Business type	Cancellations anticipated (%)	Decrease in volume (%)	Decrease in profits (%)	Staff cuts (%)	Total closure (%)	Impact duration >2 weeks/ 1 year (%)
1	64	53	47	14	05	47/26
2	28	23	22	06	05	23/12
	(0.015)[a]	(0.076)[a]	(0.1)[a]	(0.3)[a]	(0.8)[a]	(0.074)[a]

[a] level of significance.

Table 7.5. Survey C: the impacts of foot-and-mouth disease.

Business type	Decrease in visitor numbers (%)	Decrease in volume (%)	Staff cuts (%)	Impact duration > 1 year (%)	Impact still present (%)
1	98	96	22	48	30
2	91	90	33	50	25
	(0.092)[a]	(0.096)[a]	(0.1)[a]	(0.03)[a]	(0.4)[a]

[a] level of significance.

numbers, with drops of 98 and 91% in each type, respectively, indicating some sort of decrease in visitor numbers; and 96 and 90%, respectively, indicating a 'loss of business'.

When asked about specific percentages of 'loss of business', about 20% in both types of business affected identified an actual loss of business of 'more than 50%', with approximately 80% of those affected in each category identifying a loss of between 1 and 50%. Staff cuts were highest in Type 2 businesses, which differs from the findings of both Grampian surveys. A very large percentage in both types experienced the effects for more than a year, with a large number still experiencing the effects at the time of writing.

The effects of the foot-and-mouth-disease on core and peripheral areas within Grampian: Survey B longitudinal survey

Table 7.6 clearly shows that Type 1 organizations in this survey were larger and depended less on seasonal business than did Type 2 organizations. This means that the main accommodation providers were less seasonal and larger and, surprisingly, more were situated in peripheral areas, villages and remote areas. These accommodation providers, located more in peripheral areas, had a much greater decrease in volume of 53%.

Table 7.7 compares core and peripheral businesses (smaller and more seasonal), throughout the region and it seems clear that peripheral

Table 7.6. Survey B: other characteristics of businesses in Grampian.

Business type	Seasonal (%)	Size, >10 staff (%)	Peripheral (%)	Decrease in volume (%)
1	17	46	55	53
2	33 (0.1)[a]	8 (0.2)[a]	23 (0.010)[a]	23 (0.076)[a]

[a] level of significance.

Table 7.7. Survey B: peripherality and its effects.

Situation (%)	Proportion of total sample (%)	Size, >2 staff (full-time and part-time) (%)	Non-seasonal (%)	Decrease in profits (%)	Decrease in volume (%)
Core	63	63	79	28	35
Peripheral	37	35 (0.8)[a]	73 (0.5)[a]	59 (25)± (0.1)[a]	64 (0.1)[a]

[a] level of significance; [b] percentage decrease in profit.

businesses situated in Grampian experienced a greater decrease (or large decrease) than the core businesses situated in the city and towns. Sixty-three per cent of the respondents were situated in the core and 37% in peripheral locations. There was a much greater effect on profitability in the peripheral locations, with 59% experiencing some type of decrease in profitability, including a 'large decrease' in profitability (25%). There was much the same picture for impact on volume where the peripheral businesses clearly suffered the most.

Conclusions: Comparing the Data from Grampian and Cumbria

From these data, we conclude that the effects of foot-and-mouth disease on tourism business were considerable. The Grampian longitudinal studies indicate that although bad, these effects were not quite as bad as had been anticipated. In both areas the impact was immediate, manifest by dramatic drops in volume of business, profitability and reductions in staff numbers.

It was also long term, a large number of businesses taking almost a year to recover. In some cases, though we cannot be certain how many, the business actually closed. There were some unexpected results. We found that caravan sites in Grampian had an increase in business volume. Since the opposite is true of Cumbria, we deduce that visitors had deserted caravan parks in the affected areas and remained loyal to these new areas over the period.

We also found some remarkable instances where substitute products were used. These included the use of geese instead of sheep at a sheep visitor attraction. There was some evidence of specific spikes of business activity, probably related to a 'Dunkirk spirit' and a campaign to support domestic businesses and special marketing initiatives made at the time.

Peripheral businesses were more seasonal and smaller and clearly suffered the most in the disease situation, with more negative effects on profitability and volume than businesses situated in core areas. The overall effects confirm the perception of lack of security and safety in these areas (Cavlek, 2002), and these effects have rippled out into the non-affected areas (e.g. Grampian) as identified by Drabek (2000).

The data and analysis appear to support our original argument, that the attractions of otherness are fickle. Peripheral tourist areas that depend on their portrayal as appropriate places for visitors are vulnerable to any change in people's perception. As the data demonstrate, the impact of any circumstance that detracts from that attraction has serious economic consequences. Lending strength to our case about perception rather than reality is the comparison between Grampian and Cumbria. Both are peripheral places and are highly dependent upon tourism; both are rural, scenic places, so that the portrayal of otherness is symbolically dependent upon an Arcadian image. This rural otherness is a contrast to the urban, but is also bucolic, replete with the benign of rural life. Unsurprisingly, the confrontation to this imagery with media pictures of smoking cattle funeral pyres resulted in the repulsion of visitors.

However, the contrast between the two areas with regard to the presence of the disease is significant. Cumbria was very badly affected, but Grampian had no cases of foot-and-mouth. Cumbria was effectively closed to visitors, but Grampian was only marginally physically affected. Yet, broadly speaking, the impact on tourism was similar. Effects were admittedly worse in Cumbria. This seems to confirm that perceptions, rather than facts or real circumstances, create the disastrous effects of catastrophe. Within Grampian the businesses situated in peripheral areas also suffered most.

There are some serious implications for the economics of peripheral places in these findings. We know that for such places a designation of difference – the otherness of such places – is a tourism attractor. We know that peripheral places will continue to suffer from the centripetal forces drawing income into urban cores. Consequently, we realize that peripheral places are likely to become more, rather than less, dependent on remaining attractive. Globalization seems to suggest that the importance of local place is likely to be, on one hand, reduced in international convergence but, on the other, the distinctiveness of some peripheral places may become greater, simply in contrast to the convergence of others. Moreover, the massification of communication in globalization will exaggerate the qualities of peripherality. It may enhance but, as in the case of catastrophe, it may repel. Thus, peripheral places are becoming increasingly vulnerable to the fickleness of attraction. Mere facts, information alone, are unlikely to ameliorate the impact of catastrophe. Tourism decisions seem to be made in the heart, not in the head.

References

Alhemoud, A.M. and Armstrong, E.G. (1996) Image of tourism attractions in Kuwait. *Journal of Travel Research* 34 (4), 76–80.

Anderson, A.R. (2000) Paradox in the periphery and entrepreneurial reconstruction? *Entrepreneurship and Regional Development* 12, 91–109.

Anderson, I. (2003) *Foot-and-mouth Disease 2001: Lessons to be Learned Inquiry Report, HC888.* The Stationery Office, London.

Ashworth, G. and Goodall, B. (1988) Tourist images: marketing considerations. In: Goodall, B. and Ashworth, G. (eds) *Marketing in the Tourism Industry; the Promotion of Destination Regions.* Routledge, London, pp. 213–238.

Baudrillard, J. (1998) *The Consumer Society.* Sage, London.

Baum, T. (1996) Images of tourism, past and present. *International Journal of Contemporary Hospitality Management* 8 (4), 25–30.

Bigne, J.E., Sanchez, M.I. and San, J. (2001) Tourism image, evaluation variables and after purchase behaviour: inter-relationship. *Tourism Management* 22, 607–616.

Blomgren, K.B. and Sørensen, A. (1998) Peripherality – factor or feature? Reflections on peripherality in tourist regions. *Progress in Tourism and Hospitality Research* 4, 319–336.

Brown, F. and Hall, D. (1999) Introduction: the paradox of peripherality. In: Brown, F. and Hall, D. (eds) *Case Studies of Tourism in Peripheral Areas.* Report 15, Research Centre of Bornholm, Nexø, Denmark, pp. 7–14.

Carter, S. (1998) Tourists' and travellers' social construction of Africa and Asia as risky locations. *Tourism Management* 19 (4), 349–358.

Cavlek, N. (2002) Tour operators and destination safety. *Annals of Tourism Research* 29, 478–496.

Crompton, J.L. (1979) Motivations for pleasure vacations. *Annals of Tourism Research* 6, 408–424.

Crompton, J.L. and Ankomah, P.K. (1993) Choice set propositions in destination decisions. *Annals of Tourism Research* 20, 461–476.

Cumbrian Tourist Board (2002) *Cumbria and the Lake District.* Mullin Design, Kendal, UK.

Cumbrian Tourist Board (2003) *Facts about Cumbria 2003* (http:www.staruk.com, accessed 10 January 2003).

Ireland, M. and Vetier, L. (2002) The reality and mythology of the foot-and-mouth disease crisis in Britain: factors influencing tourist destination choice Working Paper, University College of St Mark and St John, Plymouth, UK.

Johnson, P. and Thomas, B. (1995) The analysis of choice and demand in tourism. In: Johnson, P. and Thomas, B. (eds) *Choice and Demand in Tourism.* Mansell, London, pp. 1–12.

Kent, P. (1996) People places and priorities: opportunity sets and consumers' holiday choice. In: Ashworth, G. and Goodall, B. (eds) *Marketing Tourism Places.* Routledge, London, pp. 42–62.

Know Your Market (1999) *Tourism Attitudes Survey 1999* (http://www.scotexchange.net, accessed 12 January 2003).

Kumar, K. (1995) *From Post-industrial to Post-modern Society.* Blackwell, Oxford, UK.

Lash, S. and Urry, J. (1994) *Economies of Signs and Space.* Sage, London.

Mansfield, Y. (1982) From motivation to actual travel. *Annals of Tourism Research* 19, 399–419.

Mathieson, A. and Wall, G. (1982) *Tourism: Economic, Physical and Social Impacts.* Longman, New York.

McKay, D. (2003) Future of tourism to be debated at Abertay. *The Press and Journal,* 13 January 2003, Aberdeen, UK.

Meethan, K. (2001) *Tourism in Global Society: Place, Culture and Consumption.* Palgrave, Hampshire, UK.

Moscardo, G. and Pearce, P.L. (1996) Mindful visitors; heritage and tourism. *Annals of Tourism Research* 23, 376–397.

Owen, R.E., Botterill, D., Emanuel, L., Foster, N., Gale, T., Nelson, C. and Pearce, D.G. (1999) Tourism in Paris: studies at the micro scale. *Annals of Tourism Research* 26, 77–97.

Pearce, P.L. (1982) *The Social Psychology of Tourist Behaviour*. Pergamon, Oxford, UK.

Pike, S. (2002) Destination image analysis: a review of 142 papers from 1973 to 2000. *Tourism Management* 23, 541–548.

Reid, L. and Reid, S. (1993) Communicating tourism supplier services: building repeat visitor relationships. *Journal of Travel and Tourism Marketing* 2, 3–19.

Selby, M. (1999) Perceptions from the periphery – the experience of Wales. In: Brown, F. and Hall, D. (eds) *Case Studies of Tourism in Peripheral Areas*. Report 15, Research Centre of Bornholm, Nexø, Denmark, pp. 15–48.

Sonmez, S.F. (1998) Tourism, terrorism, and political instability. *Annals of Tourism Research* 25, 416–456.

Sonmez, S.F. and Graefe, A.R. (1998) Influence of terrorism risk on foreign tourism decisions. *Annals of Tourism Research* 25, 112–144.

Stewart, E.J., Hayward, B.M. and Devlin. P.J. (1998) The 'place' of interpretation: a new approach to the evaluation of interpretation. *Tourism Management* 19, 257–266.

Tiefenbacher, J.P., Day, F.A. and Walton, J.A. (2000) Attributes of repeat visitors to small tourist-orientated communities. *Social Science Journal* 37, 299–308.

Tourism Attitudes Survey (2002) *Know your Market: Tourism Attitudes Survey, 2002* (http://www.scotexchange.net, accessed 12 January 2003).

Urry, J. (1990) *The Tourist Gaze*. Sage, London.

Urry, J. (1995) *Consuming Places*. Routledge, London.

Wanhill, S. (1997) Peripheral area tourism: a European perspective. *Progress in Tourism and Hospitality Research* 3, 47–70.

8

'If That's a Moose, I'd Hate to See a Rat!' Visitors' Perspectives on Naturalness and their Consequences for Ecological Integrity in Peripheral Natural Areas of New Zealand

BRENT LOVELOCK

Department of Tourism, University of Otago, Dunedin, New Zealand

Introduction

The quoted sentence in the title of this chapter may be confusing for some readers – and rightly so. To help, imagine the title being spoken in a broad Scottish accent, and you will see that the title plays on the confusion between species – in this case a moose and a mouse. It is suggested that there is a great deal of confusion over some species of flora/fauna – what they are, their role, their place, their right to exist in a certain location, and their management.

Furthermore, it is put forward that tourists may play a significant role in perpetuating and/or resolving this confusion. This chapter will explore this confusion over species, in terms of what the visitor sees as being natural or non-natural, a desirable species or a pest, and will argue that the tourist may therefore play a role in assisting or threatening a destination's naturalness, its ecological integrity or, indeed, its biosecurity.

Naturalness is Good

We are told that naturalness is good – both by the ecologists and by tourism managers, for naturalness is an essential part of the attractiveness of a destination – this may be especially so for peripheral areas, for which naturalness may be the main element of destination competitiveness. Many peripheral areas have suffered, or continue to suffer, from extractive industries such as farming, forestry or mining that impact on their ability to sell themselves on their naturalness.

Naturalness in this context is taken to equate with purity and ecological integrity, and may be defined as the extent to which the biota of the locale reflects the pre-modern level of endemism. Thus many destination managers concern themselves with efforts to maximize the naturalness of their locale – or at least to maximize the image of naturalness – as a point of differentiation from other destinations.

The question remains, however, how natural does the visitor want the destination to be? Is naturalness important to them? For example, tourists may be in favour of closing a factory that is polluting a local lake, or of halting a logging operation that is denuding a scenic vista. But does the perceived desire of visitors for naturalness extend beyond the obvious, the macro-scale landscape features, the lack of obvious pollution and extensive damage through infrastructural developments – to the level of the individual species? Furthermore, what will visitors tolerate in terms of ecosystem management practices, on a species level, aimed at achieving greater 'authenticity of nature'?

Naturalness, Purity and New Zealand

New Zealand provides an example of where the tourism industry relies strongly upon an image of naturalness. New Zealand's tourism NGO, Tourism New Zealand, has adopted the slogan '100% Pure New Zealand' and uses naturalness, or purity, as a key ingredient of its promotional campaign (Tourism New Zealand, 2004).

Sadly, the integrity of New Zealand's natural areas, critical components of the country's attractiveness, have been undermined by various geological, biological and social 'flows' that have occurred over time. Indeed, these 'biogeosocial flows' are multidimensional in that they incorporate the physical flow or movement of land masses, the flow of species, plants and animals, the flow of settlers, Polynesian and European, through colonization, and the latter-day flow of tourists.

An essential element of the flow of people is the flow of new ideas, values and practices. It can be argued that the present state of naturalness or ecological integrity in New Zealand is the result of the impact of and interaction between the five main flows that have taken place (Table 8.1). It is important to note that these flows may occur concurrently and thus interact over time.

The first of these 'biogeosocial flows' (Generation 1) is that which took place in geological time, with the separation of the proto-New Zealand land mass from Gondwanaland, creating a unique flora and fauna. It can be said that this stage established the essential attractiveness of New Zealand as a tourist destination (albeit 60 million years later).

Table 8.1. Biogeosocial flows to New Zealand.

Biogeosocial flow	Time period	Process	Components
Generation 1	60–500 million years ago	Separation of proto-New Zealand land mass from Gondwanaland	Isolation and creation of unique New Zealand flora and fauna
Generation 2	AD 700–1300	Colonization by Polynesian settlers	Introduction of some predators, radical alteration of some ecosystems
Generation 3	1769–c.1920	Colonization by mainly European settlers	Introduction of a broad range of alien plants and animals, some for tourist industry. Creation of a familiar environment
Generation 4	c.1930–present day	Establishment of conservation movement, 'expulsion' of foreign species	Recognition of impacts of introduced species, efforts at removal, eradication
Generation 5	c.1970–present day	Increased flow of inbound tourists	Tourists bring 'foreign' notions of what is natural and what is not

The next stage (Generation 2) involved colonization by Polynesians, who brought with them some predator species (e.g. Kiore, the Maori rat) and who, through their hunting, agricultural and food gathering practices, impacted upon many habitats and species. Similarly so for the Generation 3 flow of European (British) settlers, mainly during the 19th and early 20th centuries, who had an enormous impact on native species through the introduction of a wide range of exotic flora and fauna.

Both of these flows were similar in that they involved the inflow of exotic species, and also exotic ideas. The peoples involved were not familiar with New Zealand ecosystems, and were basically acting according to ideas and values imported from their lands of origin. For example, the British imported many UK birds and mammals to remind them of home, and many game species for sport and for the tourist industry. Native species were not initially valued as highly as those they were already familiar with.

By around 1920, however, a conservation movement had become established in New Zealand and, with it, recognition of the value of native flora and fauna, and the impacts that introduced species were having upon them (Hall and Higham, 2000). From this point onwards, the Generation 4 flow could be perceived as a net outward flow of exotic 'pest' species from New Zealand, as attempts were made to eradicate them from natural areas.

The last flow listed, Generation 5, involves a net inward flow, again of foreign ideas and values, with the rapidly growing flow of inbound tourists to the country. The question to ask at this point is: how does this latter flow differ from the colonizing and acclimatizing Generations 2 and 3 flows discussed above, and what impact does it have on the relationship between indigenous and introduced species? In other words, what effect does this flow have upon naturalness, purity or ecological integrity? Does this flow again value foreign (home) species above indigenous species?

In many ways, the latter flows discussed here represent core–periphery flows of humans and their values. The European colonization witnessed the imposition of core values (capitalist systems of production) upon an indigenous paradise – a Garden of Eden. These core values were expressed through the introduction of species that assist in that system of production – either directly (e.g. through producing meat, fibre or a chargeable tourist activity) or through helping create an environment 'just like home' that would continue to encourage inward migration, and thus create more profit for the fledgling nation and its protagonists.

Similarly, the Generation 5 flow of international tourists perpetuates the core–periphery flow as, arguably, New Zealand is geographically and economically (despite what Wallerstein may have said – placing New Zealand in among the core nations) peripheral and, certainly in touristic terms, this is true.

But in terms of influence upon naturalness, it could be argued that this latter flow is significantly different from the previous ones, in that visitors are better educated and living in an age of 'ecological enlightenment' – thus they would value naturalness and indeed foster the Generation 4 flow that seeks to eradicate exotic 'pest' species and thus achieve greater naturalness.

Objectives and Method

These are the questions that that this research sets out to answer. Through the establishment of a case study, the research sets out to investigate the knowledge and perceptions of visitors to New Zealand's natural areas regarding introduced and exotic species. It seeks to explore and compare whether foreign tourists in New Zealand hold different values of naturalness from domestic tourists and if they have similar or different views on how exotic 'pest' species should be managed in natural ecosystems.

It has been argued that invasive alien species are a by-product of human values, decisions and behaviours, and therefore that a focus on human beliefs and behaviour can be significant when dealing with pest issues (Reaser, undated and Mack, undated, both in McNeely, 2002). This study thus hopes also to contribute to the debate on invasive animal species in this peripheral area, by focusing upon the role of tourism as an agent of human values, decisions and behaviours. In New Zealand, previous work on attitudes towards invasive alien species is limited to that of Fraser (2001), who studied residents' views on this issue. This research will extend the scope of this line of inquiry into the tourism sphere.

The study took place on Stewart Island, in the very south of New Zealand, located at latitude 46° south. The island is the location of the country's latest national park, Rakiura, which covers most of this sparsely populated, rugged and inhospitable island. The island has traditionally supported a fishing industry, but now also attracts around 30,000 visitors per annum (approximately 60% international and 40% domestic), mainly drawn by the combination of isolation (peripherality) and natural attractions, comprising native forest, beautiful coastline and outstanding forest and marine birdlife. There is a network of walking tracks around the island that cater for longer, demanding 'tramping' trips, as well as for shorter and more accessible day walks. The only settlement, Oban (population 300), has a small tourist infrastructure.

During February 2003, within and adjacent to the park, a sample of international (160) and domestic (110) visitors were subject to a personally administered questionnaire that addressed a range of ecological management issues. The questionnaire comprised four sections. The first section tested the participant's knowledge of the New Zealand native forest ecosystem and utilized, in part, photographs of native and introduced animal species. The second section addressed the issue of ecological integrity and ecosystem management, containing 14 statements that participants were asked to respond to using a five-point Likert-type scale. The next section investigated attitudes to two mammalian pest species and their control. The final section gathered sociodemographic data.

The results presented here are discussed mainly in terms of the international/domestic visitor dichotomy. International visitors are aggregated, which may overlook cultural differences that exist among the group (Dann, 1993); however, this remains the critical avenue of analysis for the purposes of this study. It is also argued that there is a higher degree of similarity than difference among the international visitor cohort, based upon the main countries of origin revealed below.

Research conducted overseas (e.g. Hudson and Ritchie, 2001) demonstrates variation in environmental attitudes based on nationality and on culture, and previous research on international and domestic visitors to New Zealand would support the view that these groups do indeed view the natural environment differently (e.g. Dawson, 2003). For this study, it is acknowledged that other segmentation variables (e.g. gender) may be significant, in terms of the assignment of environmental perceptions but in the interests of brevity, these are not explicitly addressed within this chapter.

Results

Respondent profile

Fewer than half of the participants were New Zealand residents (39.8%), with international visitors being dominated by the UK (16.4%), the USA (15.2%), Australia (9.4%) and Germany (8.2%). Males accounted for 53.2% of the total sample. Age distribution differed between domestic and international visitors, with the 20–29 years age group dominating the international group, while older visitors (60+) dominated the domestic group.

Occupational groups were dominated by professionals in both the domestic and international visitor segments, although the domestic segment also contained quite a high percentage of manual and clerical workers. The domestic group also had a higher proportion of retirees, whilst students were more evident within the international group.

International visitors had higher rates of membership of both environmental and animal welfare organizations (Table 8.2). Overall, 28.5% of visitors were members of an environmental organization and 9.7% were members of an animal welfare organization. New Zealanders, though, were more likely to keep pets. New Zealand residents were also twice as likely to go hunting or fishing.

Ecological knowledge

Participants were asked to name five species of native plant, five species of native bird and five species of introduced animal found in the New Zealand native forest.

New Zealand domestic visitors performed significantly better in this test than did international visitors – as would be expected (Table 8.3). To further test their level of local ecological knowledge, participants were shown photographs of nine native and introduced animals, asked to

Table 8.2. Environmental and animal welfare data for visitors to New Zealand.

	NZ visitors (%)	International visitors (%)
Member of an environmental organization	22.0	32.5
Member of an animal welfare organization	5.6	12.6
Keep pets currently	59.6	37.7
Normal place of residence urban	67.9	62.5
Go hunting or fishing	54.1	22.5
Vegetarian on moral grounds	0.0	10.0

Table 8.3. Knowledge of NZ native and introduced species.

	Name five species					
	NZ visitors			International visitors		
	n	Mean	SD	n	Mean	SD	t-value[a]
Number of native plant species	109	4.52	1.21	161	2.57	1.95	10.131
Number of native bird species	109	4.73	0.77	161	3.53	1.62	8.133
Number of introduced animal species	109	4.82	0.64	161	3.84	1.56	7.114

[a]T-test is significant at the 95% confidence level.

identify each species and to state whether it was native or introduced. The species in the photographs ranged from very easily identifiable (e.g. kiwi, deer) to less readily identifiable (e.g. Kakariki (a native parrot)) (Table 8.4).

Generally, domestic visitors were quite good at identifying species and performed better than international visitors, who scored moderately well on this item (Figs 8.1 and 8.2, Table 8.5). But, as far as identifying whether species were native or introduced, there was little difference between the groups – both groups scored well on this front; however domestic visitors scored marginally higher. Although international visitors did not necessarily know the names of species, they could generally decide whether the species was native or introduced. A statistical difference between mean scores of New Zealand and international visitors was observed for both species identification and species origin scores (see Table 8.5).

Table 8.4. NZ native species identification and origin, all visitors.

Species	Identification		Origin	
	n	Correct (%)	n	Correct (%)
Kiwi	269	99.3	271	100.0
Kakapo	269	42.4	249	96.0
Possum	271	94.5	270	94.4
Fantail	269	69.5	257	91.4
Deer	271	98.2	266	94.7
Kaka	271	52.8	252	92.1
Stoat	269	71.7	265	92.8
Kakariki	268	42.5	243	74.9
Blackbird	265	46.8	243	74.9

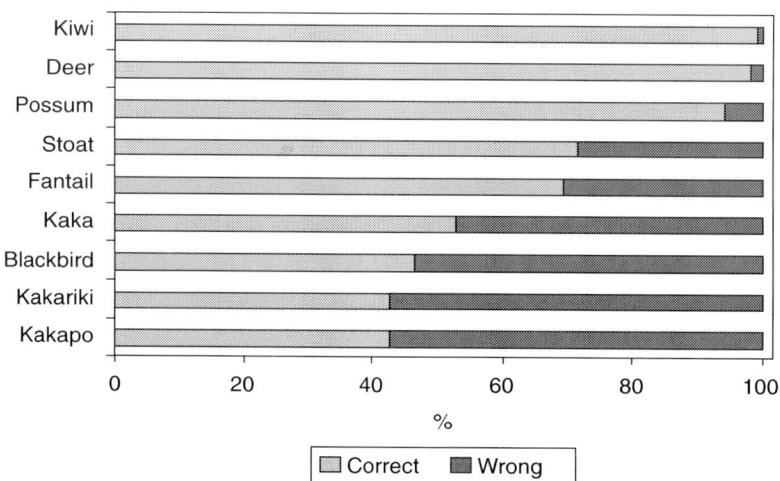

Fig. 8.1. Species identification in New Zealand: all respondents.

A further item in this section asked participants if they felt they could describe what is meant by the term 'ecosystem' to a friend (Table 8.6). Those participants who responded positively to this question were then asked to briefly define 'ecosystem', and their responses assessed with a possible score of up to three assigned.

A high percentage (89) of participants felt that they could describe what an ecosystem is. The mean score for all participants when asked to define the term was 1.7/3.0.

Generally, international visitors demonstrated a higher level of awareness of the essential components of an ecosystem, and this was statistically demonstrable at the 95% confidence level (Table 8.7).

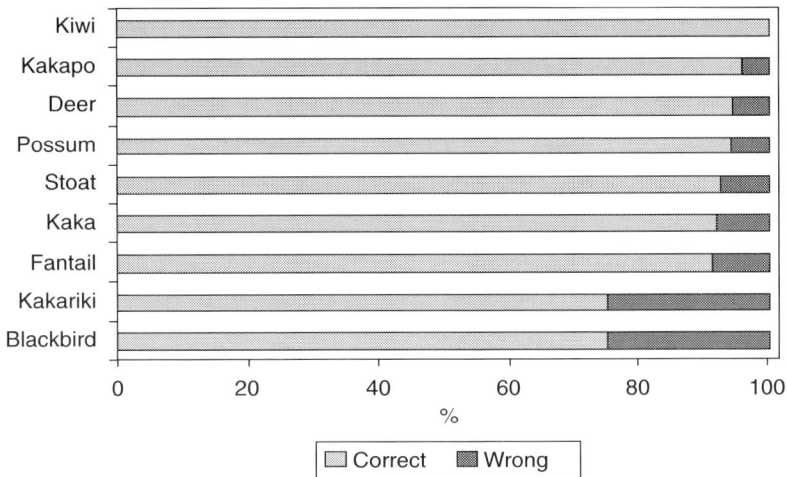

Fig. 8.2. Identification of species origin in New Zealand: all respondents.

Table 8.5. NZ species identification and origin scores, by visitor residence.

	NZ visitors	International visitors	All visitors
Species identification score[a]	7.01	5.59	6.15
Species origin score[a]	7.94	7.59	7.73

[a]T-test is significant at the 95% confidence level.

Table 8.6. Knowledge of the term 'ecosystem', by visitor residence.

	NZ visitors		International visitors	
	n	%	n	%
Yes	94	86.2	148	91.9
No	15	13.8	13	8.1
Total	109	100.0	161	100.0

Table 8.7. Definition of 'ecosystem', by visitor residence.

	NZ visitors			International visitors			All visitors		
	n	Mean	SD	*n*	Mean	SD	*n*	Mean	SD
Score[b]	94	1.45[a]	0.73	148	1.67[a]	0.66	242	1.58	0.79

[a]T-test is significant at the 95% confidence level; [b] Score out of a possible 3.

Attitudes to 'naturalness'

Response to the 14 statements related to naturalness showed that, generally, participants were highly aware of the problems facing the New Zealand native forest habitat in terms of introduced pests and predators (Table 8.8). There was only moderate agreement that the native forest habitat is highly natural or pristine, and a high level of awareness of the impacts of introduced animal pests. Participants were aware that the native forest is not adapted against the impacts of introduced pests, and that predators of native birds are not needed to make the ecosystem 'natural'.

However, when domestic and international visitors were considered separately, some differences become apparent. Eight of the 14 statements revealed statistically significant differences. International visitors tended to rate the New Zealand native forest as being more natural than similar overseas environments and seemed to be less aware of the extent of damaging animal species in the forest. International visitors also showed less support for management intervention in ecosystems, less support for extermination of plant pest species, and slightly more acceptance of the spread of pest species as part of globalization.

Overseas visitors were also less convinced that tramping/hiking is environmentally friendly, and more strongly supported caps on numbers of trampers/hikers. They also differed from New Zealanders in their view of hunting as an activity – disagreeing that hunting (which is an important means of animal pest control in New Zealand) is an environmentally compatible activity.

Further items investigated attitudes towards two significant pest species in New Zealand's native forests – deer and possums. New Zealand has seven species of deer, all introduced variously from Asia, Europe and North America, while the possum is an Australian import. To summarize, international visitors, while aware that possums are an introduced species that cause damage to native forest, were, however, less concerned about possums as a pest, and less supportive of their extermination (Table 8.9).

Participants' attitudes towards deer revealed a remarkable similarity of opinion between domestic and international visitors (Table 8.10). While visitors were aware that deer are a pest species that cause damage to native forest, they were less concerned about this, and less supportive of control or extermination than they were for possums.

Participants were asked to rate the acceptability of various control

Table 8.8. NZ and international visitors' attitudes to naturalness.

	NZ visitors		International visitors		All visitors
	Mean	View	Mean	View	Mean
The NZ native forest is generally a highly pristine habitat	2.69	Mod. agree	2.57	Mod. agree	2.45
NZ native forest is more pure than similar environments overseas[a]	3.22	Mod. disagree	2.69	Mod. agree	2.39
Natural environments sometimes need active management intervention[a]	1.63	Agree	1.92	Agree	1.79
Spread of pests into natural environments should be accepted today as part of process of globalization[a]	4.50	Strongly disagree	4.23	Disagree	4.26
There are many destructive animal species in the NZ native forest[a]	1.86	Agree	2.23	Agree	1.97
Plant weed species in the NZ native forest should be exterminated[a]	1.91	Agree	2.85	Neutral	2.35
There need to be predators of NZ native birds if the ecosystem is to be considered 'natural'[a]	4.07	Disagree	3.85	Disagree	3.80
The NZ native forest is adapted against animals such as deer and possums	4.10	Disagree	4.33	Disagree	4.08
NZ native forest ecosystems are greatly impacted by introduced animal pests[a]	1.96	Agree	1.77	Agree	1.78
Non-native animal pests should be exterminated in the NZ native forest	2.11	Agree	2.16	Agree	2.13
It is important that humans continue their role as natural predator	3.15	Neutral	3.26	Neutral	3.11
The number of trampers/hikers in the bush should be capped to protect the environment[a]	2.77	Neutral	2.18	Agree	2.40
Tramping/hiking are generally environmentally friendly/compatible activities[a]	1.97	Agree	2.37	Agree	2.20
Hunting is generally an environmentally friendly/compatible activity[a]	2.64	Mod. agree	3.33	Mod. disagree	3.04

1, strongly agree; 2, agree; 3, neither agree nor disagree; 4, disagree; 5, strongly disagree.
[a] T-test is significant at the 95% confidence level.

methods for deer and possums. These included the use of poison (including the controversial 1080 poison), biological control, trapping and shooting. For all control methods for possums, international visitors expressed a lower level of acceptability (Fig. 8.3). The differences in acceptability were statistically significant at the 95% confidence level.

One control method adopted by many New Zealanders is, when driving a vehicle at night and upon seeing a possum on the road to run the

Table 8.9. Attitudes towards possums, by visitor residence.

	NZ visitors		International visitors		All visitors
	Mean	View	Mean	View	Mean
Possums are cute animals I would enjoy seeing[a]	2.90	Disagree	2.44	Mod. disagree	2.63
Possums are a good source of fur[a]	1.22	Agree	1.71	Mod. agree	1.50
Possums are a native species and should be protected	2.99	Disagree	2.95	Disagree	2.97
Possums cause damage to the native forest	1.02	Agree	1.05	Agree	1.04
Possums are a concern to me[a]	1.09	Agree	1.56	Mod. Agree	1.37
Possums are controlled by natural predators	2.93	Disagree	2.90	Disagree	2.91
Possums should be controlled to low, manageable numbers[a]	1.69	Mod. agree	1.42	Mod. Agree	1.53
Possums should be exterminated[a]	1.10	Agree	1.53	Mod. Agree	1.35

1, agree; 2, neither agree nor disagree; 3, disagree.
[a] T-test is significant at the 95% confidence level.

Table 8.10. Attitudes towards deer, by visitor residence.

	NZ visitors		International visitors		All visitors
	Mean	View	Mean	View	Mean
Deer are beautiful animals I would enjoy seeing	1.98	Neutral	1.94	Neutral	1.95
Deer are a good source of meat and skins	1.19	Agree	1.31	Agree	1.26
Deer are a native species and should be protected	2.78	Disagree	2.88	Disagree	2.83
Deer cause damage to the native forest	1.19	Agree	1.19	Agree	1.19
Deer are a concern to me	1.68	Mod. agree	1.86	Mod. agree	1.79
Deer are controlled by natural predators	2.86	Disagree	2.90	Disagree	2.88
Deer should be controlled to low numbers	1.37	Mod. agree	1.36	Mod. agree	1.36
Deer should be exterminated	2.07	Neutral	1.87	Neutral	1.96

1, agree; 2, neither agree nor disagree; 3, disagree.

possum over. Thus participants were asked if they saw a possum in the road, would they swerve to hit or to miss it? While the majority of domestic visitors would swerve to hit the possum, the large majority of international visitors would swerve to miss (Table 8.11).

Table 8.11. Attitudes towards control of possums by the road-kill method, by visitor residence.

	NZ visitors		International visitors	
	n	%	n	%
Hit	58	54.7	31	20.1
Miss	48	45.3	123	79.9
Total	106	100.00	154	100.00

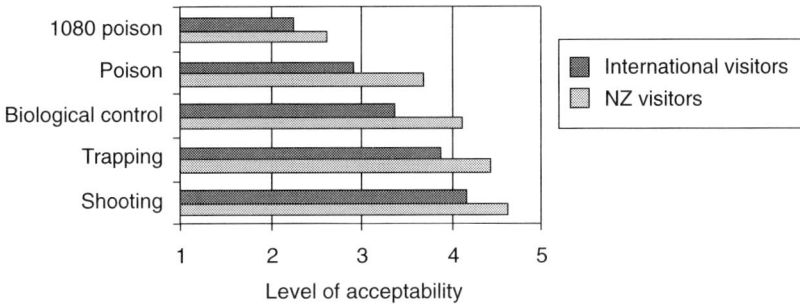

Fig. 8.3. Acceptability of control methods for possums. Levels of acceptability: 1, very unacceptable; 5, very acceptable.

Attitudes towards deer control methods were also investigated (Fig. 8.4), revealing that domestic and international visitors both held similar views about most control methods (and that this was generally lower than the acceptability levels expressed for possums). The only significant difference was that international residents were less supportive of recreational hunting as a means of deer control.

Overall, visitors were less supportive of the use of poisons for control of pests, and international visitors especially so (Figure 8.5). When international visitors were asked if they would avoid areas where poisons had been or were being used, 22–26% replied in the affirmative. However, New Zealand domestic tourists appeared to be much more risk averse when it came to visiting areas that had or were currently being poisoned, with 38–42% replying in the affirmative.

Discussion

This chapter reports on research that aimed at investigating visitor attitudes towards naturalness and towards ecosystem management aimed at achieving greater levels of ecological integrity. These issues were explored through a case study set in a natural area in New Zealand, a destination whose level of ecological integrity has been compromised through the introduction of a number of exotic pest species.

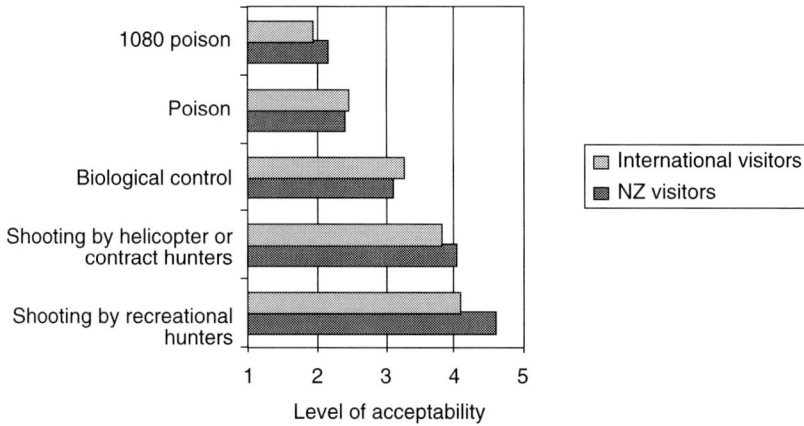

Fig. 8.4. Acceptability of control methods for deer. Levels of acceptability: 1, very unacceptable; 5, very acceptable.

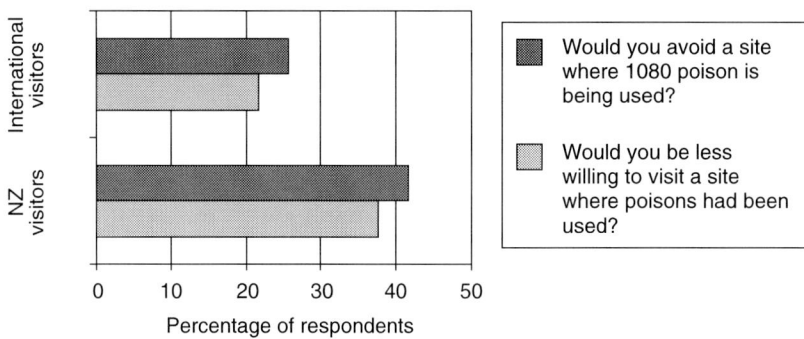

Fig. 8.5. Acceptability of visiting sites where poison had been used.

The earlier part of the chapter discusses how the current balance of native and introduced – the level of 'naturalness' – in New Zealand has been influenced by a series of biogeosocial flows. A conceptual model of these flows illustrates how, at any particular time, there has been either an inward or outward flow of exotic species from New Zealand, depending largely upon the flow of humans and their values and practices predominating at the time.

It is put forward that the current substantial flow of international tourists may be influencing the native–exotic balance and thus the level of naturalness, through the environmental perceptions and preconceptions that they bring with them. It is also conjectured that modern-day visitors (in contrast to those associated with earlier flows) would have a higher level of ecological awareness and understanding, and thus would assist in the process of destinations seeking greater naturalness, for example by supporting ecosystem management practices aimed at eradicating introduced pest species. The values of international visitors were explored in relation to domestic visitors.

The findings from this research show that international visitors have quite a high level of awareness of local ecosystems, in terms of what species are to be found, although not as high as domestic visitors. This is to be expected given that domestic visitors have a lifetime of experience within these destinations and also that, generally, New Zealanders are very outdoor-oriented with high levels of visitation to natural areas. However, international visitors demonstrated a higher level of awareness of pure ecological knowledge than domestic visitors.

International visitors are also well aware of the problems of introduced plant and animal pests in New Zealand. Despite all the above, however, international visitors are generally less supportive of interventionist ecological management – for example total eradication of pest species. They are more accepting of the spread and presence of exotic species as part of the process of globalization than New Zealanders. Ironically, international visitors are more concerned about the impact of humans in the natural environment and more supportive of measures to limit impacts.

Further investigation into attitudes towards pest species showed that the level of support for their control varies according to species. For example, support for control of the possum was strong, while support for the control of deer was less evident. This is put down to the 'Bambi syndrome', whereby people become enamoured with this species due to exposure to sensitive and moving stories involving the species during their childhood – for example the 'pro-animal genre of cartoons' from Disney (Franklin, 1999).

Unluckily for the possum, such sympathy does not extend to this species; however, international visitors did show significantly more reluctance to totally condemn the possum as a pest, worthy only of extermination. Correspondingly, international visitors showed less support for all means of control of the possum, including the 'car method' of control. For deer, international visitors held similar attitudes regarding control methods, apart from shooting by recreational hunters, for which they were less supportive. In explanation of this finding, comments by participants to the survey administrators revealed that many international visitors felt that recreational hunters may lack the skills to make a humane kill (e.g. compared with contract hunters).

International visitors appear to be less supportive of attempts to create greater naturalness in this destination. Why international visitors should be less supportive of ecosystem intervention and pest control in this environment is a question worthy of further investigation. There are characteristics of this cohort, however, that may help to explain (Table 8.2). For example, the international group is younger – and this is typically associated with a higher degree of idealism – which in turn is reflected in higher membership of animal welfare organizations than for the domestic cohort (however, ironically, fewer of the international visitors are likely to keep pets). Internationals are also less likely to go hunting or fishing compared with their domestic counterparts, and are more likely to be vegetarian.

These figures all suggest a group that is more aware of animal rights issues – and their lack of support for pest control (even if it is 'saving' other native animals) fits with this ethos. Another contradiction is that international visitors have a higher membership of environmental organizations – *and* a greater understanding of ecosystems – and are less supportive of active ecosystem intervention.

The lack of support for recreational shooting is likely to be a carryover of anti-hunting sentiments which are more highly developed in New Zealand's tourist-generating regions (e.g. the UK and rest of Europe). But the lack of support for some control measures – e.g. poison – may indeed be a reflection of the greater ecological awareness discussed above – of the possibility of by-kill of non-target species, and of contamination of the environment.

It also appears that a perception of personal risk (associated with the use of poisons in natural (tourist) areas) is also important in the lack of support for this control method – for international and domestic visitors alike. If the fear of poisons grows to any extent, it is only a matter of time before members of the tourist industry begin to question this form of ecosystem intervention, as their clients become more reluctant to venture to the destination, let alone into the forest.

The attitudes of international and domestic visitors towards animal pest control can be illuminated further by referring to the work of Franklin (1999) who, in his book on the sociological dimensions of human–animal relations, argues that different groups in society have different relationships with animals. He identifies three main ideal-type attitudes to animals (which describe the full range). Franklin's 'animal rights' group aligns with the international visitor as a group in this study, whereas domestic visitors could be seen as the less extreme 'sentimentalists' or as 'neo-Darwinians' who support a more pragmatic relationship with animals.

The animals rights group are characterized by a higher percentage of vegetarian non-pet owners, do not hunt or fish and, as the name suggests, care a great deal about the plight of animals in the modern world, arguing that animals should have complete freedom from human interference (Franklin, 1999). Franklin notes how this group may find itself at odds with environmentalists, who '… in places such as New Zealand and Australia, advocate the eradication of introduced, non-indigenous animals in favour of a preferred type of landscape and biotic community' (Franklin, 1999, p. 50).

Conclusions

We would normally associate a tourist's main threat to the biosecurity or ecological integrity of a destination to be in the form of their illegal or unknowing introduction of some foreign biota or disease. However, this study has revealed that international visitors, through the importation of their environmental attitudes, may have a profound influence upon destination ecological integrity and naturalness.

This study supports previous research (undertaken in non-touristic contexts) suggesting that different cultural groups view ecosystems and invasive alien species differently (McNeely, 2002). It has been argued that gaining public support for ecosystem intervention is critical; however, this is problematic when the 'noxious invasive' of one cultural group is the 'desirable addition' of other groups (McNeely, 2002, p. 3). Thus, invasive alien species obviously complicate our view of what is 'natural' and what is not, as human values rather than just ecological criteria come into play.

For New Zealand, the twin issues of (i) recognition of introduced species as pests and (ii) recognition of the need for their control are critical issues in the ongoing management of the ecological integrity of New Zealand's natural areas. They are also critical issues in the process of achieving greater naturalness in the destination.

However, disturbingly, international visitors seem less convinced (than domestic visitors) on both issues. This is of concern, considering the growing presence of international visitors to natural areas in New Zealand, and thus their growing significance as a stakeholder in the management of these areas (also considering that some of the most significant natural areas in New Zealand are World Heritage Areas – which, by name, imply that the international community does have a stake in the way in which they are managed).

It is important not to overstate the case against international visitors here – indeed there is a good level of awareness of the issues that New Zealand is facing in terms of maintaining naturalness, and a level of support for what the country's ecosystem managers are doing. But, in terms of the conceptual model of flows introduced in this chapter, it appears that international visitors do represent a flow of values that are, to an extent, adversative to flows of domestic origin that seek to enhance the ecological integrity of the destination through the eradication of introduced pest species.

Notwithstanding further research into this topic, it also seems likely that visitors' concerns over animal welfare, and perhaps more complex bioethical concerns over a species' right to exist (anywhere), are paramount over their concerns about destination naturalness.

Interpreted within the core–periphery framework, this is symptomatic of the imposition of tourist-sourced core values (from predominantly urban Europe and North America) upon a peripheral social and natural system. The extent to which the current ecosystem management regime will be able to defend itself against these values will depend upon how much support it gets from domestic visitors, the rest of the domestic community and the domestic tourist industry.

Acknowledgements

The University of Otago, School of Business for research funding; the Department of Conservation for advice and support for this research; Dave Palmer for research assistance.

References

Dann, G. (1993) Limitations in the use of nationality and country of residence variables. In: Pearce, D.G. and Butler, R.W. (eds) *Tourism Critiques and Challenges*. Routledge, London, pp. 88–112.

Dawson, J. (2003) *Environmental values of consumptive and non-consumptive marine tourists in the South Island of New Zealand*. Master of Tourism thesis, Department of Tourism, University of Otago, Dunedin, New Zealand.

Franklin, A. (1999) *Animals and Modern Cultures: a Sociology of Human–Animal Relations in Modernity*. Routledge, London.

Fraser, W. (2001) *Introduced Wildlife in New Zealand: a Survey of General Public Views*. Landcare Research Science Series No. 23, Manaaki Whenua Press, Lincoln, Canterbury, New Zealand.

Hall, C.M. and Higham, J. (2000) Wilderness management in the forests of New Zealand. In: Font, X. and Tribe, J. (eds) *Forest Tourism and Recreation: Case Studies in Environmental Management*. CAB International, Wallingford, UK, pp. 143–160.

Hudson, S. and Ritchie, J.R.B. (2001) Cross-cultural tourist behaviour: an analysis of tourist attitudes towards the environment. *Journal of Travel and Tourism Marketing* 10, 1–22.

McNeely, J.A. (2002) An introduction to the human dimensions of invasive alien species (http://www.iucn.org/biodiversityday/response.html, accessed 1 July 2002).

Tourism New Zealand (2004) http://www.purenz.com (accessed 12 October 2004).

9 Access, Tourism and Democracy: a Conceptual Framework and Non-establishment of a Proposed National Park in Sweden

KLAS SANDELL

Department of Geography and Tourism, Karlstad University, Sweden

Introduction

Already by 1885, the founding of the Swedish Touring Club was closely linked with an increasing interest in the Swedish mountains as a recreation area. The 'exotic' Laplanders and a poor understanding of the mountains as a cultural landscape made it a 'wilderness' for many urban people from the south. Additionally, as the Sami peoples' (the Laplanders') ownership of the land was not fully recognized, it was easy to establish relatively large areas here as national parks. Even today, tourism and national parks and their interrelationship with regional development are especially important questions for this region of Sweden.

The objective of this chapter is to present a specific case, investigated mainly using qualitative methods, of a failed national park proposal from the late 1980s in this mountain region of Sweden and to analyse the clash of interests using a conceptual framework of 'eco-strategies'. This conceptual framework, in previous versions developed for the understanding of rural resource use in a Third World context, is linked to basic questions concerning human ecology, landscape perspectives and development issues. Therefore, this discussion of different eco-strategies connects this case study with current more general issues of the links between conservation, regional development and sustainability.

The Case of a Proposed National Park

The latter part of the 1980s saw a debate concerning the possibility of establishing a large national park in the mountain area around Lake

Torneträsk, close to Kiruna in northern Sweden. It involved two smaller existing national parks, a number of marked trails, mountain huts and the Abisko tourist centre. If established, it would have been one of the largest national parks in Europe (4360 km^2). But, even though various interested parties were represented in the working group for the national park, there was such a clash of interests that the project could not be carried out by the Environmental Protection Agency (Sandell, 2000).

Looking briefly into the historical background of the current interest in tourism in this area, we may note that in 1903 a railway was opened between Narvik (in Norway) and Kiruna (a Swedish mining community, now a town of about 20,000 inhabitants with its own airport). Although the railway was intended primarily for the transportation of iron ore, it nevertheless came to play an important role for tourism as it made the 'wilderness' in the area around Lake Torneträsk easily accessible.

In 1909 the Abisko National Park (one of the first of such parks in Sweden) was established in the area, followed in 1920 by the Vadvetjåkka National Park. Trails were marked and mountain huts built, to be used for hiking in the summer and cross-country skiing in the winter. In 1976 the area was included in a list of 25 primary recreation areas in Sweden, and at the beginning of the 1980s a road was built parallel to the railway between Kiruna and Narvik. In 1986, part of the area was also designated a UNESCO biosphere reserve, emphasizing research and nature conservation (Price, 1996).

Further, it is important to note that after the road had been built, no specific 'threat' or major change with regard to status or use of the area was at hand when the plan for a new national park was presented. For general information with regard to the case and the local region, see Naturvårdsverket (1989), Bäck (1993) and Sandell (2000), and for more recent information about tourism in the mountain region in Sweden see Heberlein *et al.* (2002).

The intention behind the plan for the national park, as presented by the Swedish Environmental Protection Agency, was that: 'It is good for nature conservation if much larger groups of people than at present can be given the opportunity for genuine and first-rate experiences of nature' (all quotations regarding the proposed park are from Naturvårdsverket, 1989).

The plan further describes the area as 'unique', offering a combination of:

> mountain slopes and alpine topography and … the vast and roadless brush moors of the Swedish mountains. No other area in Europe outside Sweden offers, within an area of comparable size, both stupendous massifs and unexploited roadless wilderness-type landscape.

It is also important to note that the proposed national park involved the ambition of:

> … widening the traditional Swedish view of the national park concept … The national park is to be established … in order to strengthen the area's legal protection against exploitation, to raise its status and attraction value, and to

bring into being in a practical sense a co-ordinated administration that protects nature, is outward-looking, is locally based and generates jobs. Thus the goal is that there should be a high degree of interplay between nature conservation and regional development.

An important element of the plan for the proposed national park was the designation of six zones in order to separate different types of recreation and protection requirements. Another interesting aspect of the proposed national park was the plan to use professional 'rangers' (using the American word in Swedish as well) for information, education and guiding in addition to service and supervision. It was also planned that the tourist centre in Abisko include attractive exhibitions, shops and a cinema for 220 persons.

A clash of interests

As mentioned above, although various interested parties were represented in the working group for the national park, there was such a clash of interests that the plan was shelved for an indefinite period (Sandell, 2000). The main obstacle would appear to have been the resistance from local groups, principally in Kiruna, who were afraid that their use of the area would be curtailed, partly because of possible restrictions on such outdoor activities as fishing, hunting and the use of snowmobiles. These perspectives were argued for in the local newspapers and at local meetings, and an important channel and actor turned out to be the local hunting and fishing association.

In an appeal (containing more than 15,000 signatures!) it was asserted that the establishment of a national park in Kiruna would be a clear intrusion upon the right of public access. Here, it should be noted that local involvement in the working group was arranged through the leading local politicians – obviously not fully representative of the local majority with regard to this issue.

As part of a general scepticism regarding the intentions of central authorities (The Environmental Protection Agency), there also seemed to be a general fear that there might be more severe restrictions in the future than those initially proposed, for instance with regard to hunting and fishing. It might be noted as well that national organizations involved in tourism, conservation and the outdoors seemed to be positive to the park plan, but did not take a very active part in the discussion when the proposal was heavily criticized.

It was stated clearly in the plan that reindeer farming would not be subject to restrictions but the Sami people, although generally maintaining a low profile in the debate, seemed somewhat sceptical. The main actors in favour of the plan were the Swedish Environmental Protection Agency and the regional tourist organization, the former holding public meetings in Kiruna which, due to the conflict, turned out to be quite stormy.

From the more detailed discussion of the Swedish case study (Sandell, 2000), the following reasons for the failure to establish the park can be listed:

1. Although the Kiruna region had experienced significant problems with unemployment, this had decreased from 10.2% in 1983 to 5.7% 1989 – when the park proposal was launched – before it began increasing again. As Kiruna is traditionally a mining society, new employment prospects in the area of tourism and service were very unfamiliar to many.
2. A 'tradition' of local scepticism existed towards central authorities, due to previous tensions regarding the interest among the latter in restricting the use of snowmobiles.
3. The change from a process of a once stronger national state carrying out its intentions to a situation of more sensitivity at local level with regard to conservation and tourism.
4. The perceived local link between the concept 'national park' and a lack of local power and decreased opportunity for traditional local recreation activities such as fishing, hunting and the use of snowmobiles.

In summary, it may be argued that in the debate over the proposal there was a clash between basically very different cultural views of conservation and outdoor recreation. This clash is illustrated further below with the help of the conceptual framework of eco-strategies. First, however, the Nordic tradition of the outdoors and the right of public access is discussed to some extent, forming important aspects of these tensions around the park proposal.

The Right of Public Access

The discussion – and failure – of the proposed reserve were to a large extent underpinned by the issue of access (the need of unrestricted *versus* restricted access for different groups) linked to the tradition of the right of public access. In summary, the right of public access in Sweden is laid down in common law and can be seen as the 'free space' between various restrictions, mainly: (i) economic interests; (ii) local people's privacy; (iii) preservation; and (iv) actual use of and changes to the landscape.

For example, camping for no more than 24 hours is generally allowed, and activities such as traversing any land, lake or river and swimming or lighting a fire are permitted wherever the restrictions mentioned above are not violated. Although guidelines are provided by the Swedish Environmental Protection Agency, it is important to note that it is 'the landscape' to a large extent that tells you what is – and is not – allowed. The way the land is being used may indicate how sensitive it is to people walking on it, and the weather tells you how safe it would be to make a campfire (for further discussion on the right of public access, see Kaltenborn *et al.*, 2001 and references provided therein).

A Conceptual Framework of 'Eco-strategies'

When seeking a general conceptual framework for discussing nature, place and sustainability, we commonly identify a dichotomy of domination *versus* adaptation with regard to human views and use of nature (Sandell, 1988, pp. 47–54). A similar division with regard to regional development has been suggested by Friedmann and Weaver (1979), using the concepts 'functional development' and 'territorial development'. A major effect of this approach, in many ways a parallel between centralized and decentralized systems, is that various aspects of social integration (politics, economy and culture) are brought into focus together with the human–ecological issues.

Although the illustrations below focus on the spatial dimension, it seems reasonable to assume that the content of and potential for a more territorial development are, to a large extent, a question of permanence. The conceptual framework of eco-strategies (view and use of nature) presented here has evolved from previous work (using three main eco-strategies instead of the four now used) and takes its point of departure in human ecology and development strategies (Sandell, 1988, 1996), and has later been used for discussions of access, conservation and the outdoors (Sandell, 2000; Kaltenborn *et al.*, 2001).

The framework is now constituted as a four-field figure (Fig. 9.1), with the use of one axis illustrating the above-mentioned dichotomy between 'functional specialization' and 'territorial adaptation' as points of departure for landscape perspectives – a basic choice between functional dependence on exchange with other areas and territorial dependence on the best use of local resources.

The other axis illustrates the dichotomy between the strategies of 'active' and 'passive' usage of the landscape – in short, a choice between utilization and conservation. It should be noted that the prefix *eco-* indicates only that it is the man–nature relationship that is in focus and does not involve any normative aspects of which relationship is to be preferred.

Naturally, however, the different eco-strategies involve various crucial consequences in terms of democracy, environmental issues, views concerning nature, local development, etc. Although the different strategies may appear to be clear-cut categories in the figure, in reality it is naturally a question of tendencies and combines the involvement of a greater or lesser degree of passive *versus* active use of landscape, and of functional *versus* territorial strategies.

With a focus on conservation, outdoor recreation and nature tourism, we may summarize the four eco-strategies as follows (cf. Fig. 9.1 and the examples in Fig. 9.2):

1. The eco-strategy of 'freezing' (conserving) a specific landscape and maintaining that 'frozen' landscape, to be set aside as a *museum for external consumption*. This is done for the sake of biodiversity, nature tourism or science – priorities carried out on a national or international basis.

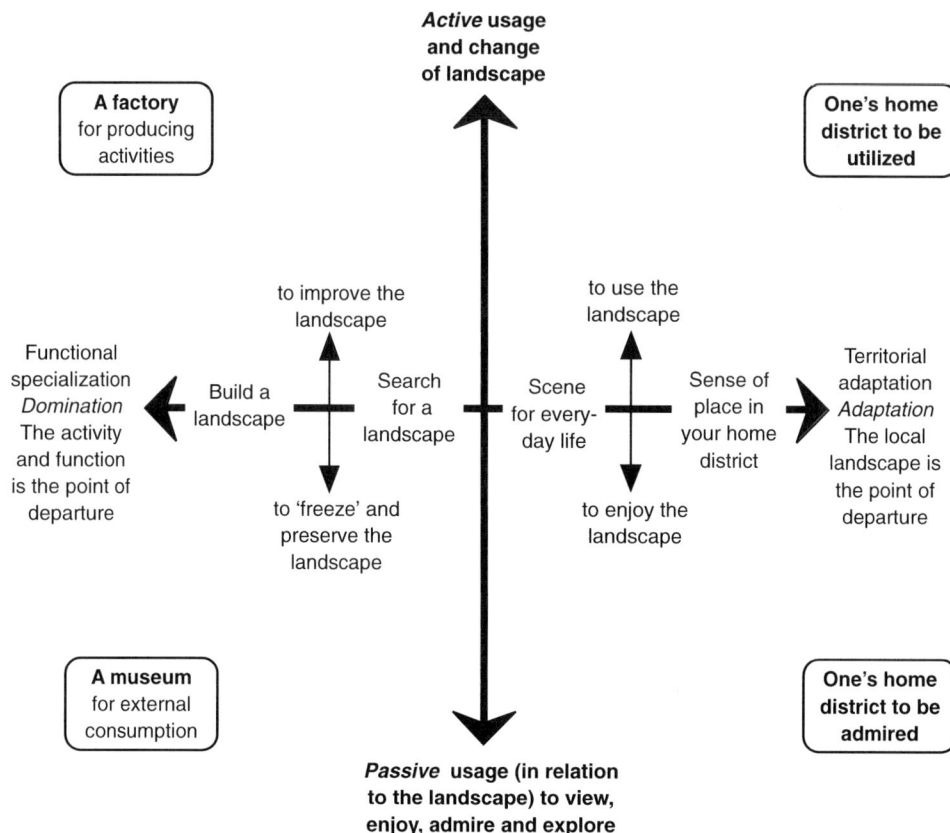

Fig. 9.1. Conceptual framework of four eco-strategies with regard to man's relation to nature and landscape (adapted from Sandell, 2000).

2. An eco-strategy in line with an active functional domination, with the point of departure in the activities searched for. Special areas, equipment and organizations are established for these specialized outdoor activities. Long-distance travel and heavy use of material resources are often involved. It could be argued that the landscape is looked upon as a *factory for producing activities* – swimming, snowboarding and climbing, and in its more extreme forms seeing these activities rebuilt indoors (e.g. climbing and swimming, computer games).

3. An eco-strategy in line with active adaptation. Here, as in the strategy of passive adaptation, interest is directed towards the features of the local natural and cultural landscapes, the topography, the season, etc. However, the eco-strategy of active adaptation also involves a direct utilization of the landscape – firewood, fishing, hunting, etc. Outdoor recreation is one of many locally integrated aspects of *one's home district to be utilized*. The area considered 'one's home district' is basically a question of identity – of feeling at home.

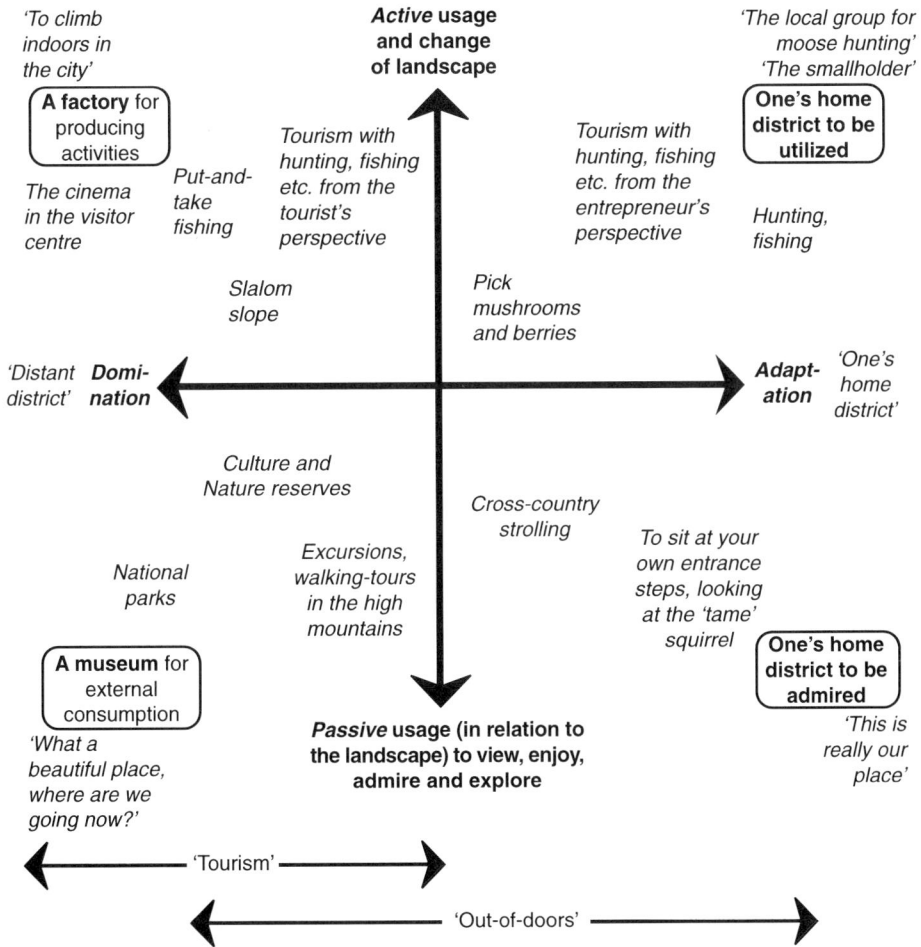

'To climb indoors in the city'

A factory for producing activities

The cinema in the visitor centre

Put-and-take fishing

Active **usage and change of landscape**

Tourism with hunting, fishing etc. from the tourist's perspective

Slalom slope

Tourism with hunting, fishing etc. from the entrepreneur's perspective

Pick mushrooms and berries

'The local group for moose hunting' 'The smallholder'

One's home district to be utilized

Hunting, fishing

'Distant district' **Domi-nation**

Adapt-ation 'One's home district'

Culture and Nature reserves

National parks

Excursions, walking-tours in the high mountains

Cross-country strolling

To sit at your own entrance steps, looking at the 'tame' squirrel

A museum for external consumption

One's home district to be admired

'What a beautiful place, where are we going now?'

Passive **usage (in relation to the landscape) to view, enjoy, admire and explore**

'This is really our place'

← 'Tourism' →

← 'Out-of-doors' →

Fig. 9.2. Conceptual framework of four eco-strategies with regard to man's relation to nature and landscape, with examples illustrating various aspects of outdoor activities and conservation (adapted from Sandell, 2000).

4. In the strategy of passive adaptation, appreciative activities such as strolling, cross-country skiing, bird watching and looking for flowers are carried out in *one's home district to be admired*. These activities are characterized by passive amusement and, on a superficial level (what is done, what type of equipment is used, etc.), it could be very much the same as the museum eco-strategy (the latter, however, is carried out without any deeper integration and identification, with the local natural and cultural landscapes separate from the special feature visited).

Additionally, in line with the two last eco-strategies – from the entrepreneur's point of view – we find many of the current attempts at ecotourism and small-scale, locally based nature-oriented recreation involving active utilization such as hunting and fishing (in line with one's home district to be utilized) or passive admiration as in hiking and photographic excursions (in line with one's home district to be contemplated). Here, tourists are 'invited' to one's home district – although the context, from the tourist's point of view, is still part of the tourist industry in accordance with the strategy of functional specialization.

The case analysed within the conceptual framework

Using the conceptual framework of the fourfold figure presented above (Fig. 9.1, exemplified in Fig. 9.2) to analyse the case of the proposed national park, we can compare the traditional national park perspective with the core point of the local opposition very much engaged in local hunting and fishing (Fig. 9.3). As illustrations of these two positions, the names of the leading institutions themselves could be used.

The Swedish Environmental Protection Agency was the central actor in favour of the proposal, opposed by the Kiruna Hunting and Fishery

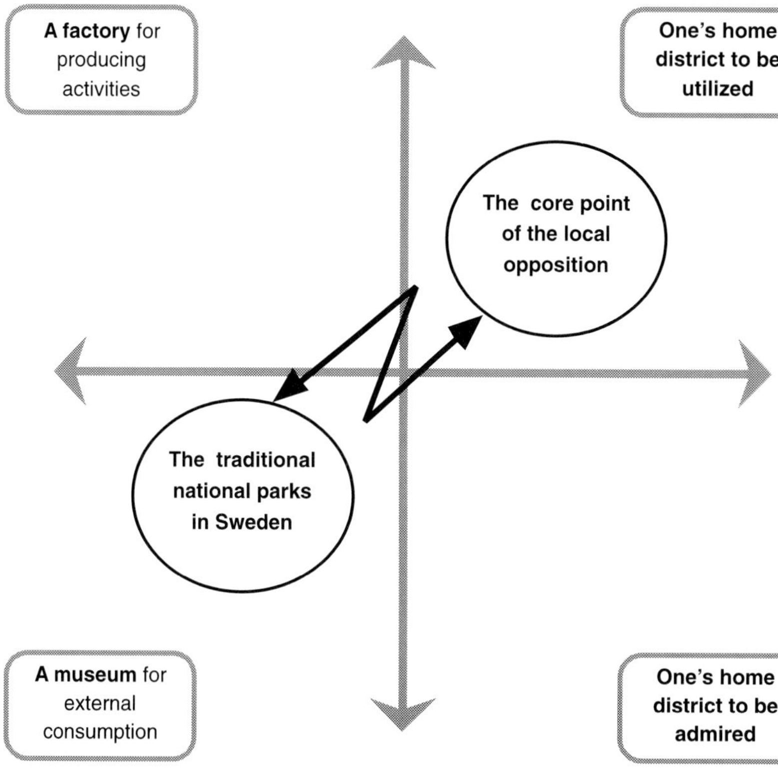

Fig. 9.3. Conceptual framework used to analyse the conflict between the traditional park perspective in Sweden and the local opposition with regard to the proposed national park.

Association. The former agency clearly indicates the central and protective view, in comparison with the perspective of local utilization by the latter. The strong local position of this latter association will also be noted, having been established at the end of the 1920s and claiming, at the time of the park proposal, almost 6000 members in a society with only slightly over 26,000 inhabitants.

As an illustration of the 'museum' perspective, the following introduction to a presentation of the park proposal in the magazine from a national mountain association could be used: 'Imagine if the whole high mountain region was a national park! … What a pipe dream! What a utopia!' (Karlsson ,1987, p. 4). This perspective can be compared with the following local statement: 'Just the word "national park" takes away the freedom to be in nature … ' (Talo, 1988).

Furthermore, we can compare the proposed extended park perspective with the traditional national parks in Sweden (Fig. 9.4), an extension inspired by international examples and argued for by tourism business. However, this has also brought opposition from a more 'puristic' preservation point of view, as exemplified in the following statement found in a history of the scientific research station in Abisko, published by the Royal Swedish Academy of Sciences (Bernhard, 1989, p. 58):

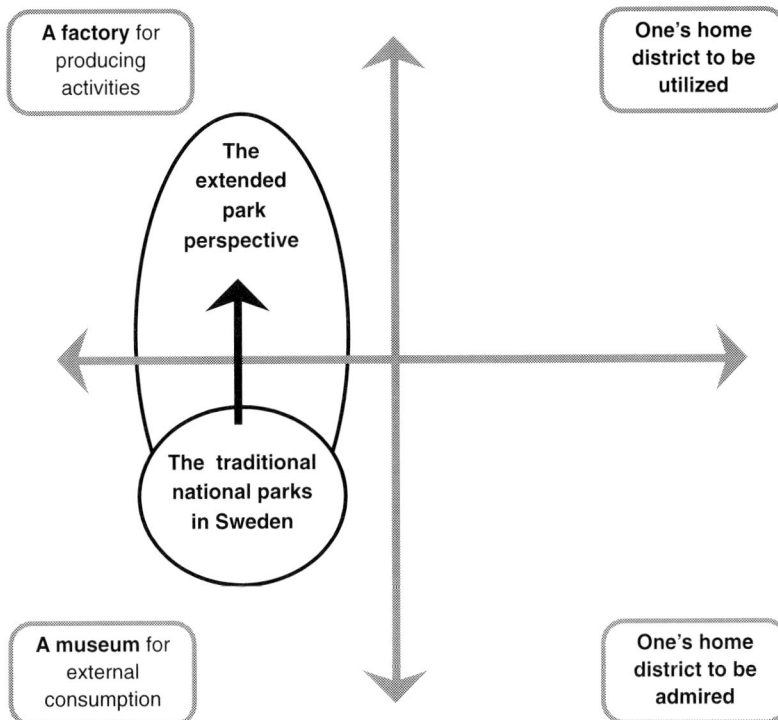

Fig. 9.4. Conceptual framework used to analyse the extended park perspective in the proposed national park.

Further [in addition to the threat to the natural environment due to the road built in the 1980s], the concept of 'National Park' is becoming increasingly tarnished since greater encroachments are planned in Abisko National Park. In the long run this means a serious threat to basic research.

Another example is how the article by Karlsson (1987), quoted above, also includes a wish for 'No lifts, no slalom slopes or other touristic infrastructure'.

Concerning the clash of interests, we can also note the lack of correspondence with the tradition of right of public access – one of the concepts used by the local opposition (Fig. 9.5). As mentioned above, the concept 'national park' as such seemed to be a main obstacle for the local population as it involved associations with authorities, external interests, regulations and the loss of freedom – a perspective very reasonable if we again look at Fig. 9.3.

Additionally, in the case study the arguments used by the different actors for and against restrictions and the various elements and statements of the final plan were analysed and the entire range of strategies and positions was found. Arguments linked to all positions in the four-field

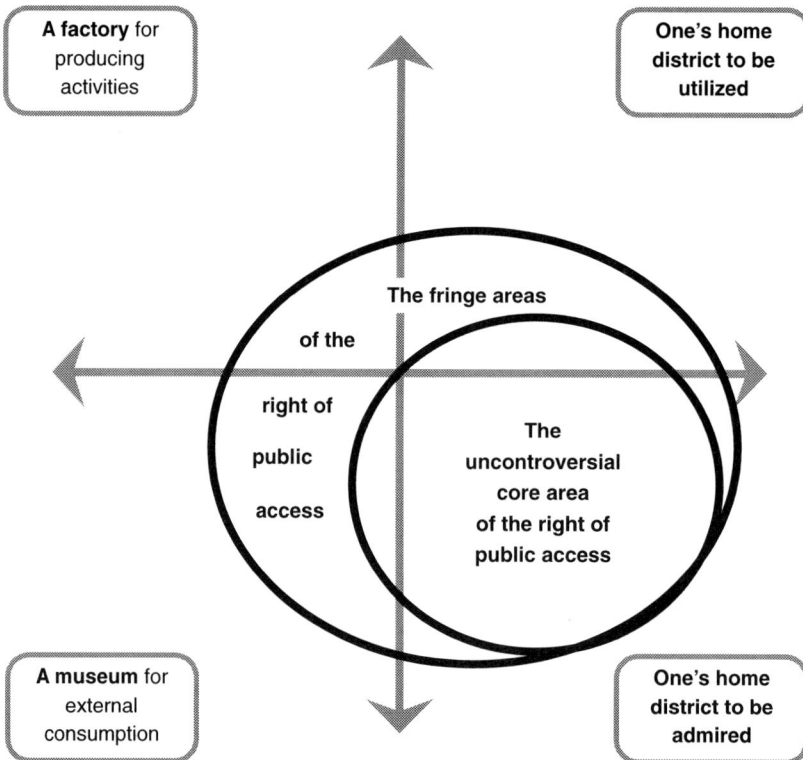

Fig. 9.5. Conceptual framework used to illustrate the Nordic tradition of the right of public access.

figure were represented in a summary of the park proposal (Naturvårdsverket, 1989). This illustrates one of the main reasons for the park proposal's failure, namely the lack of alliances – too many were too reluctant to avail themselves of the opportunities for improving their own situation and did not want to endanger what they perceived as important values. These involved various aspects of freedom, outdoor habits and attitudes regarding conservation and local self-reliance.

Territoriality, Sustainability and Regional Development

The case of the national park's non-establishment illustrates many important tensions between local, central and international interests as well as its links to various nature and landscape perspectives and activity patterns. Additionally, more basic aspects may be raised as the fact that a 'sustainable development' approach is often linked to a landscape perspective in line with 'territorial adaptation', a tradition manifested in terms of deep ecology, eco-development, green development, alternative development and an eco-regional strategy.

Simultaneously, the tradition of preservation is very much in line with a 'functional specialization' strategy. We therefore see a striking dichotomy between a tradition of linking environmental awareness with a local, place-related perspective and a tradition by which conservation and preservation in terms of reserves (national parks) come 'from above' – and, at least in the case presented here, also consequently meet severe local opposition.

In addition to this tension between functional specialization and local adaptation with regard to strategies for sustainable development, there is a debate concerning the fundaments of the traditional 'museum' strategy and its use of concepts such as 'nature', 'culture' and 'values' (Massey and Jess, 1995; Callicott and Nelson, 1998; Macnaghten and Urry, 1998; Whatmore, 2002). This makes it much more difficult to designate natural values for preservation according to the 'museum' strategy. In line with this, it seems reasonable to believe that, in the future, landscape values must be seen more as a democratic question balancing local and global perspectives.

Based on this, the question must be raised regarding the extent to which a link between national parks and sustainable development is valid; a shift towards more community-based conservation approaches is discussed. More appropriate means are sought, combining sustainable development, nature tourism, public involvement and conservation, and tools such as co-management, ecotourism and biosphere reserves are scrutinized in this respect (Butler and Boyd, 2000; Holden, 2000; Page and Dowling, 2002).

To summarize – and in line with the eco-strategical framework – it could be argued that we have neither only the tension between centralized and decentralized development strategies nor only the tension between the landscape perspectives of utilization and conservation. Instead, we have various combinations of tensions between the four primary positions in the conceptual framework of eco-strategies (Figs 9.1 and 9.2).

This means that at least six directions of tension (vertical, horizontal and diagonal) can be sought. These tensions, grounded in basic aspects of development strategies and human ecology, are naturally not linked exclusively to the past or to the Swedish context, such as in the Kiruna case, but these are obviously truly current and international issues. Kaltenborn *et al.* (1999, p. 51) say:

> While the total area so protected increases [national parks and protected areas worldwide], so do the number of associated management issues and conflicts. One of the paramount issues is how to facilitate improved public involvement in conservation tasks.

To highlight this generality, we end this article by moving from northern Sweden to the continent of Africa, where the following parallels with the main conflict in the Kiruna case between the positions of 'museum' and 'one's home to be utilized' (Fig. 9.3) are found. In favour of the former perspective, Attwell and Cotterill (2000, p. 559) argue that the shift from traditional protectionist conservation to community-based approaches influenced by postmodernist thinking 'has actively detracted from efforts to avert the crisis facing African biota and ecosystems and their associated socio-economies'.

As an example of the diagonal position in the eco-strategical framework, we note the advocacy by Jones (1999, p. 303) for conservation strategies that 'also provide the potential for the social and political empowerment of communities to gain a firmer grip on their own development'. Brockington (2002, p. 8) even argues that the traditional 'fortress' conservation policies in Africa have been harmful, unjust and unnecessary, and claims that 'only if they [the protected areas] exist with local approval can they exist at all'; however, he also indicates the frequent ambiguity with regard to whether conservation or development is the goal.

Acknowledgements

Financial support from the European Tourism Research Institute, the Mountain Mistra Programme and the Swedish Research Council is gratefully acknowledged. I would also like to express my appreciation for support and valuable comments to Martin Price, Bjorn Kaltenborn, Karoline Daugstad, Odd Inge Vistad, Hanne Svarstad, Tuomas Vuorio and Annika Dahlberg; for help with my English from Michael Cooper and Malcolm Forbes; and for informative discussions with different persons involved in the Kiruna case.

This chapter builds on an article previously published in *Scandinavian Journal of Hospitality and Tourism*.

References

Attwell, C.A.M. and Cotterill, F.P.D. (2000) Postmodernism and African conservation science. *Biodiversity and Conservation* 9, 559–577.

Bäck, L. (1993) The Torneträsk Region. In: Aldskogius, H. (ed.) *Cultural Life, Recreation and Tourism*. National Atlas of Sweden Publishing, Stockholm, pp. 106–107.

Bernhard, C.G. (1989) *Abisko Scientific Research Station*. The Royal Swedish Academy of Sciences, Stockholm.

Brockington, D. (2002) *Fortress Conservation: the Preservation of the Mkomazi Game Reserve*. The International African Institute in association with James Currey, Oxford, Tanzania.

Butler, R.W. and Boyd, S.W. (eds) (2000) *Tourism and National Parks: Issues and Implications*. John Wiley, New York.

Callicott, J.B. and Nelson, P.M. (eds) (1998) *The Great New Wilderness Debate*. The University of Georgia Press, Athens and London.

Friedmann, J. and Weaver, C. (1979) *Territory and Function*. Edward Arnold, London.

Heberlein, T.A., Fredman, P. and Vuorio, T. (2002) Current tourism patterns in the Swedish mountain region. *Mountain Research and Development* 22, 142–149.

Holden, A. (2000) *Environment and Tourism*. Routledge, London and New York.

Jones, B.T.B. (1999) Policy lessons from the evolution of a community-based approach to wildlife management, Kunene Region, Namibia. *Journal of International Development* 11, 295–304.

Kaltenborn, B., Riese, H. and Hundeide, M. (1999) National park planning and local participation: some reflections from a mountain region in Southern Norway. *Mountain Research and Development* 19, 51–61.

Kaltenborn, B., Haaland, H. and Sandell, K. (2001) The public right of access – some challenges to sustainable tourism development in Scandinavia. *Journal of Sustainable Tourism* 9, 417–433.

Karlsson, L. (1987) Ny nationalpark i fjällen? *Fjällklubbsnytt* 32 (2), 4–9.

Macnaghten, P. and Urry, J. (1998) *Contested Natures*. Sage, London.

Massey, D. and Jess, P. (eds) (1995) *A Place in the World? Places, Cultures and Globalization*. The Open University, Oxford, UK.

Naturvårdsverket (Swedish Environmental Protection Agency) (1989) *Kirunafjällens Nationalpark: Rapport från en Projektgrupp*. Report no. 3595, Naturvårdsverket, Stockholm.

Page, S.J. and Dowling, R.K. (2002) *Ecotourism*. Prentice Hall, Harlow, UK.

Price, M.F. (1996) People in biosphere reserves: an evolving concept. *Society and Natural Resources* 9, 645–654.

Sandell, K. (1988) Ecostrategies in theory and practice: farmers' perspectives on water, *nutrients* and sustainability in low-resource agriculture in the dry zone of Sri Lanka. PhD dissertation, Linköping University, Linköping, Sweden.

Sandell, K. (1996) Sustainability in theory and practice: a conceptual framework of eco-strategies and a case-study of low-resource agriculture in the dry zone of Sri Lanka. In: Hjort af Ornäs, A. (ed.) *Approaching Nature from Local Communities: Security Perceived and Achieved*. EPOS, Research Programme on Environmental Policy and Society, Linköping University, Linköping, Sweden, pp. 163–197.

Sandell, K. (2000) *Ett Reservatsdilemma: Kiruna Nationalparksförslag 1986–1989 och Makten över Fjällen som Fritidslandskap*. Report no. R 2000:5, ETOUR, Östersund, Sweden.

Sandell, Klas 2005. Access, Tourism and Democracy: A Conceptual Framework and the Non-establishment of a Proposed National Park in Sweden (Research Note). *Scandinavian Journal of Hospitality and Tourism*, Vol. 5, No. 1, pp. 63–75.

Talo, A. (1988) Vansinnig idé om nationalpark. *Norrbottens Kuriren* (letter to the editor of a daily newspaper, 31 August 1988).

Whatmore, S. (2002) *Hybrid Geographies: Natures, Cultures, Spaces*. Sage, London.

10 Visitor Management in Protected Areas of the Periphery: Experiences from Both Ends of the World

PETER MASON

Department of Tourism, Leisure and Human Resource Management, University of Luton, UK

Introduction

Managing visitors is one of the important ways of attempting to control the impacts of tourism, particularly impacts on the environment, but additionally socio-cultural and economic impacts. Visitor management has been viewed in the past 20 years or so as a significant way to reduce the negative impacts of tourism (Pearce, 1989; Hall and McArthur, 1996; Mason, 2003a).

A common approach has been through attempts to divert tourists from the so-called 'honey pots', which are areas with large volumes of tourists. Another approach has been to minimize the negative impacts at a popular site by 'hardening' (e.g. resurfacing paths and footpaths). However, there is a danger here in that by attempting to improve the site, this only encourages more visitors who, in turn, cause more damage (Swarbrooke, 1999).

These introductory statements indicate that visitor management has been used predominantly as a means of regulating visitors. Regulation has frequently involved attempts to prevent (or in certain instances allow) access to particular areas or sites. In most cases, regulations relating to tourism are unlikely to be backed up by laws and are far more likely to be voluntary and of a self-regulatory nature (Mason and Mowforth, 1996).

However, as well as regulation, managing visitors can also involve education. Education frequently involves the process of interpretation (Mason, 2003a). This educational process may involve the dissemination of information about a particular site, but is also likely to involve more general education about social and environmental factors. In certain situations, a combination of education and regulation has been used in an attempt to manage visitors.

This chapter discusses visitor management within the context of protected areas. Two specific regions of the world, Antarctica and the Arctic, provide the actual geographic focus for this discussion. These two regions share certain similarities in terms of their physical geography, which enables useful comparisons to be made between them. In addition, tourism management in the Arctic has benefited from experiences gained in managing visitors in Antarctica. Nevertheless, there are significant differences, both in physical and human terms, between the regions and these also feature in the discussion. As the examination of visitor management in these two areas is contextualized within the concept of protected areas, the nature of these areas is considered first.

Protected Areas

Protected areas have been established in a number of locations around the world. Governments at national, but also at local, regional and even international, level are the key driving force behind the establishment of protected areas. The major rationale for the setting up of such areas is to prevent the decline of the natural resource to enable it to continue to realise economic benefits (Holden, 2000).

Hence, preventing or minimizing the negative impacts of tourism (and also other human activities) is a key factor in the establishment of protected areas. Therefore, it is possible to state that protected areas have been established to protect the environments of specific areas from the development of certain types of human activity.

However, there are very few areas of the world that lack any form of human activity. Hence, in reality, protected areas range from those permitting a range of activities to those restricting almost all forms of it (WTO, 1992). Holden (2000) provided a tabulated summary of these various protected areas, in which the most restrictive in terms of human usage are at the top, with the least restrictive at the foot. These protected areas are shown in Table 10.1. For some of the protected areas shown in Table 10.1, tourism is significant as it may benefit from environmental protection and/or may actually make a positive economic contribution to that protection (Holden, 2000).

By the early 1990s, approximately 5% of the earth's surface had protected area status and over 130 countries had designated such areas (WTO, 1992). Probably the most important type of protected area in terms of tourism use is the national park, and this type is found in many countries around the world. National parks have been established with the major aims of preventing overdevelopment of natural areas and of providing access for recreationists and tourists (Holden, 2000).

The original national parks were created around the turn of the 20th

Table 10.1. Protected areas (based on the 1992 WTO classification, adapted from Holden, 2000).

Protected area	Features
Scientific reserve/strictly nature reserve	To maintain and protect existing balance
National park	Protection of natural and scenic areas for educational, scientific and recreational use; generally, extractive industries are not permitted
Natural monument/landmark	Protection and preservation of nationally significant natural features
Managed nature reserve/ wildlife sanctuary	To ensure protection of nationally significant species/biota/landscape, human manipulation is permitted
Protected landscape	Protection of landscape which is characteristic of harmonious interaction of humans and nature; recreation and tourism permitted
Resource reserve	To protect or sustain resources by prohibiting development/activities that threaten them
Naturally biotic area/ anthropological reserve	To permit the way of life for societies living in harmony with environment to continue
Multiple-use management area/managed resource	The area to be used for mix of water, timber, wildlife, pasture and outdoor recreation; nature conservation is oriented towards economic activities

century, with the very first in the USA, at Yosemite, in 1890. Others followed in the UK and mainland parts of Europe in the early part of the 20th century. It is no coincidence that parks were created in developed countries at a time of rising population and increased urbanization, with the consequent mounting pressure on countryside/rural areas (Holden, 2000). Attempting to balance competing land uses, including tourism, by nature conservation at a time of increased demand for access has been a major issue in many national parks in the developed world during the 20th century.

Visitor Management

Visitor management has been used by a number of different agencies and organizations, at different scales and in a variety of locations. In some countries it has become a major tool in attempting to control visitor flows. For example, in the early 1990s in the UK, in response to mounting concern about real and potential damage to environmental resources, a government task force produced a tourism report that included visitor management as a key strategy. This report, *Maintaining The Balance*, produced jointly by the UK Ministry of Environment, Department of Employment and the English Tourist Board (ETB), and published in 1991, focused on the relationship between the environment and the visitor and suggested there were three main ways of managing visitors (ETB, 1991):

- controlling the number of visitors – by either limiting numbers to match capacity or spreading the number throughout the year, rather than having them concentrated in a focused 'tourist season';
- adapting the resource in ways to enable it to cope with the volume of visitors, and hence become less damaged; and
- modifying visitor behaviour.

Hall and McArthur (1996), writing largely within the context of Australasia, suggested a similar set of approaches to managing visitors as that set out in the ETB report. They indicated that attempting to modify visitor behaviour, usually through some form of regulation, is common in many areas of the world. As they argued, a major aim of modifying visitor behaviour is to limit, through some form of regulation, the actual numbers of visitors to a site.

In extreme cases, there may be complete restriction of access (Hall and McArthur, 1996), although any sort of limitation may run contrary to visitors' need for freedom, self-expression and escape (Birrel and Siverwood, 1981). Shackley (2001) concurred with the views of both the ETB (1991) and Hall and McArthur (1996) on the aims of visitor management and, in particular, reported on the need for ways to reduce visitor numbers at certain popular sites within a wider context of managing visitor flows.

When discussing the control of visitor numbers, the ETB Report (ETB, 1991) suggested that the initial task should be to determine the carrying capacity. The report then cited the following threshold levels at which the ambience and character of the place is damaged and the quality of the experience is threatened. These are as follows:

- a level above which physical damage occurs;
- a level above which irreversible damage occurs; and
- a level above which the local community suffers unacceptable side effects.

The ETB report (ETB, 1991) also made suggestions on modifying/adapting the resource as a part of the process of visitor management. It indicated that this approach acknowledges there will be some wear and tear of the tourism resource. Minimizing damage through an adaptation of the resource in an attempt to promote protection is the key aim of this approach. The report suggested the following approaches:

- the use of wardens, guides and even guards to watch over and/or supervise, in order to prevent unruly behaviour, theft or deliberate damage;
- restricting the use of the site (by e.g. cordoning off areas, to prevent access, allow regrowth); and
- protective measures (e.g. reinforcement of footpaths or the building of replicas).

Hall and McArthur (1996) also suggested that modifying the resource is a common visitor management approach. They suggested that 'hardening' the site of a natural resource attraction is particularly popular, and the purpose of hardening is to limit the damage done to the tourism resource. Hence, hardening would fit within the ETB approaches under the heading of 'protective measures'.

The two major approaches of 'adapting the resource' and 'attempting to control visitor numbers' have been largely inspired by the perceived need to limit damage to environmental resources. In fact, this approach of minimizing damage to the resource would appear to be at the heart of most visitor management during the last two decades (Mason, 2002). Such an approach would seem to have evolved largely in response to the effects of mass tourism, where visitors have been conceived of as one almost entirely homogenous group and were considered as being 'guilty until proven innocent' (Mason, 2003b). Hence, in relation to mass tourism, it has been assumed that tourists either knowingly (or unwittingly) will have damaging effects on environmental resources (Mason, 2002).

Almost certainly, this view has gained credence as the numbers involved in mass tourism rose rapidly in the 1980s and 1990s. Much writing and research in the 1980s and 1990s also supported this belief of damaging effects of mass tourism on the environment (see, for example, Krippendorf, 1987; Pearce, 1989; Mason, 1990; Burns and Holden, 1995; Swarbrooke, 1999). Therefore, perhaps it is unsurprising that, particularly in rural environments, visitor management strategies during the past 20 years have tended to start from the premise that visitors will inevitably damage the very thing they have come to experience.

As a consequence of this view, many authors have produced lists of the various effects tourists can have on the environment and most of these indicate that the negative consequences are prevalent and serious (Mason, 2002). Shackley (2001) has produced a particularly interesting list as it not only shows the negative impacts of tourism but also indicates the processes (in Shackley's diagram referred to as 'agents of change') that have led to the effects. Shackley's list, presenting the negative impacts of visitors with related causal agents, is shown in Table 10.2.

Both the approaches discussed so far (that of attempting to control visitor numbers and that of modifying the tourism resource) are primarily regulatory. However, as the ETB report (ETB, 1991) indicated – and this has also been argued by others, including Hall and McArthur (1996) and Shackley (2001) – there are different ways of managing visitors. The ETB report (ETB, 1991) made a number of suggestions on 'modifying visitor behaviour', which are as follows:

- marketing and general information provision;
- promotion to bring visitors out of season, to help spread the load;
- promotion of alternative destinations;
- niche marketing, to attract particular types of visitor;
- providing visitors with specific information;

Table 10.2. Negative physical impacts of visitors (based on Shackley, 2001).

Agent of Change	Physical Impact
Theft of artefacts	Loss of resource
Vandalism/graffiti	Damage to resource
Accidental damage	Wear and tear
Pollution (fouling)	Damage to resource
Pollution (noise)	May undermine fabric
Pollution (litter)	Reduced attractiveness
Microclimate change	Fabric damage
Crowding	Leads to physical damage

- the use of signs, travel information centres and information points/boards; and
- the use of codes of conduct to enable a combination of education and regulation in the interpretation process.

The ETB suggestions above make reference to marketing and promotion, the provision of information, the use of signs, codes of conduct and interpretation. All of these activities, either directly or indirectly, involve processes of educating visitors. Therefore, unlike the predominantly regulatory approaches of controlling visitor numbers and modifying the tourism resource, the approach of attempting to modify visitor behaviour is largely educational (Mason, 2002).

Kuo (2002) discussed tourism management at environmentally sensitive sites and provided a useful summary of the approaches to visitor management that can be applied to protected area visitor management. Kuo created two major categories of visitor management and termed these 'hard' and 'soft' approaches. As Table 10.3 shows, 'hard' management strategies involve various forms of management: physical, regulatory and economic, which in summary can be stated as 'regulatory'. Kuo's 'soft' approaches to visitor management all make reference to interpretation and, in a wider sense, each can be viewed as involving educational processes.

The use of interpretation in visitor management

One of the earliest commentators on interpretation was Tilden (1957), who suggested that it is an educational process that employs objects, illustrative media and the use of first-hand experience. The aim of interpretation, Tilden claimed, is to reveal meaning and relationships. A variety of 'objects' such as urban monuments, works of art and flora and fauna – as well as media such as print and photographs – can be used to achieve this. Prentice (1995, p. 55) defined interpretation in the following way:

Table 10.3. 'Hard' and 'Soft' visitor management strategies (based on Kuo, 2002).

'Hard' approaches	'Soft' approaches
Physical management e.g. use of fences, resource hardening, limits to size of car parks	*Directorial interpretive information* e.g. signs, information on visitor safety
Regulatory management e.g. protecting wildlife, reducing traffic congestion, regulating operation of site (such as opening times), use of security staff, implementing rules/regulations	*Behavioural interpretive information* e.g. guidelines, visitor codes of conduct
Economic management e.g. charging high entrance fees, charging car parking fees, fines for littering and other misbehaviour	*Educational interpretive information* e.g. guidebooks, tour guides, maps, targeting niche groups

> ... a process of communicating to people the significance of a place so that they can enjoy it more, understand its importance and develop a positive attitude to conservation. Interpretation is used to enhance the enjoyment of place, to convey symbolic meaning and to facilitate attitudinal or behavioural change.

Interpretation can therefore be seen as part of the process of making places accessible to a public audience and providing visitors with insight. The more specific aims of an interpretation programme, it has been argued, are 'to stimulate, facilitate and extend people's understanding of place so that empathy towards conservation, heritage, culture and landscape is developed' (Stewart *et al.*, 1998, p. 257). As Stewart *et al.* (1998) indicated, a major aim of interpretation is to stimulate interest and develop understanding in visitors. Orams (1994, 1995) went further when he suggested that interpretation programmes are usually designed not just to inform, but to change visitors' behaviour.

It has been argued that visitors can respond to interpretation in two major ways. Moscardo (1996) suggested that visitors have two modes of response for dealing with new social situations: 'mindless' or 'mindful'. A 'mindless' state is characterized by mental passivity and behaviour, while 'mindful' means a state marked by active mental processing (Moscardo and Pearce, 1986; Moscardo, 1996). Moscardo (1996) argued the importance of promoting 'mindful' tourism through interpretation programmes.

Interpretation can be delivered via a number of different modes and in different formats, including books, maps and signs. It can involve the written word, but also the spoken word, where tour guides can have a major role in the interpretation process (Weiler and Ham, 2001).

The next section of this chapter discusses the environments of the two polar regions and indicates the nature of tourist attractions and activities in each. How visitors are managed in protected areas of each polar region is then discussed.

Antarctica

Antarctica is one of the last tourism frontiers. It is the remoteness of the continent combined with a unique environment that attracts some tourists (and deters others). Although the extreme climate means terrestrial ecosystems are limited, the waters around Antarctica are rich in wildlife. Polar explorers reached the South Pole only in the early 20th century. Subsequently, the isolation and extreme climatic conditions deterred continuous settlement until the second half of the 20th century.

Antarctica has a unique history and is unlike anywhere else on earth, in not being sovereign territory – it has several claimants to parts of its territory but is not owned by any one country. The continent is the only one devoted to scientific activity and only a limited amount of commercial activity is allowed, with tourism being the major commercial user of the environment.

The unusual political circumstances on the continent have led to a unique management system known as the Antarctica Treaty System (ATS), in which the legal status of all land and resources is subject to the Antarctic Treaty (AT) (Hall and Johnston, 1995). Politically, Antarctica is a neutral, demilitarized territory subject to the AT, which at the end of the 20th century had been signed by over 40 countries with interests in the continent (Mason and Legg, 1999).

The AT, created in 1961, designated Antarctic as an area to be used for peaceful purposes only, where military activities were prohibited, and gave prominence to the freedom of scientific research (Hall, 1992). The AT was created to ensure that no one single country had the right to declare any of part of the virtually uninhabited continent as its own. This unique status, in effect, means that Antarctica is the most protected area on earth.

However, Antarctica has been subjected to a number of conflicts since the creation of the AT, with seven countries (UK, New Zealand, USA, Australia, Chile, Argentina and Norway) establishing territorial claims (Prosser, 1995). The main instrument within the ATS for resolving territorial disputes that have a bearing on tourism activities is the Madrid Protocol – a part of the Environmental Protection Strategy for Antarctica – but this was only finally signed by all signatory countries in 1998 (Mason and Legg, 1999).

With its unusual and unique status, during the last two decades of the 20th century Antarctica came to have a very strong symbolic value recognized well beyond the continent itself. It symbolized (and continues to do so) the conflict between development and preservation, between the opposing agencies of 'progress' and of 'conservation' (Mason and Legg, 1999). The willingness (or unwillingness) of humans to pull back from the destruction of the Antarctic wilderness was seen as the test case of human desire and ability to avert destruction globally (Broady, 1991).

Tourism in Antarctica

A major motivation of tourists is to achieve the feeling of 'otherness' (MacCannell, 1976; Ryan, 1991). This can be otherness of culture, otherness of climate or otherness of place. Antarctica, probably more than anywhere else on earth, represents this sense of otherness, particularly otherness of place (Mason and Legg, 1999). The remoteness and isolation of Antarctica appears to make it particularly suitable for visitors to escape from their normal routine into 'otherness'.

However, Antarctica has much to attract tourists. The abundance of wildlife in the coastal margins, their habitats and the natural beauty of the setting is a major motivating factor amongst tourists. Hence, visitors come to see wildlife, particularly penguins – perhaps the symbol of the South Polar region (Hall and Johnston, 1995) – as well as whales and other marine animal and bird species. They also come to see the landscapes of ice and snow.

However, it is not just the natural world that attracts visitors to Antarctica; a key motivational factor is to see the human heritage. In particular, the huts of well known polar explorers such as Scott, Shackleton and Mawson draw tourists. In addition, other heritage sites, including scientific stations such as that at Scott Base, have become attractions. Given that the focus of most of the activity on the continent is scientific exploration, the actual work conducted by Antarctic scientists – and the opportunity of seeing it in action and meeting the scientists themselves – has become a significant tourist motivational factor.

Visitor management in Antarctica

Antarctica provides evidence that the approach of self-regulation combined with interpretation is a particularly appropriate visitor management strategy. Here, self-regulation is in the form of codes of conduct for both visitors and operators and it is the main approach to visitor management. This is coupled with interpretation, which is provided in a number of forms, including written material, although tour guides also play a very important role.

Antarctica is the one part of the earth where tourism is a major economic activity and almost all other forms of commercial activity are prevented. Until the late 1990s, tourism operations were managed almost entirely through self-regulation. This was largely possible because of the relatively small number of tourists, with approximately 10,000 per annum throughout the 1990s (Bauer, 2001), and the arrangements between the tour operators who manage visits to the continent; almost all visiting tourists until the late 1990s reached Antarctica by cruise ship.

Tourists first came to Antarctica in significant numbers in the 1960s (Hall, 1992). One of the first operators to bring tourists was Lars-Eric Lindblad (Mason and Legg, 1999). Lindblad instilled a strong environmental ethic in the visitors he brought (Stonehouse and Crosbie, 1995) and this contributed to the practices adopted by the cruise ship staff who subsequently led visits to Antarctica. In 1991, the cruise ship operators joined together to form the International Association of Antarctic Tour

Operators (IAATO). IAATO created an operator code of conduct for their own members and also devised visitor guidelines and visitor codes of conduct.

The Lindblad approach, on which IAATO based its various guidelines, involves preparatory lectures aboard ship prior to arrival by those with extensive experience of Antarctica (Mason and Legg, 1999). At these initial sessions, passengers receive copies of the guidelines and codes of conduct as well as AT recommendations on tourism on the continent. The visitor code of conduct makes reference to potential and actual impacts on the environment, as well as to plant and animal species, cultural heritage sites (primarily the huts of Antarctic explorers) and tourist safety. The guidelines accompanying the code provide the rationale for the specific instructions in the code.

As part of the Lindblad approach, tourists are taken by inflatable boat, in groups of 10–15, from their cruise ship and landed on shore accompanied by a guide. Although free to wander, tourists are required to stay close to the embarkation point, for safety reasons. Any transgression of codes of conduct/guidelines is met with an on-the-spot admonishment by the guide, and tourists can be sent back to the cruise ship. Debriefing sessions are held back on board ship, as well as discussions concerning any issues and problems, and these usually involve attempts to reinforce the environmental ethic.

The Arctic Region

The Arctic has been variously defined, but there is no single universally accepted definition (Sage, 1986). A commonly accepted approach is to use the treeline, a visible boundary that is based on climate and soil, to distinguish the Arctic from the sub-Arctic region. North of the treeline is the treeless or semi-treeless tundra which, for many people, is the true Arctic. This region, north of the treeline, has similarities with the physical/climatic features of the Antarctic. The existence of permafrost, a product of the climate, is important in definitions in Siberia and Canada (Sage, 1986). In Alaska and Europe, the Arctic Circle tends to be used as the boundary of the Arctic Region (Johnston, 1995).

In an attempt to classify areas at risk and gain protected area status, definitions combining climate and biogeographical data were first used in the early 1990s (CAFF, 1994). However, as Johnston (1995) pointed out, all definitions of the Arctic are culturally and historically based constructs. One significant construct, used in tourism marketing of the Arctic, is 'the land of the midnight sun' (Mason, 1997). However, Iceland, considered by most as being in the Arctic, and a member of the government body for the region (the Arctic Council), is almost completely south of the Arctic Circle, and much of Alaska is also sub-Arctic.

Nevertheless, the Arctic is perceived by tourists in a very similar way to visitor' views of Antarctica. The major appeal of the Arctic is that it is regarded by tourists as a vast wilderness. Allied to this is the concept of the environment as clean and unsullied by human activity (Johnston, 1995). Combining the tourist perception of a wilderness with that of an area almost devoid of population means that it is viewed as a region offering great scope for recreation, adventure and enjoyment.

Like the Antarctic, the Arctic is viewed as being metaphorically – as well as literally – at the end of the earth, and hence distant from the hectic urban existences of many visitors, where they can escape, unwind and reflect on their life (Viken, 1993). Lopez (1986) echoes this view when indicating that the Arctic is a place of retreat from alienated Western lifestyles and Johnston (1995) argued that the Arctic, like Antarctica, carries mystic symbolism and it encourages contemplation about humans, the earth and the universe.

Unlike Antarctica, there are indigenous people in the Arctic and they act as major draws for tourists, as are their artefacts and the manifestations of their activity, such as the reindeer herding of the Sami people (Mason, 1997). The indigenous people are usually viewed by tourists as living in harmony with the environment of the region, which supports the appeal of the region as a tourist attraction (Mason, 1994).

Tourism in the Arctic

Although some forms of tourist activity in the Arctic are similar to those in Antarctica, such as observing and photographic the scenery and wildlife, other types are far more consumptive of resources, including hunting and fishing. Snow-based activities such as skiing are also particularly significant in mountain and high-latitude areas of the Arctic. In sub-Arctic areas of, for example Canada, Alaska, northern Scandinavia and Iceland, hiking and walking are popular tourist activities in the short summer period.

As tourist activities are somewhat different in the Arctic to Antarctica, impacts also tend to vary. The scale of tourism, although not approaching that occurring in areas affected by mass tourism, is at a far higher level than in Antarctica. Cumulative damage caused by wheeled and tracked vehicles is significant, particularly in areas where spring and summer snowmelt expose fragile vegetation (Mason, 1997). For example, on the Norwegian island of Svalbard there have been calls to limit the expansion of tourist numbers because of alleged damage caused by the unregulated use of snow-scooters (Viken, 1995). Tourist litter and other waste has become a significant problem in the last decade of the 20th century, particularly in parts of Arctic Canada and Alaska (Johnston and Madunic, 1995).

The problem of commoditization of indigenous cultures, in which tourists view members of host populations in the same way that they view wildlife as a commodity to be consumed, has been reported in the Arctic (Hall, 1987; Smith, 1989) and appears to be growing (Mason, 1997). As tourism has expanded in the Arctic, in some locations not only has a bastardized, inauthentic pseudo-cultue been created for tou.ist consumption, but this has tended to be controlled by non-indigenous groups, which has limited the potential economic gain that could be derived by indigenous Arctic communities (Mason, 1997).

Visitor management in the Arctic

Unlike Antarctica, there is no one set of regulations relating to tourism activities in the Arctic, although a general code for visitors to the region has been proposed (see Mason, 1994). Instead, individual countries, regions and localities have their own forms of regulations that pertain to tourism. In many areas, laws are aimed at local populations and are not targeted specifically at visitors, but they have a bearing on tourist activities (Mason, 1997).

However, some regions have developed laws, regulations or guidelines. The Northwest Territories and Yukon in Canada have regulations relating to hunting as well as to access to and protection of designated sites of environmental and/or heritage value (Hall and Johnston, 1995). In the 1990s, in the Northwest Territories visitors to national parks were required to register and take part in a visitor orientation programme which involved interpretation and developing awareness of regulations, codes of conducts and guidelines (Hall and Johnston, 1995).

In some parts of the Arctic there is concern about the impacts of expeditions. Ellesmere Island is a particularly popular starting place for expeditions to the North Pole. In the early 1990s, the Canadian Government published a *Guide for Expeditions to Northern and Arctic Canada*, which acted as a form of visitor code, in that it not only gave information and practical advice, but brought together all legislation relating to wildlife and environmental protection (Johnston, 1993).

The location in the Arctic that probably can claim to have regulations that amount to the level of comprehensibility and strictness of those in use in Antarctica is the Norwegian archipelago of Svalbard. Here, the landscape is very similar to that of Antarctica and the Norwegian Ministries of the Environment and Justice have created regulations targeted at visitors that aim to protect the environment and historical remains of the islands. These regulations, which have been in existence since 1983, indicate the following: (i) conditions under which vehicles can and cannot be used; (ii) the need to remove litter; (iii) how not to disturb wildlife; and (iv) how not to damage fragile vegetation (Viken, 1995).

However, in many protected areas of the Arctic, there may be little in the way of attempts to directly manage visitors, with large parts of Siberia, for example, lacking any form of tourism regulations, visitor codes or guidelines. Nevertheless, in some Arctic locations not only has attention been paid to tourists but thought has also been given to providing information and advice to related players in tourism.

For example, in 1995 the Finnish Tourist Board produced guidelines targeted at the tourism industry. These guidelines were an attempt to promote sustainable tourism, and made reference to the following: (i) need to include environmental viewpoints in planning; (ii) the need to recognize the importance of local communities; (iii) the need to make use of local skills, services and products; and (iv) the need for the honest marketing of tourist products (UNEP, 1995).

At approximately the same time the Swedish Environmental Protection Agency, working in collaboration with the World Wide Fund for Nature (Sweden), produced guidelines for the tourism industry, which not only contained very similar statements to those produced by the Finnish Tourist Board, but suggested tour operators should employ an environmental officer, educate visitors and attempt to ensure that tourism benefited the local economy of tourism destinations (Widstrand, 1995).

Discussion

A number of comparisons have been made between Antarctica and the Arctic region in earlier sections. As this discussion section also makes a number of comparative statements about the two regions, a table summarizing similarities and differences is provided (Table 10.4).

Table 10.4 provides information on the tourism management regimes operating in each of the regions and this discussion section concentrates on this topic, with particular attention given to visitor management.

As has been indicated above, Antarctica is unique in that it is not owned by any one country, is the continent dedicated to science, is managed through the ATS and is almost in its entirety designated as a protected area. It is also the one part of the earth where tourism is a major economic activity; almost all other forms of commercial activity are prevented and it has almost no permanent resident population.

Until the late 1990s, tourism operations were managed almost entirely through self-regulation, prior to the final country signing the Madrid Protocol. In terms of visitor management in Antarctica, this has involved largely the use of IAATO codes of conduct supported by interpretation provided by IAATO tour guides who accompany visitors. According to Stonehouse and Crosbie (1995), this approach appears to have been a successful way of managing tourists to Antarctic for at least 25 years.

However, this may be to do with the relatively small number of visitors and the fact that the great majority arrives under supervision from IAATO cruise ship staff. It also seems likely that many Antarctic tourists are very well informed prior to arrival, are aware of the likely consequences of their behaviour on the continent and, although there is no hard evidence to support this, leave Antarctica as 'ambassadors' for this unique environment (Mason and Legg, 1999). In this way, they not only would appear to develop a conservation ethic that they would subsequently apply to other protected areas, but also inspire responsible behaviour in future Antarctic tourists.

It has been suggested that, to be effective, codes of codes should be targeted at different user groups in the same location and should be used

Table 10.4. Comparative aspects of tourism within Antarctica and the Arctic region in the early 21st century (based on Hall and Johnston, 1995, with more recent additions asterisked).

Antarctica	The Arctic region
Extremely harsh climate	Harsh climate, but relatively mild summers except Greenland and Canadian High Arctic
Extremely sensitive physical environment	Extremely sensitive physical environment
Disputed sovereignty over land and sea areas	Relatively clear sovereignty over land areas
Conservation operates under international management regime and almost entire continent has protected area status	Conservation operates primarily under a national management regime, including designation of national park areas
No indigenous peoples	Indigenous peoples seeking economic and political self-determination
Tourist access extremely difficult, sea and air only	Tourist access is difficult, but available by land, sea and air; northern regions of North America and Europe have well-established air routes and good sub-Arctic land routes
Range of tourists from relatively passive sightseers to recreational expeditions to Pole or traversing continent; greater proportion cruise ship-based and passive*	Range of tourists from passive sightseers to recreational expeditions to Pole or other challenges; greater proportion of tourism activity-based*
Cultural tourism relates to historic sites and current scientific/government use	Cultural tourism relates to historic sites and current scientific/government, living aboriginal culture, archaeological sites and current industry uses
Tourism operates under Madrid Protocol, signed by all signatories only in 1998*	Tourism subject to national and regional legislative control, except in disputed international waters
Tourism used as a means of reinforcing territorial claims	Tourism used as a means of reinforcing territorial claims
Visitor management primarily through IAATO operator and visitor codes*	Visitor management through various national and regional agencies, no single approach and little coordination or monitoring*

together (Valentine, 1992; Mason and Mowforth, 1996). Antarctica provides a very good example of how codes targeted at different audiences can be used together in an attempt to manage visitors. Here, it is codes for both visitors and operators that have been used at the same time. It is the unusual political and economic circumstances on the continent that enable a much clearer picture of the use and effectiveness of tourism codes than in most other parts of the world.

This example of 'soft' management (Kuo, 2002) through self-regulation used in Antarctica also reveals the links between regulation and education in tourism management. The codes and accompanying guidelines not only provide instructions on appropriate behaviour in Antarctica (the self–regulation component), but also provide a rationale for the instructions in the codes (the education component). Whether this form of self-regulation can continue to be successful in the face of an overall growth of tourist numbers to Antarctica, increasing ship size and increasing diversity of language groups from the early 21st century onwards, remains to be seen.

Interpretation is the other form of 'soft' visitor management employed in Antarctica. This takes place via preliminary discussions aboard cruise ships prior to shore visits as well is in post-visit debriefing sessions. While on shore, IAATO tour guides act as the major agents of interpretation. Combined with codes of conduct, this form of 'soft' management seems to have worked for many years in Antarctica. However, as only a limited amount of research has been conducted into its effectiveness, it is not clear how successful interpretation, as a part of visitor management, can be. Stewart *et al.* (1998) indicated that, of the few evaluation studies of interpretation that exist, effectiveness is usually determined by how much factual information visitors can recall.

Such studies, however, provide little idea of how people use interpretation to help them *understand* places they are visiting, they argued. In making the same criticism of the lack of evaluation of interpretation programmes as Stewart *et al.* (1998), Orams (1994, 1995) emphasized that such programmes are usually designed not just to inform, but to change visitors' behaviour. However, Orams (1994) added that there is little evidence to suggest that interpretation programmes will necessarily lead to a change in the behaviour of visitors.

Orams (1995) suggested that evaluation of interpretation programmes would be necessary to ascertain any changes in behaviour and advocated the use of 'cognitive dissonance' as a way of getting visitors to modify their behaviour. He argued that cognitive dissonance can be used in interpretative programmes to challenge people's belief systems (Orams, 1994). The theory of cognitive dissonance was developed by Festinger (1957), and the central concepts are dissonance, consonance and irrelevance. Festinger suggested that the existence of dissonance is psychologically uncomfortable, and hence will motivate individuals to reduce it in an attempt to achieve consonance.

The use of cognitive dissonance in interpretation, Orams (1995) suggested, would be an attempt to throw people off balance and put questions in their minds. This use of 'shock tactics' would be a way to get visitors to modify their behaviour. In addition, Orams (1994) suggested that the eliciting of emotional responses from visitors, as part of a strategy involving cognitive dissonance, may be the way to counter the problems inherent in educating tourists.

Experiences gained from managing tourism in Antarctica have been used in creating management strategies and tools for the Arctic region. For example, the generic visitor code for the Arctic, proposed by Mason (1994), drew on both the content and format of the IAATO codes. Governmental and non-governmental agencies in a variety of countries, including Norway, Finland, Sweden and Canada, have also been influenced by the principles underlying the codes and guidelines developed by IAATO, when creating regulations for their specific audiences.

A particularly good example of the experience gained in Antarctic visitor management being applied in the Arctic context can be seen in the World Wide Fund (WWF) for Nature (Arctic) Arctic Tourism Project (Mason *et al.*, 2000). The WWF Arctic Tourism Project was established in February 1995 and its key aim to link tourism and conservation. Over a period of 3 years, several project meetings took place involving tour operators, national and local government officials, local community representatives, NGO staff, Arctic scientists, Arctic tourism experts and also delegates with Antarctic experience.

At these meetings, through a process of negotiation and consensus building, tools for managing Arctic tourism were devised. The key tools were codes of conduct, supported by guidelines. The final version of these appeared in 1997. They were published in a document by WWF Arctic that contained ten principles for Arctic tourism (WWF Arctic, 1997). These are as follows:

- Make tourism and conservation compatible.
- Support the preservation of wilderness and biodiversity.
- Use natural resources in a sustainable way.
- Minimize consumption, waste and pollution.
- Respect local cultures.
- Respect historic and scientific sites.
- Communities should benefit from tourism.
- Trained staff are the way towards responsible tourism.
- Tourism should be educational.
- Follow safety rules.

The principles for Arctic tourism were accompanied by detailed guidelines. The document in which the principles appeared also contained a code of conduct for Arctic tourists and a separate code for Arctic tour operators (WWF Arctic, 1997). However, each of these codes was linked very closely to the ten principles. The document containing the principles and Arctic tourism codes was subsequently distributed to more than 5000 user groups, government bodies, NGOs and local communities in the Arctic (Mason *et al.*, 2000).

Between 2000 and 2004 a number of pilot projects were established in a variety of Arctic locations, including Arctic Canada, Alaska, Northern Finland and on Svalbard, to trial the tourism codes. Not only was this an attempt to investigate how they might function in a real context, but also to monitor how various indigenous groups react to such codes. At the time of writing these pilot projects had just ended, but results from them have not yet been published.

Managing tourism, and by implication managing visitors, in the Arctic is potentially more complex than the same process in Antarctica. The region is sovereign territory, with eight countries having at least a part of their land area in the Arctic, as well as other countries having interests and involvement in international sea areas of the region. Therefore, different parts of the Arctic are subject to different jurisdictions, with a variety of national, regional and local laws and regulations. Unlike Antarctica there is no international treaty which prevents commercial exploitation of the Arctic. In the past oil and other land-based minerals and whales and other marine species have been highly sought-after resources.

Tourism is often viewed as a preferable option for development, being considered far less consumptive than these exploitative activities (Mason, 1997). The region has also had more strategic and military importance, historically, than Antarctica – until the early 1990s the Arctic was often the focus of Cold War hostility between the old USSR and the USA.

The Arctic is also far more accessible, both geographically and from the perspective of an individual's travel budget, than Antarctica. Consequently, tourist numbers to the Arctic have been growing fairly rapidly in the last 10–15 years and the expansion is at a far greater level than in Antarctica. As a result, there has been mounting concern about visitor impacts in the Arctic and the need for appropriate and effective visitor management.

Although agencies in the Arctic have drawn on experiences of visitor management in Antarctica, the different factors at play in the Arctic could contribute to less effective visitor management. Antarctica is certainly remote and has no police force to monitor tourism management problems, but to date it has had relatively few tourists and, until the late 1990s, IAATO acted as the key regulatory force. The Arctic is also a vast, remote region, but where tourism management is subject to individual countries' jurisdiction. Tourist numbers are growing, but there are still areas little affected by tourism. The desire to gain economic benefit from tourism, like most other global locations, is strong in the Arctic. This could be good news for economically depressed or undeveloped Arctic communities. However, it could also lead to questionable practices.

It may be very tempting for tour operators, working hand in hand with local communities, to gain a competitive edge by promoting specific Arctic destinations as offering tourism experiences that are environmentally and socio-economically sustainable. Operators may be able to claim that they adhere to a particular operator code of conduct and provide tourists with a visitor code based on similar principles as a way of giving evidence to support their product (see Mason, 1997).

However, this may be little more than an operator/local community ruse to sell more holidays, which the concerned customer believes are more sustainable than other products, but are in fact potentially very damaging, as more such products are sold as a result of the promotional efforts than others. Without monitoring of the use of codes of conduct, or some form of externally imposed regulation, this type of abuse could well occur (Mason and Mowforth, 1996). Such 'green-washing' (see Fennell, 1999) is not uncommon in other global locations, so there is no reason to suspect it will not happen in the Arctic.

However, even if Arctic tour operators do act ethically and responsibly in terms of the products they sell, and communities do indeed genuinely employ sustainable practices and offer what they regard as sustainable tourism experiences, there is still an issue concerning visitors: there is no single police force in the Arctic to monitor visitor behaviour, and even if there was such a force, it would act as little more than a deterrent, as the area is so large that most behaviour would remain unobserved. If it was possible to monitor, little of the behaviour of tourists would be illegal anyway, as there are few laws relating to tourism, and visitor regulations remain largely voluntary.

Under the current political and economic conditions in the Arctic, those involved in management of visitors in protected areas such as national parks have to rely largely on tour operators acting ethically and honestly, and on tourists responding positively to advice and instructions contained in codes of conducts and information provided via interpretation. In the absence of external regulations or a monitoring force, those concerned with Arctic tourism management find themselves relying on tried and tested tools deployed in Antarctica, but in a situation where the scale of tourism activity is far larger, the impacts of tourism more significant and the rise in visitor numbers far higher.

Conclusions

This chapter has discussed and evaluated differing visitor management approaches in relation to protected areas. These can be categorized as 'hard' and 'soft' approaches (Kuo, 2002). Traditionally 'hard' approaches involving some form of external regulation, often 'borrowed' from approaches applied to managing mass tourism destinations, have been prevalent and to some extent these have been successful.

However, Shackley (1998) suggested a major problem of 'hard' visitor management approaches is that policing and enforcing any regulations will always be a problem. This chapter has indicated that enforcement will be particularly difficult in more remote areas, such as Antarctica and the Arctic region.

In particular two 'soft' approaches to visitor management have been discussed. Both of these place emphasis on the visitor experience, rather than on tourists' impacts. Interpretation has been presented as an educational process that involves not only the transfer of knowledge, but also the development of values in relation to the environment and culture of the site visited (Prentice, 1995; Stewart *et al.*, 1998). Interpretation can be used to transform visitors' thinking and behaviour, with the intention that they become 'mindful' tourists (Moscardo, 1996). However, this chapter has indicated that little is known of the effectiveness of interpretation, as it has only rarely been evaluated.

The other 'soft' approach discussed in the chapter is that of self-regulation. Through the use of IAATO codes of conduct and guidelines for both operators and visitors, it has been argued that Antarctica has a particularly effective form of self-regulation of visitors. The Lindblad approach to the management of cruise ship-based tourists in Antarctica also reveals the close link between interpretation and self-regulation and suggests that each involves processes of education. Experiences gained from the use of codes of conduct in the Antarctic have been used to develop codes for the Arctic.

However, despite a number of similarities in both the physical and human geography of each of the polar regions, conditions in the Arctic are not identical to those in Antarctica. Nevertheless, attempts have been made to develop and put into practice codes of conduct and guidelines for tourism and, as has been suggested here, the WWF Arctic Tourism Project is a particularly good example of this.

In the early part of the 21st century it appears that, globally, visitor numbers are continuing to grow. In addition to mass tourism destinations, there is also increasing pressure on protected areas, including those in both Antarctica and the Arctic region. In spite of this growth, there is still a lack of accurate data about the precise impacts of tourism at sites that attract visitors (Shackley, 1998).

If little is known about impacts of tourism in protected areas, even less is known about the effectiveness of visitor management strategies, whether these are classified as 'hard' or 'soft'. Hence, there is a real and immediate need to conduct research into both 'hard' and 'soft' approaches to visitor management, not just to assess their comparative effectiveness, but also to ensure the long-term sustainability of the earth's protected areas.

References

Bauer, T. (2001) *Tourism in Antarctica*. Harwood Press, New York.

Birrel, R. and Silverwood, R. (1981) Social costs of environmental deterioration on the Victorian coastline. In: Mercer, D. (ed.) *Outdoor Recreation: Australian Perspectives*. Sorret Publishing, Melbourne, Australia, pp. 118–124.

Broady, P.A. (1991) Antarctic: more than ice and penguins. In: Mayers, E. (ed.) *Antarctica: the Scientists' Case for a World Park*. Greenpeace, London, pp. 17–19.

Burns, P. and Holden, A. (1995) *Tourism: a New Perspective*. Prentice Hall, London.

CAFF (1994) *The State of Protected Areas in the Circumpolar Arctic, Conservation of Flora and Fauna*. Habitat Conservation Report, World Conservation Monitoring Centre, Trondheim UNEP/GRID, Arendal, Norway.

ETB (1991) *Tourism and the Environment: Maintaining the Balance*. Department of Employment/Ministry of Environment/English Tourist Board, London.

Fennell, D. (1999) *Ecotourism: an Introduction*. Routledge, London

Festinger, L. (1957) *A Theory of Cognitive Dissonance*. Stanford University Press, Stanford, California.

Hall, C.M. (1992) Tourism in Antarctica: activities, impacts and management. *Journal of Travel Research* 30 (4), 2–9.

Hall, C.M. and Johnston, M.E. (1995) Introduction: pole to pole tourism impacts, issues and the search for a management regime. In: Hall, C.M. and Johnston, M.E. (eds) *Polar Tourism*. John Wiley and Sons, Chichester, UK, pp. 1–26.

Hall, C.M. and McArthur, S. (1996) Visitor Management: Principles and Practice. In: Hall, C.M. and McArthur, S. (eds) *Heritage Management in Australia and New Zealand*. Oxford University Press, Melbourne, Australia, pp. 37–54.

Hall, S. (1987) *The Fourth World: the Arctic and its Heritage*. Hodder and Stoughton, London.

Holden, A. (2000) *Environment and Tourism*. Routledge, London.

Johnston, M. (1993) Tourism and the Regulation of Adventure Travel in the Canadian Arctic. Paper presented at the *Fifth World Wilderness Conference*, Tromsö, Norway, 24 September–1 October 1993.

Johnston, M. (1995) Patterns and issues in Arctic and sub-Arctic tourism. In: Hall, C.M. and Johnston, M.E. (eds) *Polar Tourism*. John Wiley and Sons, Chichester, UK, pp. 27–42.

Johnston, M. and Madunic, J. (1995) Waste disposal and the wilderness in the Yukon territory. In: Hall, C.M. and Johnston, M.E. (eds) *Polar Tourism*. John Wiley and Sons, Chichester, UK, pp. 85–100.

Krippendorf, J. (1987) *The Holidaymakers*. Heinemann, London.

Kuo, I.-L. (2002) The effectiveness of environmental interpretation at resource-sensitive tourism destinations. *International Journal of Tourism Research* 4, 87–101.

Lopez, B. (1986) *Arctic Dreams*. Picador, London.

MacCannell, D. (1976) *The Tourist: a New Theory of the Leisure Class*. Macmillan, London.

Mason, P. (1990) *Tourism: Environment and Development Perspectives*. World Wide Fund for Nature, Godalming, UK.

Mason, P. (1994) A visitor code for the Arctic. *Tourism Management* 15, 93–97.

Mason, P. (1997) Tourism codes of conduct in the Arctic. *Journal of Sustainable Tourism* 5, 151–165.

Mason, P. (2002) *Education and Regulation for Visitor Management*. Keynote presentation at the conference Carrying Capacity and Protected Area Management, World Wide Fund for Nature Greece, Athens, 1 June 2002.

Mason, P. (2003a) *Tourism Impacts, Planning and Management*. Butterworth Heinemann, Oxford.

Mason, P. (2003b) *Why is the Visitor always Guilty until Proven Innocent?* Presentation given at the Centre for Tourism Research, London Metropolitan University, 2 April 2003.

Mason, P. and Legg, S. (1999) Antarctic tourism: activities, impacts, management issues and a proposed research agenda. *Pacific Tourism Review* 3, 71–84.

Mason, P. and Mowforth, M. (1996) Codes of conduct in tourism. *Progress in Tourism and Hospitality Research* 2, 151–167.

Mason, P., Johnston, M. and Twynam, D. (2000) The World Wide Fund for Nature Arctic Tourism Project. *Journal of Sustainable Tourism* 8, 305–323.

Moscardo, G. (1996) Mindful visitors: heritage and tourism. *Annals of Tourism Research* 23 (2), 376–397.

Moscardo, G. and Pearce, P. (1986) Visitor centres and environmental interpretation. *Journal of Environmental Psychology* 6, 89–108.

Orams, M. (1994) Creating effective interpretation for managing interaction between tourists and wildlife. *Australian Journal of Environmental Education* 10, 21–34.

Orams, M. (1995) Using interpretation to manage nature-based tourism. *Journal of Sustainable Tourism* 4, 81–94.

Pearce, D. (1989) *Tourist Development*. Longman, London.

Prentice, R.C. (1995) *Tourism as Experience, Tourists as Consumers: Insight and Enlightenment*. Inaugural Lecture, Queen Margaret College, Edinburgh, UK.

Prosser, R. (1995) Power, control and intrusion with particular reference to the Antarctic. In: Cooper, D.E. and Palmer, J.A. (eds) *Just Environments*. Routledge, London, pp. 108–120.

Ryan, C. (1991) *Recreational Tourism*. Routledge, London.

Sage, B. (1986) *The Arctic and its Wildlife*. Croom Helm, London.

Shackley, M. (1998) Introduction. In: Shackley, M. (ed.) *Visitor Management: Case Studies from World Heritage Sites.* Butterworth-Heinemann, Oxford, UK, pp. 1–9.

Shackley, M. (2001) *Managing Sacred Sites.* Continuum, London.

Smith, V. (1989) Eskimo tourism; micro-models and marginal men. In: Smith, V. (ed.) *Hosts and Guests.* 2nd edn, University of Pennsylvania Press, Philadelphia, Pennsylvania, pp. 52–82.

Stewart, E.J., Hayward, B.M., Devlin, P.J. and Kirby, V.G. (1998) The place of interpretation: a new approach to the evaluation of interpretation. *Tourism Management* 19, 257–266.

Stonehouse, B. and Crosbie, K. (1995) Tourism impacts and management in the Antarctic Peninsula. In: Hall, C.M. and Johnston, M.E. (eds) *Polar Tourism.* John Wiley and Sons, Chichester, UK, pp. 217–233.

Swarbrooke, J. (1999) *Sustainable Tourism Management.* CAB International, Wallingford, UK.

Tilden, F. (1957) *Interpreting Our Heritage.* University of North Carolina Press, Chapel Hill, North Carolina.

UNEP (1995) *Environmental Codes of Conduct,* Technical Report, No 29, United Nations Environment Programme, Paris.

Valentine, P. (1992) Nature-based tourism. In: Hall, C.M. and Weiler, B. (eds) *Special Interest Tourism.* Belhaven, London, pp. 105–127.

Viken, A. (1993) The Arctic Tourist Experience. Paper presented at the *Fifth World Wilderness Conference,* Tromsö, Norway, 24 September–1 October 1993.

Viken, A. (1995) Tourism experiences in the Arctic. In: Hall, C.M. and Weiler, B. (eds) *Special Interest Tourism.* Belhaven, London, pp. 73–84.

Weiler, B. and Ham, S. (2001) Tour Guides and Interpretation. In: Weaver, D. (ed.) *Encyclopaedia of Ecotourism.* CAB International, Wallingford, UK, pp. 549–563.

Widstrand, S. (1995) Arctic tourism: challenges and opportunities. Interview with Staffan Widstrand. *Arctic Bulletin* 3, 8–9.

WTO (1992) *Tourism Carrying Capacity: Report on the Senior Level Expert Group Meeting held in Paris, June 1990.* World Tourism Organisation, Madrid.

Part IV
Tourism Opportunities

11 Wind Farms as Possible Tourist Attractions

ROBERT NASH, ANDREW MARTIN, DON CARNEY AND KUMARAN KRISHNAN

Scottish Centre of Tourism, Aberdeen Business School, Robert Gordon University, Aberdeen, UK

Introduction

Tourism is now the world's largest service industry, worth £4.4 billion to Scotland alone, attracting over 18 million tourists per year (VisitScotland, 2003). Doswell (1997, p. 1) suggests that:

> Tourism is not really an industry sector in itself. It is economic activity that runs through society involving many different sectors and there are clearly benefits for tourism economic activity allied to a high quality visitor attraction created around a wind farm development.

Certainly wind power and wind farms are on the international political agenda and at a local level both the British and Scottish political institutions recognize the need for an environmentally friendly energy source and are investing heavily in wind power. Following the Kyoto Energy Summit,

> The UK Government pledged to produce 10% of its electricity from renewable sources by the year 2010. The Scottish Executive is currently pursuing a renewable energy target for Scotland of 18% by 2010, and they are consulting the feasibility of generating 40% of Scotland's energy from renewable sources by 2020. Scotland has particular potential for the development of renewable energy, especially wind energy, due to its geography and climate.
>
> (VisitScotland, 2004a)

Against this background of enthusiasm for the development of renewable energy sources, there are the issues related to tourism and the likely impacts on the tourism product, especially in areas that rely on the environment as a key component of their tourism product (such as Scotland). This is because wind farm development tends to generate controversy in connection with the likely visual impacts, possible noise and detrimental affects on accommodation businesses within the locality. 'This is of particular importance to Scotland where the importance of the Scottish landscape as an attraction for visitors, whether for passive sightseeing or active outdoor pursuits, has been reinforced by every visitor survey' (VisitScotland, 2004a).

A Mori poll commissioned by the Scottish Executive (2002) showed overwhelming support for wind generation, with only 12% of respondents saying that wind farms spoiled the landscape (British Wind Energy, 2002c). However, there is increased public opposition to such developments and as this opposition comes to the fore on both the political and social agendas, the momentum of debate in the UK will gather impetus.

The Scottish Executives Climate for Change programme (Scottish Executive, 2000) highlights how the executive is firmly committed to the Kyoto agreement and, as such, it must approve wind farm developments as part of a portfolio of strategies for energy production. On 1 April 2003 the Executive put in place the Renewable Obligations (Scotland) Act. This places a legal obligation on every electricity supplier in Scotland to supply increasing amounts of electricity from renewable sources.

Public Attitudes to and Press Comment on Wind Farm Development

Between 1990 and 1996, 13 different research studies were carried out by different research groups into public attitudes to wind power. In total, these surveys canvassed the opinion of 3549 people who were living close to the existing or proposed site. Every study shows that the overwhelming majority of residents in areas with a wind project are in favour of wind power, both in terms of renewable energy source and in being located in their area. On an average, eight out of ten supported their local wind farm (British Wind Energy, 2002d).

When questioned about the design of the windmill, over half of the respondents (56%) in the Taff-Ely area of Cardiff, Wales, UK, thought that the turbines looked 'all right', a quarter (28%) thought they looked ugly and over a tenth (15%) thought they looked 'graceful'. Another survey auditing 3000 visitors at seven wind farm open days found that the proportion of those who approved (or approved strongly) of wind power rose from 80 (before) to 92% (after) the visit. In the Cemmaes study in mid-Wales, UK, 91% agreed that wind is a good alternative source of energy (British Wind Energy, 2002c).

In a Scottish context *The Scotsman* (2003), suggested an alternative in its article 'Wind farms to hit Scottish Tourism, protestors claim', states that the Stop Wind farms in Moray Action Group have identified that there are 135 identified sites in Scotland either under development or awaiting planning approval in Scotland. Today there are 270 turbines in Scotland but, if all the proposed sites get approval, there will be 5000.

The *Aberdeen Press and Journal* (2004a) pointed out that Frank MacAveety (the then tourism minister) had commented that wind power is an imperative for the executive and all offices of the executive had to facilitate meeting the targets set. He assured the public that the communities involved would always be consulted in an effort to find the best solution and that the Scottish Executive's commitment to renewable energy would be met.

In a further article in 2004, the *Aberdeen Evening Express* (2004) commented that the National Trust for Scotland (NTS) had met the previous week in Inverness and unanimously agreed a motion calling for the Trust to provide this wake-up call to champion Scotland's landscape against the badly sited and intrusive development of wind farms. The NTS also pointed out the inadequacy of the Scottish Executive's planning guidelines and declared them to be inadequate.

MSP (Member of the Scottish Parliament) Murdo Fraser, in *The Courier* (2004), called 'for a moratorium on any further wind farm developments until clearer guidelines are issued by the executive'. He cited a lack of a national strategy in this area. Finally, the *Aberdeen Press and Journal* (2004b) commented that: 'If developments for wind farming went ahead in Thurso it would destroy the area's world-famous tracts of blanket bog known as the Flow Country.' There were questions raised about the justification that wind framing was actually 'green friendly'.

It has to be recognized that there are wide-ranging views and ongoing debate on the subject of wind farm developments and it is unlikely that there will ever be total agreement as to the development issues. These issues will be returned to again in the conclusions section.

Wind Farms as Tourist Attractions

Wind farms across the world have proved attractive to tourists. For example, California (the world's most populated site for windmills) attracts millions of tourists who take a ride through the locations in electric cars. There are specialist tourist operators who take these visitors around; 'Windmilltours' is an organization which offers guided tours of the wind farms in California (Windmilltours, 2002).

One of the concerns for the anti-development lobby is that wind farms drive tourists away. However, in Tararua (New Zealand), the wind farm has provided a unique opportunity for the region's rapidly growing tourism industry. Several of the farms surrounding the site are diversifying into tourism to accommodate the higher numbers of people wishing to visit the site. Public access and various tour and adventure activities are also available (Tararua, 2002).

In the UK context, Causeymire wind farm is an example where the farm provides a focus for tourism in the Caithness area in the far north of Scotland. In April 2002, the Blayney Shire Council completed the construction of a wind farm viewing platform to cater for the growing number of tourists. Another example is the case of Delabole wind farm in north Cornwall, south-west England. This wind farm has established itself as a visitor centre in its own right. A purpose-built visitor centre provides year-round focus for tourists. On opening ten years ago, the wind farm attracted around 100,000 visitors. Now around 30,000 people a year visit this facility (British Wind Energy, 2002b).

Strachan and Lal (2003) commented that, drawing on the experience of Denmark, the UK Government and the wind power companies claim that wind farms have no negative effect on tourism and indeed have the potential to be significantly beneficial to Scotland's tourism industry. VisitScotland (2004a) published a survey on the likely impacts of wind farm development on tourism in Scotland in 2004 in which they pointed out that, in general, respondents in their survey were more positive than negative towards the impact of wind farms on tourism.

Some of the positive impacts suggested were the possibility of the wind farms as an attraction in themselves, the potential they offered in terms of attracting new markets, positive employment opportunities as well as greater access to rural and remote areas. There was some concern in connection with the number of possible wind farm developments but, overall, the VisitScotland survey suggested that as long as the wind farms were sensitively sited then there were relatively few negatives associated with their development.

A survey conducted by The British Wind Energy Association (BWEA) suggested that tourists were not negatively disposed to wind farms. The study found that nine out of ten tourists visiting some of Scotland's top beauty spots say the presence of wind farms makes no difference to the enjoyment of their holiday. In fact, twice as many people would return to an area because of the presence of a wind farm than would stay away, dispelling the belief that wind farms and tourism cannot co-exist, according to a poll carried out by MORI Scotland (British Wind Energy, 2002b).

The poll supports a recent Scottish Executive survey of residents near wind farms whose opinion of the sites became more positive after they became operational (Scottish Executive, 2002). When asked whether the presence of wind farms had a positive or negative effect on their impression of Argyll as a place to visit, over half (55%) of the respondents maintained that it had a generally or completely positive effects, while one in three were ambivalent (32%). Less than one in ten (8%) felt that it had a negative effect (British Wind Energy, 2002a).

Almost half of the respondents (48%) stated that they were visiting this area due to its beautiful scenery and views. Eighty-three per cent of the respondents cited that countryside and landscape were the major aspects that had attracted them and 71% of the respondents did not find anything unattractive. When asked whether the presence of wind farms had a positive or negative effect, 43% maintained that it had a positive effect. Less than one in ten (8%) felt it had a negative effect. When the tourists were asked to what extent they would be interested in visiting a wind farm if it were opened to the public with a visitor centre, the majority (80%) would be interested with over half (54%) 'very interested'. Around one in five were not interested (British Wind Energy, 2002a).

Aberdeen and Grampian Tourism Strategies

Tourism is Scotland's fourth largest employer, directly employing 197,000 (9%) of the workforce. Economically, it is one of Scotland's most important industries, injecting £4.5 million annually into the Scottish economy (VisitScotland, 2004b). Despite having Aberdeen, Scotland's third largest city, within the region, it could be argued that Aberdeen and Grampian has not reaped a proportionate share of the tourism spend. This area has relied on trails as a draw for tourists, the most successful of these being the world-famous malt whisky and castle trails. Each of these trails is promoted through joint marketing and sponsorship. Although arguably these trails are not unique, they offer visitors a high-quality experience not widely available throughout the world.

There is also a shortage of leisure facilities, in terms of recreational amenities for the host community; in the form of swimming/leisure pools – including water-slides, sauna and hot tub facilities, etc. – across the whole area. This does present an opportunity for the wind farm attraction. Leisure provision could be provided (has a link to energy) to satisfy pent-up local demand for such facilities.

Certainly, the oil and gas industry has been of pivotal importance to the Aberdeen and Grampian economy since the early 1980s. There are conflicting projections as to how long the oil and gas sector will continue to dominate the regional economy, and it is accepted that the $ barrel oil price influences regional economic activity; however, the reality is that these natural resources will run out, and from here on their influence will decline. Prior to the oil and gas era, the regional economy relied on strong fishing and farming industries. Both of these are now in decline.

Following the 'scenario planning' exercise instigated by Aberdeen City Council in 2001, it has been accepted that new sources of economic activity are important in sustaining the economy, and tourism is seen to be the industry that can fill the gap that will be left when the oil does eventually run out.

While business tourism in the city of Aberdeen has sustained a buoyant 4-day market, with hotels in the Aberdeen Hotel Association reporting full occupancy on mid-week dates, this is in stark contrast to the low occupancy being reported for the 3-day weekend market. It is this weekend and leisure market which presents the best opportunity for tourism growth in the region.

VisitScotland has devised a two-tier campaign to increase UK-based visitors, which leads with 'The Senses' and follows up with 'Live It'. (VisitScotland, 2004c). This aims to attract the experience-orientated visitor. Aberdeen and Grampian is well placed to win increased visitors with this campaign, as castles and whisky will feature. A well-conceived wind farm attraction could complement this drive to increase more experience-orientated visitors, giving them another reason to visit, stay longer and potentially to return.

England and Scotland are the most important markets for Aberdeen and Grampian (as well as for Scotland), accounting for 87% of visitors (VisitScotland, 2004b). Visitors from these local markets need to have reasons to visit the region and make return trips. Certainly, there is an increased vibrancy within the local hotel association, but it is year-round attractions that are needed. Steps have been taken in the winter/spring of 2004/2005 to have one (NTS) castle open, albeit with reduced hours, to address the issue.

More is needed to sustain arrivals throughout the shoulder and winter periods. A wind farm attraction open on a year-round basis would fit well with current strategies geared towards enticing leisure tourists located within a few hours' travelling time of the region. However, the current strategy of the local enterprise company favours focusing on tourism attractions that already exist in the region rather than funding or developing new ones. This is an issue because the majority of the existing attractions are run by the local authorities and they struggle to break even, let alone make a profit (Nash and Martin, 2003).

Research Methodology

The first stage involved secondary data collection from published sources such as journals, the Internet, company policy documents and minutes as well as issues relating to wind farm development and perceptions associated with wind farms and tourist attitudes to the development of such farms.

The second stage involved primary data collection. Twelve in-depth interviews were conducted between 31 October and 12 November 2002, as well as three focus groups (consisting of eight respondents in each group). The aim of the primary research was to identify problems and issues associated with wind farm development and tourism provision in this peripheral area of north-east Scotland. During the respondent selection a list was drawn up using key informants. The snowball technique was utilized in this research and Fink suggests that: 'This type of sampling relies on previously identified members of a group to identify other members of the population. As newly identified members name others, the sample snowballs' (Fink, 1995, p. 19).

The focus during the data collection was mainly on the public sector and, as a consequence, all local authorities, local enterprise companies and area tourist boards were interviewed. The respondents were all involved in tourism and were chosen because of their expertise and knowledge in relation to the subject area. Several were managers from the public sector, attractions managers, educationalists and members of the voluntary sector, others being members of the consultant team and topic experts from Robert Gordon University, Aberdeen.

There were many options for the collection of the necessary primary data needed for this research, but the options most likely to enable this research to achieve its objectives were focus groups and interviews. The method of data collection was qualitative in nature because there are certain kinds of data that can be best obtained by asking questions about consumers' experiences, feelings, attitudes and reactions (Nash and Martin, 2003).

Face-to-face interviews were used as opposed to telephone interviews because these allowed the interviewer to pick up on non-verbal cues and to follow-up ideas, responses and feelings, which the questionnaire does not allow for. A questionnaire was used during the interview to ensure that the questions were standardized and, where appropriate, explanations in relation to specific questions was provided.

Focus groups were also used as a means of brainstorming potential ideas and suggestions for wind farm development, as well as identifying examples of best practice. The participants all had a common interest, knowledge or experience (tourism and the area) and the focus group provided the opportunity to engage with other respondents to discuss issues suggested by the research team.

Findings

The issues outlined below were identified as headings as a result of respondent feedback:

- Impressions of wind farms.
- Facilities at the site.
- Advertising, promotion and community involvement.
- Potential external funding and partners.
- Likely number and range of visitors.

Impressions of wind farms

A majority of the respondents felt that Scotland was a perfect location for setting up a wind farm. The respondents believed that this alternative source of energy is an excellent concept of environmentally friendly power generation and that it is very much in line with the Scottish Executives strategy on renewable energy, as well as being in line with global trends. There was consensus over the need to develop the energy source, because it is a free and sustainable resource that can benefit both the community and the environment.

However, there were concerns that although wind energy has an enormous potential, there still remains an element of stigma associated with it in the minds of the general public. There was also concern that there were issues to do with public perceptions associated with wind farm effectiveness, efficiency and visual intrusion and that these issues have to be addressed.

Despite the fact that visual impact and noise were cited as key issues, almost all the respondents expressed the view that the attitude of the general public has been changing dramatically in favour of wind farming since it was first introduced. Some of the respondents referred to the MORI Scotland report on assessing public attitudes towards wind farming and stated that public resistance to setting up wind farms is changing in favour of development. That said, the respondents favoured the continuation of effective communication, which should depict the long-term benefits for the community and the environment.

Other respondents mentioned that the structures are interesting in engineering terms and that, with advances in technology, the noise level has been considerably reduced. This is in line with the research report mentioned earlier by the BWEA (British Wind Energy, 2002a). Some of the respondents felt that wind farms should be developed in isolated barren landscapes or at sea.

When questioned about the effectiveness of wind farms as tourist attraction and their appearance, there were mixed reactions. Several of the respondents commented that the structures themselves were 'elegant', 'aesthetic' and 'not ugly', but few of the respondents felt that wind farms were impressive enough as structures to create a 'must-see desire' amongst the general public. The consensus was that they would not be a crowd-puller on their own, and that they would have to be combined with visitor attractions or visitor centres.

Facilities at the site

When questioned about this issue, a range of answers were generated, from clear signposting and adequate car parking through to a leisure centre development. A few respondents mentioned access to a remote site (such as any wind farm development) would be problematical and that this might require the development of a single-track access road for the traffic; however, it was pointed out that this would be difficult to manage. If a visitor centre were to be set up at the wind farm, it would have to provide facilities that complemented the attraction. Examples of facilities that were suggested are outlined below:

- Clear signposting.
- Road access.
- A gift shop.
- Hands-on-type exhibition.
- Computer work stations which offer descriptive and photographic details about energy, alternative sources and wind farming in particular.
- Educational facilities and display units with enough information.
- Ample number of places for parking and turning buses.
- Classrooms for organized talks.
- Food and beverage facilities; the food should be thematic and focus on local organic produce.

- Toilet facilities.
- Disabled access.
- Display units with information available.
- Visitor centre.
- Tourist information centre for the Grampian region.
- Company merchandise.
- Integration of infrastructure and local services.
- Active element to keep children occupied.
- Leisure facilities (locals) market – national research suggests that this will continue to be a growth market, and there is a need in the region.

Advertising, promotion and community involvement

Advertising and PR activity are key components when attempting to reach the public and arouse an interest and desire to visit any new tourist attraction. When questioned about the various forms of advertising, the respondents came up with ideas such as: (i) printing leaflets and maps; (ii) advertising in local newspapes; (iii) information boards; and (iv) setting up an interactive website.

In order to attract more people, the respondents felt that the proposed centre could be a part of the region's portfolio of attractions and link with other attractions and trails. The site should focus on attracting repeat visits and should consider options such as family saver or loyalty tickets.

Community involvement is one of the most important aspects for sensitive developments such as wind farms. It was pointed out that many communities still feel that setting up a wind farm has a negative impact on their community and their local economy. One of the respondents pointed out that 'Community involvement would have to be handled extremely carefully given the experience of anti-wind farm protesters in Morayshire, where the local press have given considerable coverage to the people who are fighting against wind farms being developed'.

It was suggested that local clubs and associations, schools and local community councils should be contacted and engaged in the process at an early stage.

Potential external funding and partners

In order for a project to be successful, the respondents identified that the proposed centre should align itself with possible partners, which would provide the necessary number of visitors. When questioned about partnerships and alliances, the respondents came up with a number of bodies who could be targeted. The possible organizations suggested included the following: (i) Aberdeen Maritime Museum; (ii) the NTS; and (iii) Aberdeen airport. The proposed centre could also provide links into the national parks set up such as at Cairngorm and Loch Lomond. Involvement with regional trust attractions and development of theme trails were suggested as ways forward.

It was identified that there was a need for the proposed development to attract external funds and assistance. When asked about the sources of potential external funding bodies, the respondents came up with a list of agencies and organizations such as: (i) the Scottish Executive; (ii) the Office of Science and Technology; (iii) Aberdeen City Council; (iv) the European Union; and (v) Scottish Enterprise Grampian, as well as several others. Some of the respondents also suggested that oil companies could be approached for collaborative purposes and financial support.

Likely numbers and range of visitors and possible scenarios for development

There were several suggestions regarding groups to be targeted, such as: (i) young families; (ii) active elderly groups; (iii) university groups; (iv) visitors to friends and relatives; (v) walking and rambler groups; (vi) eco-enthusiasts; (vii) adult education groups; (viii) special needs groups; (ix) locals; and (x) school parties.

The overwhelming consensus was that school parties had the most potential in terms of any wind farm development. Focusing the product on schools would ensure a regular flow of visitor numbers. Wind farms and electricity generation are areas that fit well with modern educational requirements, and schools are keen to find an interesting and interactive way of developing their teaching. The environment policy document is something that schools must address as part of their curriculum. Conservation, sustainability and development are all areas that could be addressed by wind farm tours that would fit within social science, as well as within science- and technology-based subjects.

Several possible development scenarios were suggested by the respondents and these are listed below. The aim was to suggest tourism initiatives that could be used and incorporated with a possible wind farm development to either raise income for the site or to positively change public attitudes and perceptions associated with wind farm developments.

- Sensory gardens aimed at special needs.
- Rural theme and environmental centre.
- Garden centre and local artists' gallery/workshop.
- Power-oriented theme.
- Industrial heritage centre.
- Sustainability/green centre for renewable/alternative forms of energy.
- Children's activity centre and adventure playground.
- Recreational attractions and leisure centre.
- Viewing platform with panorama boards.

Conclusions

Harnessing wind power is not a new idea; nevertheless, in the current political climate, with the need for governments to achieve renewable energy targets, Scotland is considered to be a perfect location for wind farms. This alternative source of energy is an excellent form of environmentally friendly power generation, which has found favour internationally.

Despite the enormous potential of wind farms, there still remains an element of resistance amongst the general public. Although through reasoned debate some of the issues could be addressed, it is fair to say that the research points to a public who are 'not negatively' disposed towards wind farms, in which case there is still a job to be done in promoting a very positive opinion on wind farm development (VisitScotland, 2004a). This could partly be addressed by providing a visitor attraction that is perceived as valuable to the host community.

The work found that, in terms of wind farms as tourist attractions there were mixed reactions. Several felt that they are impressive structures and they have a curiosity factor associated with them that could serve as a visitor attraction. However, the majority of the respondents suggested that they would need to be combined with a visitor attraction or a visitor centre. There are international comparisons to be made, and certainly the Californian model providing a unique visitor experience appears to be the ideal. Within Scotland, repeat visits in Argyll have been attributed to a viewing tower.

A wind farm as a tourist attraction located in the Aberdeen and Grampian area does offer the potential to increase leisure visitors from the main weekend market (UK-based visitors). There is a need to increase weekend leisure visitors to the region, and a wind farm attraction would fit well with the 'Live It' national campaign, supporting the whisky and castle attractions at a regional level. As Aberdeen and Grampian seeks to increase leisure and conference tourism collaborations such as the Hotel Association/Tourist Board and Ryanair, this would bring more weekend business to the area and a unique attraction (in the form of a wind farm) could provide a draw for these markets.

However, it has been found that the wind farm as an attraction on its own is not thought to posses sufficient tourist pull. There is acceptance that the concept of an attraction themed with the wind farm is sound, but a cluster of activities is required for the site to work. There was a divergence of ideas in terms of what constitutes an ideal tourist attraction featuring the wind farm. As community involvement will be crucial to the success of the proposed development, the scenarios reflected this need.

This work has shown that any development will need to offer a leisure amenity or experience of value to the host community. This is not a problem as it is this host community that wind-power developers wish to win over and, in reality, an increase in tourism and the economic benefits to the region are not their goal. This is potentially in conflict with national and regional tourism aspirations to grow tourism. By giving tourists more reason to visit, stay or return, a more ambitious magnet attraction is required. In this case the development would have more in common with the Californian interpretation than the viewing tower development in Argyll.

The location of a wind farm attraction is particularly crucial. The chosen location for any development will need to be acceptable to the local host community, and to offer them perceived benefits beyond regional economic regeneration. No local community will accept intrusion without benefit. Beyond this hurdle is the issue of finding the right location to maximize year-round visits.

In essence, then, the wind farm attraction will have to be accessible to tourists and located in an area with a low density of population. The geography of the Aberdeen and Grampian region has the potential to meet the first location requirement – by using a site in one of the forests. By choosing such a location, however, the wind farm attraction becomes less accessible to tourists, resulting in the need for the attraction to be truly unique to exert enough pull on potential visitors.

A window of opportunity currently exists for the creation of a wind farm tourist attraction in the Aberdeen and Grampian area. There is a feeling amongst potential visitors that wind farms hold some novelty value at present (VisitScotland 2004a). Should the tourism stakeholders in Aberdeen and Grampian truly have the courage and conviction to create a visitor attraction of a national scale then time is of the essence. Once another part of the UK has created a truly unique wind farm visitor attraction the opportunity will have been lost.

References

Aberdeen Evening Express (2004) Why we have to save our lovely landscape. 10 July 2004, Aberdeen, UK.

Aberdeen Press and Journal (2004a) Challenge to minister over islands tourism. 23 August 2004, Aberdeen, UK.

Aberdeen Press and Journal (2004b) Bellamy urges halt to wind turbines. 25 November 2004, Aberdeen, UK.

British Wind Energy Agency (2002a) British wind energy (http://www.britishwindenergy.co.uk, accessed 30 October 2002).

British Wind Energy Agency (2002b) Tourism (http://www.britishwindenergy.co.uk/view/news/tourism.html, accessed 29 October 2002).

British Wind Energy Agency (2002c) Mori briefing (http://www.britishwindenergy.co.uk/pdf/mori_briefing.pdf, accessed 31 October 2002).

British Wind Energy Agency (2002d) Frequently asked questions (http://www.bwea.com/ref/faq.html, accessed 30 October 2002).

Doswell, R. (1997) *Tourism: How Effective Management Makes a Difference.* Butterworth-Heinemann, Oxford, UK.

Fink, A. (1995) *How to Sample in Surveys.* Sage, London.

MORI (2002) *Public Attitudes to Wind Farms: Research Findings.* The Scottish Executive No. 12, 2003, Edinburgh, UK.

Nash, R. and Martin, A. (2003) Tourism in peripheral areas – the challenges for Northeast Scotland. *International Journal of Tourism Research* 5, 161–181.

Scottish Executive (2000) *Climate for Change Programme*. Scottish Executive, Edinburgh, UK.

Scottish Executive (2002) *Building a Sustainable Scotland: Sustainable Development and the Spending Review 2002*. Scottish Executive, Edinburgh, UK.

Strachan, P. and Lal, D. (2003) Wind energy policy: planning and management practice in the UK. Paper presented at the *Business Strategy and the Environment Conference*, 16–17 September 2003, University of Leicester, Leicester, UK.

Tararua (2002) Wind farm (http://www.tararua.com/container_pages/wind_farm.asp?level1=Wind_Farm, accessed 30 October 2002).

The Courier (2004) Backing for wind farm freeze rising. 9 March 2004, Dundee, UK.

The Scotsman (2003) Wind farms to hit Scottish Tourism, protestors claim. 22 January 2003, Edinburgh, UK.

VisitScotland (2003) Know your market (http://www.scotexchange.net/KnowYourMarket/knowyourmarket.asp, accessed 30 October 2003).

VisitScotland (2004a) Wind farms (http://www.scotexchange.net/KnowYourMarket/kym-windfarm, accessed 13 December 2004).

VisitScotland (2004b) Scotexchange (http://www.scotexchange.net, accessed 13 December 2004).

VisitScotland (2004c) *Annual Report and Accounts*. VisitScotland, Edinburgh, UK.

Windmilltours (2002) Windmilltours (http://www.windmilltours.com, accessed 30 October 2002).

12 Sporting Events as Tourist Attractions in Canada's Northern Periphery

TOM HINCH AND SUZANNE DE LA BARRE

Faculty of Physical Education and Recreation, University of Alberta, Edmonton, Alberta, Canada

> It is said in the earliest days that the Northern Lights were caused by people spending their afterlife in the sky regions … they are constantly playing ball, the favorite game, laughing and singing, and the ball they play with is the skull of a walrus. […] It is this ball game of the departed souls that appears as the aurora borealis, and is heard as a whistling, rustling, crackling sound.
>
> (Heine, 2002, pp. 1–3)

Introduction

The aurora borealis has long been one of the tourism icons of northern Canada. It is featured in promotional images and forms the central attraction of a popular line of specialized tours to the region. The fact that the Northern Lights are described as a 'ball game of the departed souls' by the indigenous people of the north also highlights the relevance of sport and games in northern cultures.

It is this relationship between sport, culture and tourism that is the subject of this chapter. Sporting events are seen as having the potential to function as culturally based tourist attractions in northern Canada but, like most culturally based attractions, a variety of challenges exist if this potential is to be realized in a sustainable fashion.

The chapter begins with a discussion of sport as a culturally based tourism attraction. This is followed by a description of three distinct types of northern-based sporting events: traditional, contemporary (mediated) and contemporary (introduced). Finally, the chapter closes with an assessment of the underlying issues associated with the positioning of each type of event as a tourist attraction.

Sporting Events as Culturally Based Attractions

Leiper (1990, p. 371) defines a tourist attraction as 'a system comprising three elements: a tourist or human element, a nucleus or central element and a marker or informative element. A tourist attraction comes into existence when the three elements are connected.' From a sport tourism perspective, the tourist or 'human element' consists of persons travelling to the attraction to the extent that their behaviour is motivated by sport. Hunters and fishers travelling to engage in these activities represent a popular type of sport tourist currently found in the north.

'Markers' are items of information about the attraction (Leiper, 1990). Examples of consciously placed markers featuring sport in the north include travel advertisements showing visitors involved in destination-specific sporting activities such as snowmobiling and dog-sledding. Similar images may be communicated with no conscious tourism objectives but which, none the less, serve to mark the northern periphery as a destination.

The central element of Leiper's (1990) tourist attraction system is the nucleus, which is where the tourist experience is produced and consumed. In the context of the previous examples, the nucleus includes those aspects of the northern landscape that facilitate the activities of fishing, hunting, snowmobiling or dog-sledding. Sport is unique as an attraction nucleus in at least three ways. First, each sport has its own set of rules/practices that articulate spatial and temporal structures such as the physical parameters of the game or its duration (Bale, 1989). In the northern periphery, these rules are influenced by the immense scale of the land and by extreme seasonal cycles.

Secondly, sport is characterized by competition relating to physical prowess. In a southern-based context this dimension encompasses the goal orientation, competition and contest-based aspects of sport (McPherson *et al.*, 1989). In the north, this dimension of sport is strongly influenced by indigenous values related to cooperation and community. Practical realities like the relative isolation of communities have also served to moderate this aspect of sport in the north. Finally, sport is characterized by its playful nature, which is certainly in evidence at the various sporting festivals found in the north. This element also includes the notions of uncertainty of outcome and sanctioned display.

In this chapter, culture is viewed as a way of life in the north. It consists of the values, feelings, and behaviours of northern residents. Culture is the way that northerners understand and give meaning to their lives (After McGregor, 1983). Northern culture is imbedded in the way northern people live, inclusive of the sports and games played in the north.

In a tourism context, sporting events allow a visitor access to the backstage of a community. This access is rendered more powerful by the authenticity of sport. Getz (1998) has argued that community-based festivals provide a window on the living or authentic community. He suggests that 'an "authentic cultural experience" is not a commodity negotiated between visitor and community, but a realization of the visitor that the experience truly reflects local values' (Getz, 1998, p. 426).

Sport-based festivals can function in this way. The experiential nature of sport, with its unique ability to engage participants physically, cognitively and emotionally, goes a long way to ensuring this sense of authenticity. Even spectators at a sporting event are cognitively and emotionally engaged. While their physical engagement may be limited, their overall engagement in the event is evident by the way they react to the sporting action and its final outcomes.

While there are potential economic advantages to positioning sporting events as tourist attractions in Canada's northern periphery, there are also challenges – especially in a cultural context. If these sporting events are seen as genuine expressions of local culture, then their commodification as tourist attractions may threaten the local meaning associated with them (Greenwood, 1989). Similarly, to the extent that sporting events are part of a larger process of globalization, positioning them as tourist attractions may contribute to the homogenization of place and activity (Rowe and Lawrence, 1996).

Finally, positioning sporting events as tourist attractions is challenged by the difficulty in developing working partnerships between and within the sport and tourism industries (Weed and Bull, 2004). All three of these challenges need to be considered in the context of the unique features of northern-based sporting events.

Case Studies

The number of sporting events that take place in the north is increasing. In fact, the Yukon government announced their 'decade of sport and culture' initiative in 2003. This initiative was meant to maximize potential benefits in the Yukon from both the 2007 Canada Winter Games (Whitehorse, Yukon) and the 2010 Winter Olympics (Whistler, British Columbia) (YTG, 2004, p. 12). The Canada Winter Games are being positioned as a tourism attraction and include both pre- and post-Games sporting events that are aimed at bringing visitors to the Yukon (YTG, 2004). However, not all Northern sporting events are equal in terms of their suitability as tourist attractions.

Three sporting events are examined in the context of their potential for serving as tourist attractions in northern Canada, and each event is distinct. Table 12.1 highlights the key characteristics of these events using the attraction framework presented in the previous section. This will be followed by a description of the nature of each event in more general terms, prior to commenting on their potential as tourist attractions in the context of key development issues.

Traditional: the Northern Games

Traditional games, also known as 'Arctic Sports', are intimately tied to the land. They include games such as the aptly named 'One Foot High Kick', the

Table 12.1. Summary of sporting events as tourist attractions.

Dimension	Traditional Northern Games	Contemporary (Mediated) Arctic Winter Games	Contemporary (Introduced) Fulda Challenge
Human element	Northern athletes • Primarily native • Open competition	Northern athletes • Primarily non-native • Competitive selection	International two-person teams • Primarily non-Northern • Competitive selection
	Cultural performers/ coaches/officials	Cultural performers/coaches/ officers	Coaches/officials
	Few spectators • Family and friends • Northerners	Many spectators • Family and friends • A few non-Northerners	Few spectators • Broadcast audience • Some locals
Nucleus Rules	• Aboriginal practical consciousness • Minimally organized • Flexible	• Euro-Canadian practical consciousness • Highly organized • Rigid	• European/international practical consciousness • Highly organized • Rigid
Physical	• Open participation • Cooperation • Process over results • Traditional sports • Integrated with nature	• Performance qualification • Adversarial but good sports • Results and process • Euro-Canadian and Arctic sports • Nature as friend	• Performance qualification • Adversarial • Results over process • Extreme activities • Nature as enemy
Play	• Informal • Social • Achievement rarely outlasts the occasion	• Formal • Athletic achievement • Qualification for national competitions	• Serious • Financial rewards • Career advancement
Markers	• Local focus • Cultural renewal and traditional activities • Word of mouth	• Northern sport organizations • Local and national media coverage • Website	• International media coverage • Extreme sport broadcasts • Website • Yukon tourism • Fulda sponsorship

'Knuckle Hop' and the 'Finger Pull'. These games embody traditional cultural meanings associated with a subsistence lifestyle. Traditional games were important for learning how to live on the land and for developing strength, endurance and skills with applications in areas such as hunting (Heine, 2002).

The games were originally intertwined with other daily activities in the north, as there was little separation between work and play (Paraschak, 1997). Thomas Siatalak, an Inuit survey respondent for a Sport North Arctic games training manual, says 'Inuit culture and the Inuit way of making a living in the North (hunting, trapping and so forth) [*sic*] is one and the same' (cited in Heine, 2002, pp. 1–49).

The Northern Games are composed of 'native-derived' sporting activities. This refers to a 'customary, native-derived lifestyle', including traditional activities that have survived to this day due to northern natives' 'relative isolation from Euro-Canadians and their majority status in terms of numbers relative to Euro-Canadians' (Paraschak, 1997, p. 5). The Committee for Original Peoples Entitlement (COPE) argues 'these sports are not a novelty – they are generations old – and are taken very seriously by the athletes. They still serve to test the mettle of the men and women who live in the High Arctic' (COPE, 1978, p. 2).

The Northern Games Association was formed in 1969 as a response to the exclusion of traditional 'sporting' activities from the original Arctic Winter Games. Their conception by community-based native people outside of government was a direct response to the initial exclusion of games by AWG organizers (Paraschak, 1997). Since 1970, the Northern Games have operated as a distinct northern sport/culture event, shifting between a variety of smaller northern communities each summer. Participation levels vary, but are normally measured in the hundreds rather than in the thousands.

Today, the Northern Games are part of a movement to revive the traditional arts and to enhance contemporary aboriginal relationships with the land (COPE, 1978). As one northern sport survey respondent put it: 'Sport is part of nature – it is a bodily, physical thing. Caring for physical nature and caring for nature itself go hand in hand' (Sport North Federation, 1995).

Organizations like the Northern Games Association have facilitated the revival and assured the contemporary role that traditional sports have in northern environments. Forums that put traditional games on display serve a social purpose by allowing traditional cultural meanings to find expression in modern aboriginal society.

Traditional games focus on participation over performance in local and informal settings, and rely primarily on 'word-of-mouth' for promotion. Results from the competition garner less attention than the process of play, and the opportunity to join in with a cultural and social gathering. Rules are flexible and accommodate the native-derived origins and purpose of the games. The games take place with little or no consideration for spectator needs and make few concessions to detailed scheduling as understood in Euro-Canadian practical consciousness (Paraschak, 1997).

The informal and relaxed nature of traditional games is not particularly well suited for high performance or organized sporting events. None the less, a recently created Arctic sports training manual (Heine, 2002) describes ways in which certain traditional games can be transformed into performance sports, especially for coaches and athletes who want to participate in the Arctic Winter Games. Finally, with the exception of the Northern Games Association, the Games have relied on informal, community-based involvement rather than on formalized organizations and facilities (COPE, 1978, p. 66).

Contemporary (mediated): the Arctic Winter Games (AWG)

It may be ironic, but just as the Northern Games Association was created in reaction to the exclusion of traditional sports in the first Arctic Winter Games; the latter were created in reaction to the limited opportunities afforded northerners for competing in southern-based athletic competitions. The Arctic Winter Games Corporation was formed in 1968 in response to low northerner achievement at the 1967 Canada Winter Games in Quebec City. The Arctic Winter Games were initiated in 1970 to afford northerners the opportunity to compete in athletic competitions against other northerners (Arctic Winter Games, 2003).

As an organized event replete with its own internal justification and structure, the AWG mission is to facilitate athletic competition, cultural exhibition and social interchange between northerners. Where sport competition is concerned, its underlying values include the following: (i) cultural awareness and understanding; (ii) fair play; (iii) access and equity; (iv) integrity; (v) respect for self and others; (vi) partnerships; (vii) personal development; and (viii) community development (Szabo, 2003).

Specific activities can be divided into these categories: (i) contemporary northern sports like snowboarding; (ii) traditional sports such as the Knuckle Hop; and (iii) emerging hybrid sports like the snowshoe biathlon. Competitions are held on a biennial basis, with the most recent being the XVII Arctic Winter Games in 2004 hosted by Fort McMurray, Alberta. The AWG have grown from a modest beginning of 500 athletes, coaches, mission staff, officials and cultural performers in the inaugural 1970 Games in Yellowknife to over 1600 participants in 2002. Participating regions have included the Northwest Territories, Yukon, northern Alberta and Quebec, Alaska, Greenland and Russia.

The AWG's success as a sporting event has been at least partially due to its capacity to make the compromises necessary in representing natives and non-natives, to engage large and small communities and to encourage widespread participation. The Games are intended to foster the development of sport in the north and to prepare northern athletes for southern-based competition. In so doing, the AWG are meant to complement north–south competitions rather than replace them (AWG Corporation, 1982).

Notwithstanding this complementary relationship with southern sporting competitions, there has been a recognized need to retain the 'uniqueness of north' (AWG Corporation, 1982). Given the distinctive communities of the north, it is only reasonable for the sport development system to have significant variations from southern-based systems. For example, the AWG fosters broad-based participation, exhibiting more flexibility in the selection process for athletes than is found in southern Canada (AWG Corporation, 1982). Another distinction is that traditional, indigenous Arctic Sports were added as an official component in 1974 and were expanded in 1990 (Paraschak, 1997).

Contemporary (introduced): the Fulda Challenge

With its invitation to 'fight the elements!' and participate in the 'world's hottest adventure madness', the Fulda Challenge is clearly positioned as an extreme sporting event. This challenging contest is sponsored by the Fulda Tire Company, which positions its products metaphorically as champions in a competition with a harsh 'driving' environment. While women make up approximately one-half of the participants, the discourse about the race features 'hypermasculine' narratives that are consistent with extreme sports cultures throughout the contemporary world.

Held in late January/early February each year since 2002, the 10-day extreme event challenges ten teams from Canada, the USA and Europe to compete across '2000 km of Arctic Hell', and promises to make them 'sweat at minus 50 degrees' (Fulda Challenge, 2005). The teams compete with other in a variety of winter sports on a wilderness course that follows the famous Goldrush Trail from Whitehorse (Yukon) to the Arctic Coast. Sport challenges include skiing, snowshoeing, snowmachining, ice-climbing and dog-sledding.

Competition is focused on performance and receives international media coverage through television, the press and on the Internet. It is highly organized and is supported by a rigid rule structure. Participants must qualify to participate and must make a significant financial investment. Results are valued over process and the rewards for competition outlast the performance. Winners leave the north with a financial prize and improved ranking as extreme athletes.

The Fulda Challenge is a sporting event that pits the athletes not only against each other, but also against the environment. It is unlike the Northern Games and the Arctic Winter Games, as it is not infused with local culture. It does, however, rely on the mythical north. It is a north that is admired, while simultaneously being presented as harsh, unforgiving, desolate, barren and 'not fit for humans'. The last characterization contrasts sharply with aboriginal views of the natural environment, which celebrate and respect the land as part of the living fabric of northern communities.

Issue Analysis

While all three sporting events have the potential to function as regional, national and international tourist attractions, they also face a variety of challenges. These include operational challenges related to access and a lack of tourism infrastructure. Of particular interest in this chapter, however, are the challenges associated with culture.

Commodification and authenticity

Wang (2000) claimed that almost every item of culture is 'touristifiable' and can be turned into a consumer good. Yet, in this process of commodifying local culture for tourism, there is a danger that the practices and places associated with this culture will lose their meaning – that the very qualities that make them unique and valuable for residents and guests alike will be lost. When culture, place and sport embody powerful meanings for residents, there is a need to critically examine the potential changes that tourism development may bring to them.

In the case of the Northern Games, while the traditional games may be a strong attraction for visitors, the small scale and community focus of the Games may make them very sensitive to an increased number of 'outside' spectators. Scheduling concessions that would be required by tour operators so that they can guarantee a specified experience would also compromise the authenticity of the event. While structured schedules may address the needs of the tourists and of the tour operators, they would undermine the aboriginal practical consciousness as reflected in a very flexible schedule in tune with the natural rhythms of northern life.

The AWG would face a similar issue but to a much lesser extent. The Games themselves are relatively large in the context of northern events, so a few hundred extra spectators would not have as large an impact. The fact that the AWG are already operating on a southern-based sporting event organizational model means that the scheduling demands of tourism could be more readily accommodated. The traditional games component of the AWG would, however, still be threatened by further erosion and care would have to be taken to avoid turning these events into simple demonstrations for the entertainment of spectators rather than genuine contests with a focus on the competitors.

The Fulda Challenge, on the other hand, is not derived from local cultural practices, at least not directly. Arguably, it is a product of popular culture with commodification at its core. As an introduced activity, there is little direct risk of undermining locally held cultural meaning. Even traditional activities such as dog-sledding have already been modified to such an extent that there is little likelihood of eroding cultural practices in the north.

In the context of the Fulda Challenge, authenticity is likely to be judged on the basis of whether the climate and environment prove to be as 'harsh' and 'unfit for humans' as the promotional campaigns promise. In this sense, the Fulda Challenge seeks out Northern characteristics to provide drama for an extreme production. In effect, it relies on the 'north' to confirm the hypermasculine nature of the event and the sponsorship product. While not posing a major direct threat in terms of commodification and authenticity, it does influence the image of the north as a tourism destination for better or worse.

Globalization

Globalization is characterized by growing spatial and temporal linkages. It is also characterized by the threat of standardization of place (Mowforth and Munt, 1998). Notwithstanding the contribution of tourism to this process, it has been argued that 'Attachment to place and territory remain important in modern society despite [and possibly because of] the increased mobility of the population and the production of standardized landscapes' (Geertz, cited in Entrikin, 1991, p. 41). In fact, travel to peripheral areas may actually reflect a search for individual meaning in a postmodern world (Urry, 1995).

For aboriginal peoples, travel was traditionally experienced through subsistence-based and nomadic relationships to the land: 'People used to travel widely when they were following the migratory animals. That's how they got to meet people from different areas' (Cecilia Angutialuk in Heine, 2002, pp. 1–12). Some impacts of early aboriginal travel include a decrease in regional and local differences for what and how traditional games were practised.

Heine (2002) claimed: 'Visitors might introduce games that the hosts had not played before, and now the hosts would begin to play those games as well. In this way, many games came to be played by all of the regional groups' (pp. 1–5).

Given the tremendous pressures on aboriginal cultures, it may be to their advantage that some aspects of cultural life in the north are shared by many groups and communities, and not held in trust by a few people in each location. Therefore, whatever possible negative impacts may have resulted from a decrease in types of games played, or manner in which they were played, should be considered in light of the empowerment that comes with being able to share games with regional groups.

A similar argument can be made in the context of regional tourism in the north; that is, travel from one northern location to another. Furthermore, homogenization processes within the north have offered a type of 'cultural refuge' for aboriginal people at local or regional levels. In so doing, regional tourism has enhanced place capacities and cultural vigour in local communities throughout the north.

Richards and Hall's (2000) discussion of 'neotribalism' is useful in both the creation of 'tourism development as well as [...] the potential for resistance to modernization and the effects of globalization' (p. 4). In some significant ways, the growing importance of Arctic Sports in the informal and regional Northern Games, and their inclusion in more formal ways in the AWG, is already fostering northern pride and reinforcing a 'sense of place' for northern residents.

Northern identity, as promoted in part through these sporting events, may offer some resistance to the assimilation agents that characterize globalization. Tourism could build on this by reinforcing local identity. If developed carefully, product sustainability in terms of product longevity and community support may be achieved.

The Yukon Government is also pleased by the opportunity to further position the Yukon as a wilderness environment fit for extreme and adventure sports enthusiasts even though, or perhaps because, the Fulda Challenge is an externally introduced popular cultural activity (YTG, 2004). This event relies on very specific northern and periphery markers (e.g. weather and isolation) in order to dramatize performance and to build credibility as an extreme competition. The event is not tied to the landscape or the environment in the context of local culture or place identity. In fact, other northern landscapes could function just as well as a backdrop for its event and activities. The long-term sustainability of the event is therefore vulnerable to the discovery of other – and more extreme – environments.

Control and partnerships

Where northern sport is concerned, it would appear that the more informal the sporting activities, the more likely they will be intertwined with local culture. Historically, and currently, the more informal Northern Games reflect subsistence lifestyle activities of local people. They represent a celebration of the traditional ways of living in the north and a bridging between the past and the present. In recent years, increased awareness of intellectual property rights for aboriginal cultural 'products' has made it increasingly difficult for non-aboriginal groups to unilaterally exploit these Games as tourist attractions. Increased consideration related to these intellectual property rights and Land Claims Agreements make tourism partnerships with local peoples a necessity.

The Arctic Winter Games are controlled primarily by northern sport organizations. They reflect a mandate to foster and develop sport in relation to northern values of community, healthy living, cooperation and respect for the environment. Increasingly, however, given the growing needs of sport competition in the north, and perhaps also due to the positioning of the AWG as a tourism attraction, formal partnerships are being negotiated (Hinch and de la Barre, 2004).

These partnerships may eventually challenge northern control of the Games as southern-based tourism operators enter any such agreement on the basis of their own and their clients' needs. Notwithstanding, the mutual trade-offs inherent in this type of agreement, the underlying integrity of the sporting event must be retained in the interests of sustainability.

The Fulda Challenge is quite distinct given that it is controlled by Fulda Tire, the German-based tyre-making corporation. It is subject to the destination's laws and regulations, such as those regulations that exist in parks, conservation areas, and on First Nations' land through Land Claims Agreements. In most other ways, the Fulda Challenge is controlled by a non-northern – indeed a non-Canadian – entity. Northern communities have little say in how the event takes place. Furthermore, it is likely that if northern communities or governments made it difficult for the Fulda Challenge to operate the way its sponsors prefer, they would simply find another extreme environment where their activities could take place.

Conclusion

The three northern-based sporting events described in this chapter are all currently functioning as tourist attractions. In the case of the AWG and the Northern Games, participants and spectators regularly travel great distances from throughout the north to join in with the sporting celebrations in the host community. In contrast, the Fulda Challenge caters to a smaller number of visitors but with the majority of these coming from other countries, many of which are not located in the higher latitudes.

Further potential exists for each event to be positioned as national and international tourism attractions. Much of this potential rests on the fact that these events provide visitors with a window on authentic, northern-based sporting culture. By attending these events, visitors can obtain a taste of the real north.

Yet, the very thing that makes these events so attractive is also threatened by tourism development. Of the three events described, the Northern Games would be the one that is most at risk given its small scale and its celebration of local culture. Northern culture associated with the Fulda Challenge is minimal and therefore the development of this event as tourist attraction presents few threats to local culture. This development is, however, limited by the movement of the event along a 2000 km course and its made-for-broadcast emphasis.

Taking all three events into consideration, the AWG appears to have the most potential for tourism development. It combines a significant cultural core in terms of sporting activities with an organizational framework that encompasses a southern-based practical consciousness. It also tends to be hosted in the larger communities of the north, which are characterized by a higher level of tourism infrastructure.

The decision to pursue this potential is not an easy one, however. The AWG organizers would have to work closely with tourism organizations and the host community to ensure that the cultural celebration of sport was not lost in the rush to meet the demands of visiting tourists. While not ever likely to match the powerful draw of the Northern Lights, sporting events do offer the potential to function as sustainable cultural attractions by tapping into the 'living soul' of the north.

Acknowledgement

This chapter builds on earlier work by the authors that explored the potential of the Arctic Winter Games as a tourist attraction (Hinch and de la Barre, 2005).

References

Arctic Winter Games (2003) Arctic Winter Games Homepage, (http://www.arctic wintergames.org, accessed 10 July 2003).

Arctic Winter Games Corporation (1982) *The Arctic Winter Games 1972–1982: an Analysis.* Makale & Kyllo Planning Associates Ltd., Calgary, Canada.

Bale, J. (1989) *Sports Geography.* E & FN Spon, London.

Committee for Original Peoples Entitlement (COPE) (1978) In: Shewan, S. (ed.) *Inuvialuit: 1978 Special Edition Northern Games.* Campbell Printing, Hull, Ottawa, Canada.

Entrikin, J. (1991) *The betweenness of place: towards a geography of modernity.* MD thesis, John Hopkins University Press, Baltimore, Ohio.

Fulda Challenge (2005) Fulda Challenge Homepage (http://www.fulda-challenge.com, accessed 2 January 2005).

Getz, D. (1998) Event tourism and the authenticity dilemma. In: Theobald, W.F. (ed.) *Global Tourism.* 2nd edn, Butterworth-Heinemann, Oxford, UK, pp. 410–427.

Greenwood, D.J. (1989) Culture by the pound: an anthropological perspective on tourism as cultural commodification. In: Smith, V.L. (ed.) *Hosts and Guests: the Anthropology of Tourism.* University of Pennsylvania Press, Philadelphia, Pennsylvania, pp. 17–31.

Heine, M. (2002) *Arctic Sports: a Training and Resource Manual. Traditional Aboriginal Sport Coaching Resources: Volume 2.* 2nd edn, Sport North Federation & MACA (GNWT), Yellowknife, Northwest Territories, Canada.

Hinch, T. and de la Barre, S. (2004) Culture, sport and tourism: the case of the Arctic Winter Games. In: Higham, J.E.S. (ed.), *Sport Tourism Destinations: Issues, Opportunities and Analysis.* Butterworth-Heinemann, Oxford, UK, pp. 260–273.

Hinch, T. and de la Barre, S. (2005) Culture, sport and tourism: the case of the Arctic Winter Games. In: Higham, J. (ed.) *Sport Tourism Destinations: Issues, Opportunities and Analysis.* Butterworth-Heinemann, Oxford, UK, pp. 260–273.

Leiper, N. (1990) Tourist attraction systems. *Annals of Tourism Research* 17, 367–384.

McGregor, C. (1983) *Pop Goes the Culture.* Pluto Press, London.

McPherson, B.D., Curtis, J.E. and Loy, J.W. (1989) *The Social Significance of Sport: an Introduction to the Sociology of Sport.* Human Kinetics Books, Champaign, Illinois.

Mowforth, M. and Munt, I. (1998) *Tourism and Sustainability: New Tourism in the Third World.* Routledge, London.

Paraschak, V. (1997) Variations in race relations: sporting events for native peoples in Canada. *Sociology of Sport Journal* 14, 1–21.

Richards, G. and Hall, D. (2000) *Tourism and Sustainable Community Development.* Routledge, New York.

Rowe, D. and Lawrence, G. (1996) Beyond national sport: sociology, history and postmodernity. *Sporting Traditions* 12 (2), 3–16.

Sport North Federation (1995) *The Benefits of Sport in the Northwest Territories: an Assessment.* Iqualuit and Yellowknife, Northwest Territories, Canada.

Szabo, C. (2003) The Arctic Winter Games are hot. *Parks and Recreation Canada* 60 (5), 38–44.

Urry, J. (1995) *Consuming Places.* Routledge, London and New York.

Wang, N. (2000) *Tourism and Modernity: a Sociological Analysis.* Pergamon Press, Oxford, UK.

Weed, M.E. and Bull, C.J. (2004) *Sports Tourism: Participants, Policy and Providers.* Elsevier Butterworth-Heinemann, Oxford, UK.

Yukon Territorial Government (2004) *Marketing Plan 2004–2005.* Department of Culture and Tourism, Whitehorse, Yukon.

Part V
Future Perspectives

13 Tourism Research in Greenland

Danish Centre for Forest, Landscape and Planning, KVL, Hørsholm, Denmark

Introduction

Tourism has increased significantly in Greenland in the past decade and is a focus area of development in Greenlandic society. Along with this growing tourism activity, the need for knowledge about the socio-cultural, economic and environmental impacts and benefits of tourism has increased. This study assesses the existing knowledge on tourism development in Greenland and identifies a range of research needs and criteria to help guide future tourism research and development in Greenland.

Background

Greenland may be characterized as peripheral in several ways. Its location in the North Atlantic makes it remote from both the European and North American continents. Although it is the world's largest island, its cold climate limits living conditions and infrastructure as the inland ice covers 81% of the land, leaving only 410,449 km^2 (19%) of ice-free coastal lands. With a disperse population of only 56,854 (Statistics Greenland, 2004a) – mostly Inuit and some Danes – many communities are peripheral.

The Inuit culture has traditionally been linked closely to the unique Arctic nature and climatic conditions, but has for some decades been undergoing major transitions to meet the challenges of the postmodern global world. Since the Greenland Home Rule Government was established in 1979, the country has been gradually building up its own capacities and institutions while maintaining strong ties with and continuing to receive economic support from Denmark.

Tourism Trends in Greenland

Touristically as well, Greenland represents a peripheral area, both in its tourism image as a remote, unexplored Arctic wilderness inhabited by Eskimos and by actual tourism visitation being limited by high prices and difficult access. Organized tourist travel to Greenland began in 1959 with flights from Copenhagen and 1-day tourist flights from Iceland (Thalund, 2000), but tourist numbers remained quite low and tourism has become a significant societal factor only within the past decade.

In 1991, tourism became one of three key issues in a commercial development strategy established by the Greenlandic Home Rule Government. The intentions were to supplement income from the declining fishing industry with incomes from minerals and tourism, and substantial public funds were allocated to tourism development. Consequently, Greenland has become an emerging destination for tourists. As seen in Fig. 13.1, tourism has grown substantially since the early 1990s from approximately 4000 tourist arrivls in 1993 to over 32,000 in 2001 (Statistics Greenland, 2002). After a slight drop to 27,603 in 2002 – most probably due to the worldwide decline in tourism associated with 9/11 – the numbers increased to just under 30,000 in 2003 (Statistics Greenland, 2004b).

The majority of tourists to Greenland (84%) come from Scandinavia – primarily Denmark. Seven per cent come from other Northern European countries, 5% from Southern or Central Europe while only a few per cent come from non-European countries – primarily 2% from North America (Statistics Greenland, 2004b). Just under half the tourists (45%) are on holiday, a quarter are on business trips (25%), 18% are primarily visiting family and friends while the remainder come to study (4%), attend

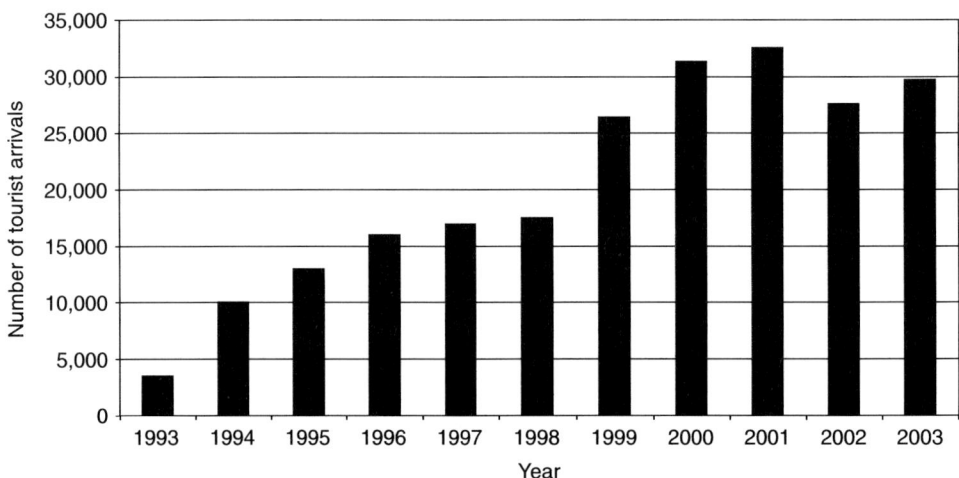

Fig. 13.1. Tourist arrivals in Greenland 1993–2003, based on estimates from Greenland Tourism, 2001 and Statistics Greenland, 2002, 2004b.

conferences or seminars (3%) or to participate in other activities (5%) (Statistics Greenland, 2004b). On average, tourists stay for 15 days.

Tourists primarily stay overnight in hotels (37%), private homes (31%) and youth/sailor hostels (16%), while 6% stay in tents, 3% on cruise ships, 6% on boats and 1% in huts/on sheep farms (Statistics Greenland, 2004b). Due to climatic conditions tourism is highly seasonal, with most tourists arriving in July and August (Statistics Greenland, 2004c). Tourists tend to be older, with the age group of > 50 years constituing the dominant group – possibly because of the high price of travel to Greenland.

Greenland Tourism divides Greenland into four tourist regions (Fig. 13.2) although, statistically, north Greenland is subdivided into the popular Disco Bay area and the remote North Greenland. Each tourist region offers a variety of attractions and activities, all of which tend to focus largely on nature qualities. Disco Bay, west and south Greenland in particular are popular tourist destinations, while east and north Greenland are more remote and have fewer established tourism facilities and a less developed infrastructure.

Tourism in Greenland is strongly linked to nature and nature-related activities, while cultural experiences include visiting the historic remains of the early Inuit and Norse cultures as well as present-day culture. This is strongly reflected in marketing materials, such as brochures and elaborate Internet information presenting Greenland to tourists. Knowledge about tourists has increased, as Statistics Greenland now systematically collects and publishes results of exit surveys, providing important data to the tourism industry. However, more detailed data on tourist activities, motives and preferences in Greenland are needed.

While the first Greenlandic tourism plan focused primarily on increasing tourist numbers, income and job creation, the tourism strategy plan 2003–2005 (Greenland Tourism, 2003) focused on sustainable tourism development, capacity building and alliances. Further knowledge about the operationalization of sustainable tourism to Greenlandic conditions is needed.

Cultural Resources in Greenland

The cultural resources of Greenland are part of the tourism marketing and attractions. Greenland has been inhabited periodically for the past 4500 years (Grønnow, 2000), since the first wave of Inuit migration from Canada in approximately 2500 BC. Remains from different cultural periods (Independence I & II, Saqqaq, Dorset I & II) can be found in Greenland. The last major wave of immigration by the Thule Culture – around AD 1200 is the origin of the current Inuit population (Gulløv, 2000). Most of the prehistoric remains seen in Greenland today originate from the Thule Culture.

Around AD 985, an immigration group of Norse farmers from Iceland settled in the fjords of southern Greenland (Arneborg, 2000). Remains and

North Greenland (3%)

Attractions:
• Nature, flora and fauna
• Inuit hunting culture
• Inaccessible and untouched
• Expeditions, hiking, dog-sledding
• Midnight sun

Barriers of access, transport conditions, military restrictions

Disco Bay (29%)

Attractions:
• Nature, flora and fauna
• UNESCO World Heritage Site
• Ice and glaciers
• Midnight sun, Northern Lights
• Hiking, boating, year-round dogsledding, angling, whale watching
• Handicrafts

Barrier of overnight capacity

West Greenland (53%)

Attractions:
• Nature, flora and fauna
• Nuuk – the capital, handicrafts
• Hiking, boating, horseback riding, angling, whale watching, musk ox safari, heli-skiing
• Northern Lights

Relatively weak area in activities, experiences and attractions

East Greenland (3%)

Attractions:
• Hunting and fishing culture
• Hiking, dogsledding, boating, climbing, angling, camping
• Handicrafts
• Northern Lights

Barriers of access, overnight capacity, product development, length of stay, helicopter rides a bottleneck

South Greenland (12%)

Attractions:
• Nature, flora and fauna
• Ice fjords and hot springs
• Sheep farms, seal watching
• Norse history
• Angling, hiking, boating
• Horseback riding
• Big-wall climbing
• Northern Lights

Barriers of boat access by ice-locked fjords in early summer

Map labels: Kap morris Jesup; Qaanaaq; National park; Upernavik; Ittoqqortoormiut; Uummannaq; Qeqertarsuaq; Ilulissat; Aasiaat; Qasigiannguit; Kangaatsiaq; Sisimiut; Maniitsoq; NUUK; Tasiilaq; Paamiut; KALAALLIT NUNAAT; 1:10 mio; Ivittuut; Qaqortoq; Nanortalik; Kap Farvel; 100 0 100 200 300 400 500 km; Geodætisk Datum WGS 84, projektion UTM zone 24

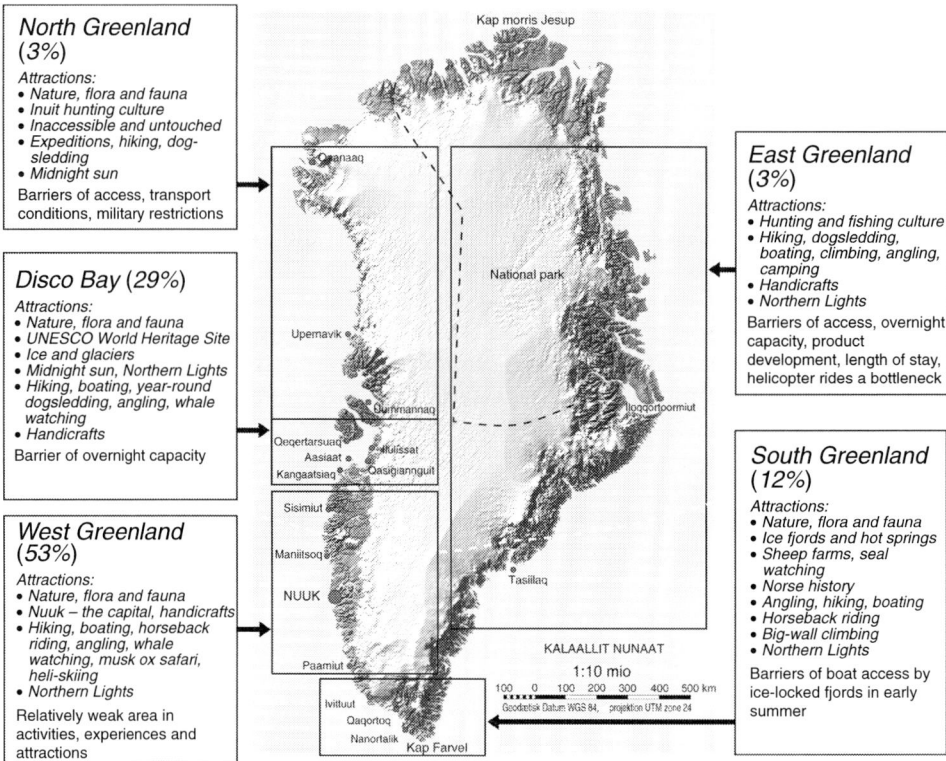

Fig. 13.2. Percentages of tourists, key attractions and barriers to tourism in the five tourism regions of Greenland. Underlay, copyright Kort og Matrikolstyrelsen.

reconstructions from this era are among the tourist attractions today. The 1000-year celebration of Leif den Lykkelige's discovery of America and introduction of Christianity to Greenland was celebrated in the year 2000 and integrated as part of the tourism activities.

However, some time after 1408, the Norse settlers disappeared, possibly also due to climatic changes. In 1721 the priest Hans Egede arrived in Greenland in search of the Norse settlers, but when he was unsuccessful he became a missionary among the Inuit and started to establish trading posts.

This initiated a process of colonization that lasted until 1953, when Greenland became an equal member of the Danish Kingdom with two representatives in the Danish Government. The Greenlandic Home Rule Government was established in 1979, and continues its representation in the Danish government. The strong ties between the two countries are reflected in the fact that the majority of tourists come from Denmark.

Many of the cultural remains from the various prehistoric and historic periods in Greenland, as well as present-day culture, are part of the tourist attractions in Greenland. More knowledge is needed on the links between culture and tourism, such as tourist perceptions, impacts of tourism on cultural sites and interpretation.

Natural Resources and Nature Protection in Greenland

Arctic nature has unique landscapes, ice formations, wildlife and plant communities that are highly attractive to tourists. Nature in Greenland includes habitats that are closely adapted to the high, low and sub-arctic conditions and are generally more sensitive than habitats in temperate areas. Although Greenland has a low population density, the use of natural resources is a key factor in Greenlandic society and is increasingly affecting the sensitive nature areas (Due and Ingerslev, 2000).

The North East Greenland National Park, established in 1974, is the world's largest national park. Furthermore, Greenland has five smaller protected areas and 11 Ramsar areas (areas protected by the Ramsar Convention). In 2004, the Ilulissat Icefjord in Disco Bay became a UNESCO World Heritage Site (UNESCO, 2004). However, it is primarily areas in the high arctic zone that are protected, while the low and sub-arctic zones (where most current and future changes and impacts from hunting, fishing, agriculture, mineral extraction, recreation and tourism occur or are expected to occur) are the least protected areas (Due and Ingerslev, 2000).

The transition of Inuit culture also influences the use and perceptions of natural resources in Greenland. While traditional Inuit culture dictates a deep respect for nature and the use of only the resources necessary for sustainable living, Hansen (2001) suggests that this has changed and that overhunting and wasteful use of natural resources are taking place, which may deplete the Greenlandic fauna within a few decades. In addition, a status report on the biodiversity of Arctic flora and fauna points to the threats from global warming, introduction and invasion of non-endemic species, and pollution from industry and cars, which accumulates in the Arctic ecosystems (CAFF, 2001).

The impacts of tourists on nature and culture in Greenland remain largely unexplored. However, an inter-Nordic project involving Greenland, Iceland and Svalbard mapping the environmental impacts of the Arctic tourism industry indicates that impacts on nature in Greenland originate as much from local residents as from tourists. Furthermore, the project has found that visual pollution greatly influences tourists' perceptions and the quality of their experience (Nordic Council of Ministers, 2001).

Tourism is closely linked to Greenland's natural qualities and may provide an alternative to more extractive uses of nature. Consequently, more knowledge on the interrelations – such as tourist perceptions, nature impacts, nature management and potential changes towards higher sustainable practices – is needed.

Objectives of the Study

The main objective of this project is to review existing knowledge of the links between tourism, natural resources and local communities in

Greenland. This includes identifying barriers and opportunities for tourism in contributing to creating a platform for conservation of natural resources and to sustainable development of Greenlandic society. Another objective is to suggest criteria to guide the Danish Environmental Support to the Arctic to prioritize future research projects related to tourism.

Methods

This project is based on literature reviews and internal report documents on tourism, natural resource management and local communities in Greenland. Materials were collected from libraries, the Internet, research institutions and government administrative units in Greenland and Denmark and have been compiled in an annotated bibliography. Furthermore, 20 qualitative interviews were conducted with key informants in Greenland and Denmark to identify research and information needs. An analysis of barriers and opportunities in relation to existing knowledge has been performed and a number of criteria are suggested as possibly guiding future research efforts.

Existing Research on Tourism and Nature

Research environments/institutions

A number of research institutions in Greenland and Denmark carry out research and investigation on nature and environment, tourism and humanistic and social sciences. Some institutions – especially universities – conduct studies (often student projects) that are somewhat broader in scope. This varies depending on how embedded the various researchers are in Greenland and the extent of cooperation and partnership with institutions within and outside Greenland.

Research on natural resources is carried out at The Nature Institute of Greenland, The Danish and Greenlandic Geological Institute, a section of the Danish National Environmental Research Institute and ASIAQ, the Greenlandic survey institute. Most research is highly focused on the natural sciences, and a few documents are found with brief links to tourism or local communities. Greenland has a long tradition of natural science research related to fields including geology, glaciology and biology. As early as 1878, the Commission for Management of Geological and Geographical Investigations in Greenland was established, today named the Commission for Scientific Research in Greenland (KVUG, 1998).

Research on local communities and culture is carried out at Greenland University, Greenland National Museum and Statistics Greenland. In Denmark, research is undertaken at the Institute of Eskimology at the University of Copenhagen, Aalborg University, a division of North Atlantic Regional Studies at Roskilde University and at the Center for North

Atlantic Studies (CNS) at Aarhus University. The focus is often on the links between humans and the natural environment in the past and present, while tourism is only vaguely addressed.

Research on tourism is carried out by Greenland Tourism, the Trade Section of the Greenlandic Home Rule Government, the Copenhagen Business School and a large number of consultants based primarily in Denmark. Most focus on traditional tourism business, development and marketing issues.

Research cooperation between these three research spheres appears to be limited. Generally, research in Greenland is dominated by research in the natural sciences, with few connections to studies of human activities – including tourism. In 1995, only 17% of the total funding for research in Greenland was allocated to social sciences, statistics, humanistic sciences and health sciences combined, while at least 67% was allocated to natural science research; the remainder was allocated to institutions and programmes with a strong focus on the natural sciences (Statistics Greenland, 1997).

The limited attention to research on socio-cultural aspects in Greenland was also mentioned by KVUG (1998) and Dahl and Sejersen (2000), who attributed this to isolation, closed research environments and lack of funding. A research programme on cultural encounters conducted in Southern Greenland did not involve present-day culture or tourism.

Tourism research in Greenland focuses primarily on business aspects, marketing and development of tourism, with limited integration of natural resources and local communities. However, as tourism is becoming an increasingly important factor in Greenlandic society, the focus seems to be shifting. The latest proposed tourism strategy by Greenland Tourism is focused less on tourism numbers and more on increasing local capacity building and sustainability aspects.

In addition, the statistical tourism data collection by Statistics Greenland has been significantly upgraded since 1998. Tourism is also emerging as a prioritized topic in the National Strategy for Polar Research 1998–2002, in which investigations of the social and cultural basis for sustainable development of various industries – including tourism – are deemed important. Furthermore, analysis of the economic, social and cultural effects of new industry projects at the local, regional and national levels, as well as comparative studies with other arctic regions, are important (KVUG, 1998).

Additionally, several Nordic/Arctic research projects/programmes and NGOs (Arctic Council, Nordic Council of Ministers, WWF Arctic Program) are beginning to focus more on tourism in the Arctic region. Greenland is participating in work on developing a Nordic strategy for sustainable tourism (Nordic Council of Ministers, 2001). Thus, there seems to be great interest in finding new ways of establishing a balance between nature, culture and tourism. This is also reflected in a higher integration of community and natural resources in tourism appearing in more recent reports and student projects.

However, a major barrier to increased research activities, cooperation and funding is the lack of overview of previous research and data collections within the field of tourism in Greenland. As the Danish Cooperation for Environment in the Arctic has started receiving an increased number of applications for funding of tourism studies, the programme decided to conduct the present study. Their intent is to provide an overview of research documents, institutions, examples of best practices, current tourism strategies, research needs and suggestions for criteria for future projects.

Knowledge analysis of written sources

The literature study identifies over 170 documents related to tourism in Greenland. Some have tourism as their primary topic and include documents on natural resources and local communities when they mention tourism in Greenland. More documents than expected were identified, but most are internal reports and student projects unavailable through libraries or the Internet.

The Body of Knowledge

The literature review indicates that broad ranges of topics related to tourism are addressed. As seen in Fig. 13.3, the main category is marketing and tourism development documents, while a large number of tourism policies and strategies are also found. The tourism category (T) also includes transport studies and education materials/manuals.

The second category includes studies on nature and nature management with direct or indirect links to tourism. Some mention only briefly touristic use of nature or other human impacts, while others address hunting, nature protection and management strategies. Approximately ten sources focus on sustainable tourism, while a few address codes of conduct, integration of environmentally friendly practices in tourism or similar topics.

Within a third socio-cultural category, projects on culture/local knowledge often focus on the relationships between local residents and natural resources, while links to tourists are very limited. A few links between local communities and tourism were found, mostly in theoretical student projects.

Generally, most of the identified projects and reports are very applied and little highly 'academic' research is found. Altogether, the literature review shows several characteristic trends. Most projects are mono-disciplinary; the tourism documents are very business oriented, with limited integration of nature and local communities beyond the attraction level.

The studies on nature and nature management also focus within this

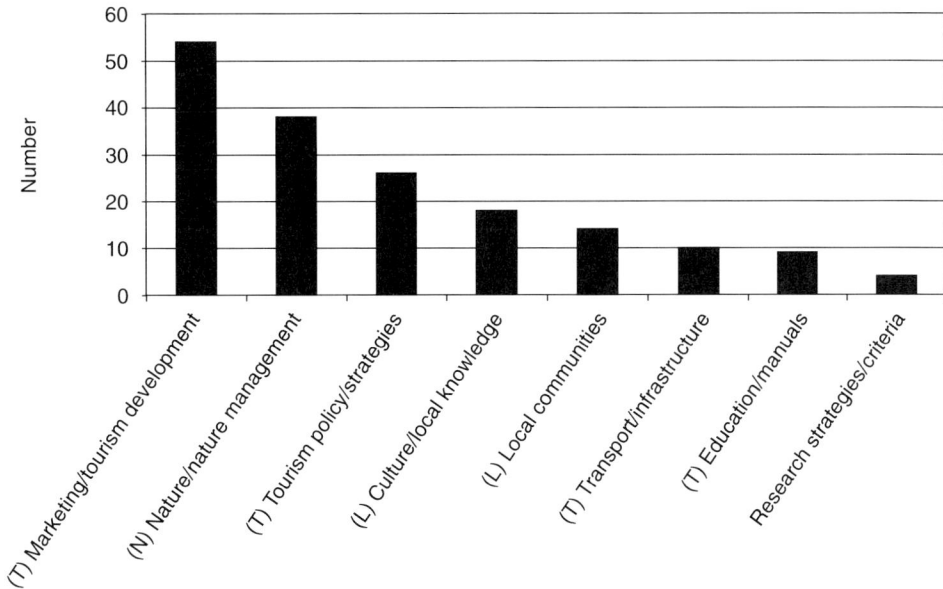

Fig. 13.3. Main topics of the 173 written sources on tourism (T), nature management (N) and local matters (L) in Greenland. The remainder relate to research strategies and criteria.

field, and treat tourism and local communities only as secondary issues. In social and humanistic research, the focus is on people and local communities and their relationships to nature, but rarely involves tourism. Consequently, there is a lack of projects with a cross-disciplinary approach involving tourism, nature and local communities. However, there is a trend of the more recent projects on sustainable tourism having broader approaches. Nevertheless, the concept of 'sustainable tourism' needs operationalization and adjustment to Greenlandic conditions to make it applicable to the tourism industry as well as to other groups.

Geographical distribution of knowledge

Many projects are conducted by external consultants and institutions, mainly from Denmark, and some are conducted by students without having previously visiting Greenland. Most student projects and some consultants' reports are physically located in Denmark, while documents from Greenland Tourism, the Greenlandic Home Rule Government and some consultants are found primarily in Greenland although most are unpublished, internal documents. Generally, a large amount of the knowledge and expertise being gathered concerning tourism in Greenland finds its way out of the country, contributing little to the accumulation of knowledge and competency in Greenland.

Access to knowledge

Another problem is the internal character of many reports and documents, which makes them unavailable to institutions such as libraries. Access to the documents becomes limited to researchers and others with connections. A small collection can be found at the Danish Polar Centre library in Copenhagen. Some universities also have small collections of student projects, but these are often for internal use only. Most reports are published in Danish, a few in English, and a few include summaries in Greenlandic. This limits access to established knowledge for people in Greenland, Denmark and other countries.

Expressed Research Needs

This study identifies knowledge needs related to tourism, local communities and natural resources. Information was collected through 20 interviews with key informants from local government agencies, interest organizations, researchers and tourism outfitters in Greenland and Denmark. Many of the expressed needs are linked to applied hands-on projects or initiatives rather than 'academic' research. However, as many of the needs represent problems needing both action and research, all suggestions are included and caregorized into eight topics:

1. Tourism product; more knowledge and data are needed regarding the motives, preferences and activities of tourists in Greenland, the present provision of attractions and interest in changes in tourism attractions and services.

2. The conditions for touristic use of nature; more knowledge is required on the pressure and disturbances tourism activities inflict on the natural environment, including wildlife. Projects to improve nature management and planning are also requested, as well as more information for tourists on nature and management restrictions.

3. The conditions for touristic use of culture; more knowledge and regulation of popular cultural sites are requested, as well as improved trails and regulation of conflicts between local *versus* touristic uses (e.g. snowmobiles *versus* dogsleds).

4. Logistic requirements; both the role of accessibility and transport for tourism on a countrywide scale and locally in relation to safety of tourists in nature and how local people can meet safety standards to qualify as tour operators.

5. Preconditions for support and involvement of local residents in tourism; in particular, concerning how to integrate tourism as an alternative opportunity in local communities and to raise awareness and acceptance of tourism among local residents. Further interests are: (i) upgrading local resident qualifications to meet the needs of the tourism industry; (ii) integrating local resources and traditional knowledge in tourism; and

(iii) overcoming barriers of internal competition to deal with cultural differences in understanding between Western tourists and the Inuit culture.

6. Expectations by tourists; of high-quality experiences, projects to clean up nature, interpretative facilities and expansion of the system of overnight shelters.

7. Tourists' understanding of experiences in Greenland; through projects comparing and interpreting the European and Inuit understanding of culture and nature, as well as by providing pamphlets for tourists.

8. Long-term follow-up requirements; including needs for the tourism industry to increase knowledge on tourists' satisfaction, activities, experiences and suggestions, and to increase data collection on tourism, nature and local communities. Nature management must develop methods and monitoring systems to follow tourism's use of and pressures on natural resources. Finally, the overall dissemination of knowledge on tourism, nature and local communities must be revised to ensure exchange of and access to knowledge, local accumulation of knowledge, exchange of knowledge with other Arctic regions and dissemination of popular versions of research results to the local population.

Conclusions

When comparing the written sources and the needs expressed through interviews, there is a strong focus on 'applied' research rather than on 'academic' research, but both are needed for the building of knowledge and capacity.

As sustainable tourism – involving economic, socio-cultural and nature aspects – is the basis of the tourism strategy in Greenland, there is a need for more attention to the overlapping between tourism, nature management and socio-cultural community aspects. Only a small number of existing projects address all three of these issues.

A number of barriers and opportunities for tourism research in Greenland have been identified (Table 13.1). Barriers include a predominant focus on natural science research and single disciplines, limited research environments and lack of integration between the tourism industry and academic institutions. Within tourism research, there is a traditional focus on economic and marketing studies, while integration with nature management and community issues is more limited. Additionally, the limited cooperation and exchange of knowledge between Greenland and neighbouring Arctic countries is a barrier.

Suggested criteria for allocation of environmental support

This project involved the provision of suggestions for criteria to contribute to the priorities of the Danish Cooperation for Environment in the Arctic

Table 13.1. Barriers to and opportunities for current research and collection of information on tourism in Greenland.

Barriers	Opportunities
Overall research in Greenland is dominated by natural sciences (e.g. geology, glaciology, biology)	Increased research on touristic, social and humanistic matters and cross-links to natural resources
Research on tourism, nature management and local communities is conducted within single disciplines	Cross-disciplinary research focusing on the links between tourism, nature and local communities; use of pilot projects and action-research to ensure high applicability to Greenlandic conditions
Small, isolated research environments with too few researchers to reach a 'critical mass'	Larger research environments with 'critical mass'
Limited integration of research and data collection between research institutions and the tourism industry	Increased research cooperation between the tourism industry and academic institutions
Traditional tourism focus on increasing tourist numbers and income	Focus on sustainable tourism – environmentally, socially and economically
Studies and data collection focus primarily on tourism industry development (e.g. marketing analyses, market strategies, feasibility studies of new facilities and infrastructure)	Broader focus on sustainable tourism, with research and data collection on environmental, social and economic aspects
Geographical focus on Greenland and local areas/cases	Circumpolar focus with increased exchange of knowledge, research results and tourism experiences with other Arctic regions (e.g. Canada, Svalbard)

when evaluating the growing number of applications for projects on tourism in Greenland. It was suggested that the following six criteria be given priority in applications:

Cross-disciplinary research

Most research and data collection on tourism, nature management and local communities are conducted within isolated disciplines. However, sustainable tourism – a primary objective in the latest suggested tourism strategy (Greenland Tourism, 2003) – is based on a combination of economic, socio-cultural and nature-related aspects of tourism. Consequently, a higher focus on cross-disciplinary research on the links between these three fields is needed and priority should be given to cross-disciplinary projects. Some of the more recent reports and student projects show a tendency in this direction and can be of some inspiration.

Increased operationalization of 'sustainable tourism'

Sustainable tourism development – in harmony with nature and local communities – is one of the aims for tourism in Greenland. However, existing research on tourism still focuses on a traditional approach including market analyses, economic development strategies, feasibility studies and infrastructure expansions to increase tourist numbers and revenue. Although a stated objective, sustainable tourism is a concept that must be operationalized and adapted to Greenlandic conditions. Consequently, attention should be given to projects involving operationalization of 'sustainable tourism' into actions that the tourism industry and others can implement more directly.

Increased cooperation between the tourism industry and academic institutions

The tourism industry and academic institutions need to increase their cooperation to establish a mutual understanding of the economic, socio-cultural and nature-related aspects of tourism and to share knowledge. Currently, the tourism industry focuses on business aspects and often uses external consultants to conduct studies. Contact with universities and similar research environments conducting studies on the socio-cultural and environmental aspects of tourism is rather limited. All groups could benefit from increased cooperation and coverage of broader sustainability issues. Consequently, projects including cooperation between the tourism industry and academic institutions should be given priority.

Local integration

Local integration into projects is important for capacity-building in Greenland. Most projects are conducted by Danish consultants or as student projects at Danish institutions. Consequently, analyses of tourism, nature and local communities lack insight from local knowledge and preconditions in Greenland. This is a weakness, but is also a strength as it brings in new ideas from outside, as well as solutions independent of local political interests.

However, the acquired knowledge and capacities of a project are lost from Greenland when researchers return to Denmark after completing a project. Consequently, it is suggested that projects integrating local partners be prioritized.

Education and capacity-building in Greenland

Education and knowledge exchange are important tools for changing actions and raising awareness of both local residents and tourists regarding issues on tourism, nature and local communities. It is highly relevant to educate more local residents to take part in the tourism industry, including interpretation for tourists. It will increase local employment and provide tourists with more authentic experiences when guides are Inuit rather than Danish or other from other European countries. The established Danish Nature Interpretation Education Program may possibly contribute to the education of more Greenlandic nature and culture guides.

Educational efforts at the academic level are also relevant, and if more Greenlandic researchers and project managers are educated more tourism data collection and analyses can be undertaken locally in Greenland. The Danish Cooperation for Environment in the Arctic may consider sponsoring Greenlanders undertaking such studies abroad. This means giving priority to a long-term educational and capacity-building effort.

Cross-national/circumpolar projects and knowledge exchange

Most existing studies of tourism in Greenland only include Greenland or local case studies. Only a few – mainly Nordic – projects integrate experiences from other countries and/or polar regions. However, this being a new field in Greenland, knowledge and experiences accumulated in other Arctic regions on tourism, nature and local communities could be highly valuable to Greenland. Consequently, priority should be given to projects with a cross-national or circumpolar focus and to the exchange of knowledge, research results and experiences.

These suggested criteria may contribute to the prioritizing of future projects by the Danish funding programme for the Arctic. Furthermore, compilation and review of existing knowledge provide a platform for researchers and data collections in Greenland. As a first step, it is suggested that the annotated literature review from the present project be converted into a database on the Internet and be made available to researchers, tourism planners and others. This can provide an overview of existing knowledge and facilitate new research efforts.

Secondly, it is suggested that a tourism library section be established at the Greenland National Library in Nuuk, containing copies of existing literature and other references. This will make the currently diverse sources much more available to researchers, students, tourism planners and other persons interested in Greenland, and it will be requested that those carrying out new projects provide copies for the collection. When existing knowledge is made widely available, new projects can be better directed to add to knowledge and capacity-building in Greenland.

The attention to cross-links between tourism, nature and local communities through this project may contribute to a higher focus on these key issues of sustainable tourism by Greenland Tourism, the Greenlandic Home Rule Government and other decision-makers in future tourism strategies and development.

Given the socio-cultural transitions of Greenlandic society, the decline of traditional industries and changing relationships with the natural environment as well as the increasing role of tourism, it seems timely to increase research on how tourism interrelates with and affects local Greenlandic communities and nature.

References

Arneborg, J. (2000) Nordboerne. In: Jakobsen, B., Holm, B., Bøchner, J., Nielsen, N., Guttersen, R., Humlum, O and Jensen, E. (eds) *Topografisk Atlas Grønland, Atlas over Denmark* Bd.6. The Royal Danish Geographical Society Publications, Copenhagen, pp. 54–55.

CAFF (Conservation of Arctic Flora and Fauna) (2001) *Arctic Flora and Fauna – Status and Conservation* (http://www.caff.is/sidur/sidur.asp?id=18andmenu=docs, accessed 22 September 2005).

Dahl, J. and Sejersen, F. (2000) Der skal flyttes grænsepæle. Debat om samfundsforskningen i Grønland. *Polarfronten* 2000 (1), 15.

Due, R. and Ingerslev, T. (eds) (2000) *Naturbeskyttelse i Grønland. Grønlands Naturinstitut*, Teknisk Rapport No. 29 (http://http://www.natur.gl/dokument/Følsomme%20områder.pdf, accessed 22 September 2005).

Greenland Tourism (2001) *Estimates of number of tourists to Greenland 1993–2000*. Nuuk, Greenland.

Greenland Tourism (2003) *Tre Vigtig år – Oplæg til Strategi og Handling for Turismen i Grønland 2003–2005*. Nuuk, Greenland.

Grønnow, B. (2000) Palæo-eskimoerne – de første mennesker i Grønland. In: Jakobsen, B., Holm, B., Bøchner, J., Nielsen, N., Guttersen, R., Humlum, O. and Jensen, E. (eds) *Topografisk Atlas Grønland, Atlas over Denmark* Bd.6. The Royal Danish Geographical Society Publications, Copenhagen, pp. 46–51.

Gulløv, H.C. (2000) Thulekulturen. In: Jakobsen, B., Holm, B., Bøchner, J., Nielsen, N., Guttersen, R., Humlum, O and Jensen, E. (eds) *Topografisk Atlas Grønland, Atlas over Denmark* Bd.6. The Royal Danish Geographical Society Publications, Copenhagen, pp. 52–53.

Hansen, K. (2001) Til den bitre ende. *Polarfronten* 2001 (2), 15.

Kommissionen for Videnskabelige Undersøgelser i Grønland (KVUG) (1998) *National Strategi for Polarforskning*. Copenhagen.

Nordic Council of Ministers (2001) *Towards a Sustainable Nordic Tourism*. TemaNord, Copenhagen, p. 546.

Statistics Greenland (1997) *Greenland Statistical Yearbook 1997*. Nuuk, Greenland.

Statistics Greenland (2002) *Flypassagerstatistikken 2001*. Turisme 2002 (2), Nuuk, Greenland.

Statistics Greenland (2004a) *Nøgletal* (http://www.statgreen.gl, accessed 22 September 2005).

Statistics Greenland (2004b) Flypassagerstatistikken 2003. Turisme 2004 (2), Nuuk, Greenland.

Statistics Greenland (2004c) *Overnatningsstatistikken 2003*. Turisme 2004 (2), Nuuk, Greenland.

Thalund, S. (2000) Moderne turisme i Sisimiut. In: Jakobsen, B., Holm, B., Bøchner, J., Nielsen, N., Guttersen, R., Humlum, O. and Jensen, E. (eds) *Topografisk Atlas Grønland, Atlas over Denmark* Bd.6. The Royal Danish Geographical Society Publications, Copenhagen, pp. 236–237.

UNESCO World Heritage Centre (2004) *World Heritage List – Ilulissat Icefjord* (http://whc.unesco.org, accessed 22 September 2005).

14 Epilogue/Prologue

BRUNO JANSSON AND DIETER K. MÜLLER

Department of Social and Economic Geography, Umeå University, Sweden

Introduction

Giving an overview of tourism in peripheral areas is a vast undertaking. The concept of peripheral has many facets and the areas claimed to be peripheral are enormous. Thus, there is no simple interpretation of the concept, and the meaning depends on the context. This book may thus seem somewhat scattered, since there are so many facets of the central concept. Peripheral is, in a way, a misused concept. One place is in fact always peripheral to the other.

Periphery implies that the viewer looks upon a place from a central position. The periphery as a concept is just far away from the centre, but it also encompasses rurality, since most peripheral areas have a strong rural component and the periphery most often has a sparse population and a lagging economy.

The hinterlands of the urban centres are peripheral and sparsely populated. Lagging areas are peripheral since the economic centre is not, by definition, peripheral. There is really no information regarding the distance from the centre at which a site becomes peripheral: it is all in the eye of the beholder. When a tourism scholar says peripheral, it is likely that he/she means something like a rural, lagging, sparsely populated area far from the centre. The Arctic is remote in relation to all urban areas, sparsely populated, economically lagging and really far away. The Swedish mountain areas are remote in relation to the Stockholm area; the economic capital of Sweden. North-western Scotland is remote in relation to London or Edinburgh.

Most chapters in this book address rural areas, and all areas looked upon are sparsely populated. Thus, the northern and southern peripheries are bearers of manifold attributes, as well as a number of ongoing processes and a wide spectrum of activities. All peripheral places mirrored in this

© CAB International 2007. *Tourism in Peripheries: Perspectives from the Far North and South* (eds D.K. Müller and B. Jansson)

book are unique in the sense that the tourism sector has different aims and directions locally. The book is thus to be taken as a smorgasbord with various dishes, all of which are in some way or another related to the characteristics of periphery as described above.

The peripheral areas are strongly linked to the general development of the economy. A boom in the economies of the countries is normally also positive for economic development in peripheral areas, but the rural periphery too is undergoing a rapid economic restructuring, a swing from the basic sector to a more service-dominated economy. The fall of the historically strong sectors followed by out-migration to economically stronger regions inevitably destroys the population structure and gives way to the expansion of service industries. The tourism sector is often considered as a vehicle for development. In the most remote areas, tourism in a way represents modernization and is sometimes even believed to create something that has never existed in the previous 50, years: an economic boost.

Tourism and Regional Development

In an effort to provide means for development in peripheral areas it has, over the last few decades, become an issue for central governments and even the EU to support tourism development within their regional support or other undertakings. These contributions have not been successful in creating sustainable tourism jobs, however. The idea that tourism is the vehicle for development in troubled areas with a lagging economy and socio-economic problems is widespread, but challenged by Hall (Chapter 2), who connects to earlier works on the subject.

He is rather sceptical about giving tourism a role as the saviour of peripheral areas and he makes a strong point that policymakers most often have a poor understanding of the real nature of tourism. Thus, he calls for 'more realistic assessment of what tourism can bring to the periphery'. Saarinen (this volume) agrees with that and even Zillinger's work (Chapter 4) points in the same direction.

However, even if tourism development is not the saviour of peripheral areas, successful examples like alpine resorts, ice-hotels and Santa villages will involve governments putting further effort into developing destinations into pleasure peripheries. Müller and Ulrich (Chapter 6) provide some evidence showing that tourism employment has, in fact, increased in many areas and, hence, it can be expected that other municipalities desire a similar development. Nevertheless, it appears that this is not necessarily because governments are convinced that tourism will be the best solution; instead, support of tourism development is at least some action in a problematic situation, but may be clutching at the last straw.

Naturally, not all peripheries dispose of assets such as natural scenery, adventurous activities and man-made attractions capable of luring tourists from all over the world. However, governments obviously have difficulties in eliminating areas in favour of more promising destinations. Hence, resources are spread out rather than concentrated.

Tourism development is not only an issue for governments. Private enterprises seize business opportunities and are equally important stakeholders in developing tourism in peripheral areas. However, Zillinger (Chapter 4) clearly indicates that cooperation is crucial, but nevertheless difficult to achieve. This is also addressed by Hall and Saarinen (Chapters 2 and 3, respectively), who argue for a more comprehensive approach to development, featuring tourism as one of many integrated strategies.

Access to skilled staff is further identified as a problem (Saarinen, Chapter 3). Nevertheless, Löffler's contribution (Chapter 5) clearly indicates that rural communities have a great deal to gain from tourism development, because tourist consumption contributes to sustaining a contested service supply in peripheral areas.

Managing Peripheral Tourism

Even in cases where tourism contributes to local and regional welfare, it is obvious that there are threats that can easily erase the existing structure. Irvine and Anderson (Chapter 7) illustrate this risk in the context of the foot-and-mouth crisis in Scotland; although not directly affected, all rural areas were hit hard. The image of a pristine environment was wiped out overnight, clearly demonstrating the impact of media in creating stereotypical and undifferentiated representations of areas beyond the major demand markets.

Struggles over touristic amenities and resources occur not only between centres and peripheries, however. In fact nature conservation, which is often promoted as a facilitator of tourism development, can be perceived as an intrusion into the affairs of local communities. Sandell (Chapter 9) exemplifies this by pointing to the different interests of various stakeholders regarding the use of the environment. Similarly, Lovelock (Chapter 8) detects differences between different groups of tourists. He states a core–periphery movement of both elements in nature and perceptions of nature.

Thus, foreign visitors are against the extermination of pest species, viewing the spread of different species as an art of globalization. Although most tourists appreciate the local views on the spread of species, this is nevertheless an example of tourists' values as a force for changing the periphery's flora and fauna. Hence, even if tourism development is successful, it is not to be seen as unproblematic.

Peripheral municipalities, although often small, are complex and gather heterogeneous interests and wills. Thus, planning is crucial as is the integration of stakeholders into the planning process. However, as has been argued by Hall and Boyd (2005), peripheral municipalities often lack political control and governance over their territory and, thus, they are objects of political decisions and power struggle at the regional, national and international levels. The case of the non-establishment of the Kiruna National Park is thus the exception to the rule (Sandell, Chapter 9).

The difficulties in planning are also addressed by Mason (Chapter 10), who argues that planning and management schemes are rarely evaluated. They are often taken from mass tourism destinations and transferred into the context of peripheries. Hence, little is known about how to manage increasing amounts of visitors to protected areas which, according to Kaae (Chapter 13), can also be explained by anecdotal and natural science dominated research, particularly in the polar regions.

Tourism Opportunities

Current stereotypes of peripheries usually include the notion of pristine environments and landscapes. These amenities of interest for tourists traditionally comprise the landscape, and thereby mountains, waterfalls, beautiful sights and other freaks of nature. However, tourism has long been considerable in urban areas, and man-made attractions dominate in these areas.

Windmills, or wind farms, hydroelectric installations with their high dams and nuclear power plants are characteristics of urban society, although they most often appear in rural and rather remote areas. Thus, these often unintentional modern creations of amenities can be based on industrial activities. Major buildings such as wind farms have become interesting to tourists as well as castles and other buildings from earlier centuries. Not only is the wind farm attractive to tourists, but so even are, surprisingly, nuclear power plants, due to their impressive size and slight feeling of controlled danger. The modern development of amenities mirrored by Nash et al. in their chapter on wind farms in Scotland (Chapter 11) is an interesting account of this development.

Besides the environment and man-made attractions such as those discussed above, indigenous cultures are important attractions within peripheral areas. Here, sustaining culture is mandatory, but this does not necessarily always imply that tourism development should be avoided or limited. Hinch and de la Barre (Chapter 12) point to the role of tourism as a facilitator of cultural development and means to stimulate the maintenance of indigenous traditions and skills. However, access and timing of events are crucial factors that must be solved to really develop tourism around an indigenous theme.

Looking Forward

As pointed out in the introduction to this book, tourism in peripheral areas has accumulated a considerable body of literature (e.g. Hall and Johnston, 1995; Price, 1996; Butler et al., 1998; Brown and Hall, 2000). This book is therefore an additional contribution. Still, both Kaae and Mason (Chapters 13 and 10, respectively) argue that knowledge of tourism in peripheral areas is crucial but rare.

This can certainly be explained by more than one factor. First, peripheries, although in the context of this book all located in the 'developed' world, comprise very different physical and socio-economic and political conditions. Secondly, research has been rather *ad hoc* and uncoordinated.

However, there are – as has been seen here – common problems arising from declining economies and disappearing communities. Moreover, shared experiences of weakness in relation to economic and political centres make tourism developments comparable and worth studying, not least with regard to peripheral communities struggling for their survival.

However, it should be noted that Christaller's (1964) notion of peripheries as resorts for the core regions' urbanites has never become real, at least regarding the northern and southern peripheries which lack amenities such as a Mediterranean climate and warm water. However, the recent increase in nature-based tourism as noted by Saarinen (Chapter 3) and a growing interest in indigenous cultures indicate that tourism development in peripheries is possible.

Societal changes in the main demand markets such as ageing populations, increased health and welfare and the rise of budget airlines all seem to promise brighter futures and good prospects even for peripheral destinations. Moreover, fear of terrorist attacks and epidemic diseases also ironically work to the advantage of perceived safe and pristine areas in the northern and southern periphery.

Nevertheless, global environmental change is an issue threatening all positive prospects (Gössling and Hall, 2006). As pointed out by Johnston (2006), it is not only the emissions of travelling as such that are critical for a future development of peripheral tourism. Instead, emissions from core areas also contribute to deteriorating environments in the polar regions and elsewhere. Hence, even peripheral areas, sometimes depicted as slow and almost apathetic, are in constant change, not only regarding their environmental conditions but also regarding the societal and political frameworks conditioning their future development. Thus, there will be reasons for continuously revisiting peripheral tourism development, even in the uncertain times to come.

References

Brown, F. and Hall, D. (2000) *Tourism in Peripheral Areas.* Channel View Publications, Clevedon, UK.

Butler, R., Hall, C.M. and Jenkins, J. (1998) *Tourism and Recreation in Peripheral Areas.* Wiley, Chichester, UK.

Christaller, W. (1964) Some considerations of tourism location in Europe: the peripheral regions – underdeveloped countries – recreation areas. *Papers in Regional Science* 12 (1), 95–105.

Gössling, S. and Hall, C.M. (2006) *Tourism and Global Environmental Change: Ecological, Social, Economic and Political Interrelationships*. Routledge, London.

Hall, C.M. and Johnston, M.E. (1995) *Polar Tourism: Tourism in Arctic and Antarctic Regions*. Wiley, Chichester, UK.

Hall, C.M. and Boyd, S. (2005) *Nature-based Tourism in Peripheral Areas: Development or Disaster?* Channel View Publications, Clevedon, UK.

Johnston, M. (2006) Impacts of global environmental change on tourism in the polar regions. In: Gössling, S. and Hall, C.M. (eds) (2006) *Tourism and Global Environmental Change: Ecological, Social, Economic and Political Interrelationships*. Routledge, London, pp. 37–53.

Price, M. (1996) *People and Tourism in Fragile Environments*. Wiley, Chichester, UK.

Index